RUTH MARTIN

Sweet Charity

*Office politics, teamwork, anger management,
redemption, love and everything*

First edition

ISBN: 978-1-7397634-3-5

Cover art by Debs Waters

This book was professionally typeset on Reedsy.
Find out more at reedsy.com

I dedicate this book to anyone who works or has ever worked in comms anywhere, in any office, who loves what they do, who strives to do good, and who approaches their work with just the right amount of serious.

"Where people aren't having fun, they seldom produce good work."
– David Ogilvy

Intro

'And what do you do?'

'I work for a charity in central London.'

I kind of knew what was coming next. Sort of impressed eyebrows, and a perfect, round, slow-nodding 'Oh.'

The woman's eyes narrowed, and she leaned in with a serious expression. Serious, but not at all confident in the subject. Like when someone tells you they're moving to Pinner, and you don't know if that's a good thing or a bad thing. I could see her searching her mind for the 'Did you mean this?' information. Her eyes widened.

'When we were in Namibia last year, we met a young chap from Rwanda. A really nice chap – *clever*. He and his wife lived just outside of Geneva. And he worked for the United Nations, you see, in some area of human rights, I think it was. They were amazing people. *Very interesting.*'

Her reference was wide of the mark ... or maybe it wasn't, really. You see, working for a charity *is* about human rights. But you learn that just because you're working for a charity or any organisation that does good, really, it doesn't mean you're amazing, or interesting, or clever. You're doing good work and everything, but you're still human, you work in an office, and everyone's flawed. And boy, you and your colleagues can be so annoying. But, as Warren says, not in a bad way. When Warren says 'not in a bad way', this is what he really means: in a bad way.

Prologue

I walk into my room. I haven't been there for years. I've been robbed.
Everything looks different. It's all been rearranged.

Someone's moved my chest of drawers. And my bicycles have been
wedged under the window. I try to move everything back to where it
should be. It's all too heavy, and I can't do it. I can't find anyone to
help me. I want my room back the way it was.

I go outside to the bus stop. I sit in the middle of the road and my
body heaves with sobbing and everything. I can't breathe. I stick all
my fingers into my mouth and try to chew off all my fingernails at
once. I sob and chew and sob and chew. My life is unravelling.

I wake up. It's a relief not to have to sob any more. It was a nightmare,
but it's been my life too.

I have a job interview this afternoon. It's the second interview for a
job I really want. Well, *any* job is one I want, really. I've had about four
million interviews, and a lifetime's worth of rejections and everything.
I'm not sure I can stand. My shoulders are tight, my heart feels heavy.
I look across at Jamie and he's still sleeping. I climb out of bed.

Chapter 1

I had that nightmare six months after we'd arrived in London. I'm glad that sorry story's all behind me and everything, I have to say. Let me tell you about it.

This is the third country Jamie and I have lived in since we got married fifteen years ago. We lived in Zimbabwe (where we were born and got married), South Africa, and now the UK. Each of the moves has meant getting used to a new way of life, new jobs, and making new friends and everything.

Three things to know about Jamie and me:

1. We always try and *carpe* as much as we can out of every *diem*, even if it scares us.
2. We're at our happiest when we're going to concerts or movies or travelling or just *carpe*ing the *diem*. The cost has been not making many new friends here in London, but that's also a feature of living in London. I might be wrong, but that's how it seems to me anyway.
3. We don't have any children; it's something that makes us feel sad, but it's just never happened. I'm telling you upfront, in case you were wondering about that. People often do wonder. And people do ask, which can be annoying and everything. But we just try to ignore the pain, I guess.

Jamie and I went to the same university and met each other in real life (irl, as Mason would say), in the days before online dating and using Google as a verb. Jamie and I have slightly different ideas of when we met.

My version is that we met at a cheese and wine evening during Freshers' Week, when he was standing with some other Zimbabwean guys my friend Debbie knew. Jamie had the bluest eyes I'd ever seen and he was staring deep into my soul. It turns out he couldn't see anyone because he wasn't wearing his glasses that night.

Jamie's version is that we met at a local pub a month or so after Freshers' Week. He was wearing his glasses that night and says he looked over at me and, for some weird reason, knew I was *the one*. It was a premonition or something. Maybe he was drunk but he says he couldn't have been – he'd spent all his cash during Freshers' Week.

When he looked at me, I waved and he walked over to our table.

'Hi, Jamie! Come sit with us,' I said, patting the chair next to mine.

'Who, me?' he said.

'Yes!' I said.

'Um, okay, sure. And you are …?'

'Morag! Remember? We met in Freshers' Week? It's so lovely to see you again!' I said, immediately regretting this silly level of enthusiasm.

'We did? I don't remember, I'm afraid.'

I was so embarrassed; I'm such an idiot.

'To be honest, I don't remember much apart from the cheap beers! Nothing personal, promise,' he said, as he sat down next to me.

My heart fluttered. Debbie appeared behind us and put her head on my shoulder.

'Hey Jamie! Do you have a light?' she said, holding her unlit cigarette.

'No, but I've got an Anglepoise lamp you can borrow, if you like,' he said.

'Would she have to travel the entire bulb for that?' I said.

'No, she'd just have to plug up the courage,' he said.

'And get herself amped,' I said, feeling stupid again.

Jamie's big, generous laugh was the best sound I'd ever heard.

'You guys! I'll get a light from someone else,' said Debbie.

I over-laughed. It was either nerves, or the joy of finding someone else with a love of terrible puns. Or the joy of meeting someone as wonderful as Jamie. We became inseparable from that moment; I was nineteen, he was twenty-one.

It's super lame and everything, but we tell everyone we were *just light* for each other.

Jamie and I lived in Cape Town after we got married. And when Jamie felt his job was going nowhere and he wanted a change, he started looking elsewhere. When he found a job in London he liked, he asked me what I thought. It seemed to be a good time for a change, we were heading too fast towards our forties, and we decided to give London a go.

We were both burnt out, to be honest. We'd had some big challenges to deal with, including losing both of my parents in quick succession and all of our failed attempts at getting pregnant and everything. If anything, London would give us a chance to try something new (see point 1), and Jamie and I promised each other we'd make an adventure of it.

So we left our lives, our home, our family (Jamie's, anyway), our friends, our security, our jobs, our summer, our world. We left everything that was safe and familiar.

We sold our house, reduced our belongings into two suitcases and leapt into the unknown. Well, into a Boeing 747, to be honest. We'd booked a cheap bed and breakfast in London until we could find a place of our own. That, and Jamie's job, were the only sure things we had. Oh, and of course our sense of adventure and point 1. Everything else we'd have to figure out when we got there.

It began with an early-morning arrival at Heathrow. No welcoming party, no fanfare. It was quite weird arriving in London and to our new lives, all alone and everything.

It took us two weeks to find a flat that we liked and could afford, and once Jamie started his new job at the university, I thought it would take me only a few weeks to find a job. Not that I'm amazing or anything, but because the odds would be in my favour. There'd be lots of jobs in a city like London, hey? And the UK was starting to emerge out of a major recession, so there'd be loads of new jobs around too, hey? Boy, was I wrong. Not about the recession or loads of jobs and everything, but about the odds being in my favour. I totally overestimated my chances.

I spent six months job hunting. It kind of became my full-time job – not that you get paid for doing it or anything, obviously, but because I spent about eight hours a day at it. I applied for any job that looked suitable.

Some of my cover letters were ridiculous, really, because I've never really known how to demonstrate my competence or anything. Rejection emails came flying in faster than my applications went out, making it difficult for me to stay positive and keep applying for more jobs.

Here's something to know about me and applying for jobs:

1. I'm completely useless.

The rejection letters had reasons like:

1. There were other candidates whose experience matched the job requirements more closely.

2. The employer has decided not to go ahead with the appointment.
3. We're going out again to recruit the right candidate for this role.
4. You don't have any local experience.
5. You're too nice for this role.

No offence taken for numbers 2, 3 and 4, but number 5 was my favourite rejection reason. I'd applied for a job in a large charity, and the HR person invited me for an interview in a coffee shop inside a gym in Chelsea. Why the hell would she want to interview me there? She asked me questions and "listened" to my answers while she slurped a frothy cappuccino and tore apart a flaky croissant with her fake fingernails. If she'd asked me to show her my not-so-nice side, I could have done so, easily. But you don't think about doing that in an interview, do you?

This is how I feel about interviews, if I'm honest:

1. I can't fucking stand them.

(Please excuse the language throughout – living and working in London can sometimes make you a bit sweary and everything. Although I miss my parents, I'm glad they're not around to read this book. They'd just hate my language. You'll understand when you find out more about them later.)

Some interviews felt like I was back at school. For one job, the HR Officer met me in the reception area and she was breathless.

This is how our interaction went:

HR Officer: 'Sorry I've kept you waiting. Will you walk this way, please?'

I followed her up the stairs and did my best at copying her walk.

Me, trying to break the ice: 'It looks like you're having a busy day.'

HR Officer: 'You're just trying to find out how many people we've interviewed today, aren't you?'

Me: 'No ... I was just noticing you were in a hurry, and you seem busy and everything, bitch.'

(I didn't really say that last word, although I wish I had. She made me feel so stupid and, well, what she said was just unnecessary.)

She showed me into the test room, pointed to the desk and the clock on the wall. She slapped the test paper down.

'Look, you have thirty minutes for this test. I'll turn the paper over at 3pm, and come back to take you to the interview at 3.30pm. Am I clear? Any questions?'

This is what I thought:

1. 'Piss off. What am I, eleven?'

This is what I said:

1. 'Okay, no worries. That's fine. Thank you.'

(Something else I should tell you about me is that I quite often say 'no worries' when I'm thinking completely different thoughts.)

I did the test. To be honest, I find those tests quite enjoyable. When you're left on your own to think, your writing flows more easily. Why can't interviews be more like that, with less pressure? I might do better in them. Or not. Who knows?

At 3.30pm on the dot, the HR person opened the door and escorted me and my test into a giant boardroom, with six interviewers spread around a table the size of a small farm. There was no microphone to answer the questions that came to me from all directions. Is that what it feels like to sit before a select committee? I didn't get that job, *obviously.*

'Unfortunately your voice wasn't loud enough. And there were other candidates whose walk matched our requirements more closely.'

In truth, when the HR person called to turn me down, she offered me 'some advice, for free', she said. She told me what I needed to do to get a job, like she'd just got a word of inspiration from the great beyond and everything.

'What you need to do is this: you need to build up some *local* experience because that's what employers are looking for when they interview candidates for jobs. *Local* experience. Okay?'

Sometimes you just want to punch people in the face and everything when they say such stupid things and disguise them as insight.

I grew to hate the word "unfortunately". It's now one of my worst words. Here are my top three worst words:

1. Unfortunately.
2. Autumnal.
3. Nom-nom.

I also grew to hate the advice people gave you, and the pitying looks you got from interviewers when your answers weren't the right ones. And every unsuccessful interview you had – especially when you'd built up a whole collection of them – chipped away at your already withering confidence. You'd sometimes sob and sob and sob in desperation, when you felt you just couldn't get a job. You felt stupid, useless, anxious and everything.

(You know when you've been living somewhere for about six years or something and you suddenly realise you've picked up some local habits? Well, sometimes you say 'you' when you mean 'I'.)

In my worst interview ever, |I found the interviewers to be cold, unfriendly and, to be honest, quite horrible, and I was messing up my answers anyway. When one person asked me if I could give an example of a project I'd led that had gone well, they all sat back, stone-faced and arms folded, trying to stare the answer out of me.

The whole experience had been awful and I knew I'd hate to work there anyway. Nothing to lose, hey?

'No, I can't, actually. Nothing. Zero comes to mind. Sorry, I don't think I should waste any more of our time. I'm just going to leave, if that's okay,' I said.

The panel was shocked. They looked at each other and at me and back at each other again. None of them knew how to respond, and not one of them smiled. One asked me if I was okay, and if there was anything they could do. I said I was okay. I stood up, packed my notebook and pen back into my bag, thanked them, waved goodbye to their gaping mouths and walked out of the room.

I cried most of the way home – partly relief, and partly frustration and everything. But then deep down I felt proud of myself. I'd taken back a bit of power after I'd thrown it away in every single other job application and interview situation. Plus, what I'd just done was brave, maybe even pioneering. Well, maybe not pioneering if you think about the true sense of the word and everything, but it was brave. It was the bravest thing I'd ever done.

It was a bit of a tragic comedy, really, and if I'd told any of my friends I'd done that, they wouldn't have known whether to laugh or cry or high-five me. I don't know which I'd have wanted them to do either. But I also knew that one day I'd look back on that experience and laugh, because it is pretty funny if you think about it and everything. I guess that's what I'm doing right now.

So really, I was getting nowhere. You grow to hate it when people ask you how the job hunting's going, because people don't really know what to say when you say it isn't going well. Sometimes people look terrified when you tell them news that isn't good. They want you to feel better and they don't want to feel uncomfortable or anything.

Or they just go silent and never reply to your emails or messages or anything.

You try to remain stoic and optimistic and everything but boy, it's hard keeping up that front. You end up feeling useless and it feels like you'll never ever get a job again in your whole life. Never, ever, ever, amen.

I felt like I just didn't have the right script. You have your own innate shorthand and everything, where you don't have to explain what you mean because you know how things work in the world you know. It doesn't always work in another country. You don't know where to start, how to build the right kind of experience, or how to create a career path for yourself. You don't have that insider knowledge. That's what I was missing; that's what I told myself, anyway.

You have to work it out as you go along and it's not easy. You don't know what you don't know and, for a long time, you don't even know how to find out what you don't know.

But you just have to force yourself to keep going and to stop expecting you'll get another "unfortunately", otherwise you'll never ever be able to apply for another job again. Never, ever, ever, amen.

Chapter 2

When the job of storytelling manager at a charity called The HAMP (Helping you deal with Anger Management Problems) popped up in one of my searches, I steeled myself and applied for it. You get that kind of sick feeling when you press "send" because you know there's nothing more you can do. This is what can happen next:

1. You can get invited for an interview.
2. You can get an "unfortunately" email.
3. Absolutely nothing.

To date, I'd gathered about seven point 1s, three-thousand five-hundred and eighty-one point 2s and approximately seventy-one-thousand point 3s. Well, maybe not quite, but you know what I mean.

So I was chuffed but only a little optimistic when I got a point 1 from The HAMP, a week after I'd applied. An *actual* interview. But, after my seven interviews to date – of which I'd been successful in a total of approximately zero – I wasn't holding my breath or anything.

A few more things to know about me:

1. I've never been outstanding at anything. Not one single thing. I'm okay at a few things, but I'm mostly mediocre at everything, and I've never achieved anything major. Ever.

2. I don't often feel sorry for myself; I just know where I stand. Some people are destined for greatness, while the rest of us are here to make up the numbers. Only one person was born to be Nelson Mandela.

3. This might be a bit ironic, when you think about what I've said in point 2 and everything, but there are times when I wish the universe would just give me a frigging break.

My first interview was with Ruby Stanfield, The HAMP's Head of Communications at the time. (This is what we call communications: *comms*.) She welcomed me at the reception desk, was super friendly and everything, and made me feel relaxed straightaway. She asked me a few things about my CV and my experience, and then gave me a proofreading and writing test. After I'd finished the tests, she took me back to the interview room. I assumed she was going to ask me some more questions or ask me to run through the tests with her, but she just sat me down for a bit of a gossip.

She asked me where I'd got my dress (she went, 'Ah no!' when I told her I'd got it at a shop at the Waterfront in Cape Town – she hadn't even heard of the Waterfront, let alone the shop or anything, and she'd never even been to Cape Town). She asked what I was doing that evening, told me all her weekend plans, and told me a bit about her housemate. She overshared a bit, which I found a little embarrassing, but then Ruby was like that. She was lovely and everything, but this is approximately how many boundaries she had: zero.

I was over the moon when The HAMP invited me for a second interview. This time I met with Ruby and Mr Mathews, the Chief Executive. (This is what we call the Chief Executive: *CEO*.) They'd asked me to prepare an outline of features I thought would work well in their supporter magazine. I talked them through my ideas and answered their questions okay, I think. I was a bit more relaxed than

I had been in previous interviews and everything, not only because this was the first *second* interview I'd ever had, but also because now I knew quite a lot more about Ruby since my first interview.

Mr Mathews was quite formal and did a lot of unnecessary fact-sharing in his questions.

'I like your idea about featuring sports people who have previously made use of our services. Did you know that "eidolon" is a synonym for role model?' he said.

'No, I didn't,' I said.

'Who would be the first eidolon you'd feature?' he said.

He carried on asking what seemed to be trick questions like that and everything, and then asked if I knew where the terms "cut and paste" came from, or "crop", or that years ago people used to type out copy straight on to actual paper?

It was a bit unnerving, really. I knew some of the things he was talking about, but I wasn't sure if I was I supposed to know all the facts he'd gathered for the interview, or if he was just kind of showing off. He seemed to be the kind of person who would have good general knowledge, but maybe he also just bloody loved Google. He also told me how long he'd been the CEO at The HAMP.

'I can imagine how intimidating it must feel to have someone like me interview you, Morag. But let me tell you something that will astonish you: I can indeed still remember a time when I, like you, wasn't the boss,' he said, as he went on, and on, and on. And on.

It wasn't clear if that was part of the actual interview, so I tried to demonstrate my competence by putting on my very astonished face. How could I bring Mr Mathews back to the point, though? I was so glad when Ruby looked at her watch and brought the conversation to a close. Mr Mathews had left Ruby about this many minutes to say anything: one.

Ruby used that minute to tell me they had one more person to see that afternoon, and that they'd make a decision about the job after that. She said they'd get back to me the following week to let me know their decision.

I left really not sure if I'd get the job or not; it had been less of an interview, and more like a conversation you'd have at a wedding if you get stuck at a table with your friend's boring uncle, to be honest.

Anyway, on the bus home I went over and over the interview in my head and thought about all the ways I could have answered the questions better. I always do that, and then I obsess and dream about it the whole night and drive myself crazy worrying that I've made a complete idiot of myself. Because most of the time I have. So far I haven't proved myself wrong on that front, to be honest.

I was just starting to drive myself crazy when my phone rang. I thought it might be Jamie to ask me how the interview went, but it was Ruby. She told me they'd just finished interviewing the other candidate and they'd made a decision: they wanted to offer me the job. She didn't want me to wait the whole weekend for their decision, so she thought she'd call me straightaway.

I waited for a "but" but there wasn't one. When I realised she was actually offering me the job, I over-thanked Ruby. I can't remember how many times I thanked her; it was a bit embarrassing, really, but when you think about it, I'd just got a job. An *actual* job. In London. A real job. A full-time job. In *my* field and everything.

I'd waited *so* long to hear those words. So many interviews had ended with a "no", that I hadn't really allowed myself to think any interview – let alone this one – might end in a "yes". That's at the top of my list of favourite words. These are my top three favourite words:

1. Yes.
2. Disingenuous.
3. Whimsical.

So getting that "yes" after all those "nos", and all that time of waiting and everything, was amazing. It was the best feeling ever. I screamed and shouted and punched the air. (After making sure no one was watching.) I'd been tackling this huge beast called London for more than half a year, never able to wrestle it to the ground. Not even once. Not even close. And now I had.

This was the score:

1. Big Smoke: seven.
2. Morag: one.

I'd only needed one to win. That was six years ago.

Chapter 3

On my first day at The HAMP, I arrived at the reception desk in the lobby of our building and the guy I now know to be Richard Pilkington signed me in and told me where The HAMP's offices were.

'Third door to the left down there and all. Morag, is it?' Richard said, pointing at the sign-in sheet. He stood, yanked his trousers up, jerked his tie straight, and pointed me towards the corridor.

When I walked through the front door of The HAMP's offices, Ruby was waiting for me at the front desk. She made me a cup of coffee and took me into a meeting room for a quick catch-up. She ran through the sorts of things I'd be doing every day, told me about the comms team, showed me an organogram of the whole charity, and told me who I'd be working most closely with. And then she told me not to worry about remembering anything she'd just told me.

'You'll have induction meetings with all the people you'll be working with anyway, so don't stress about remembering everything,' she said.

To me it seemed quite funny and a complete waste of time, really, but it made sense if you thought about it and everything. After that, she took me on a walk-round to introduce me to my new colleagues. Our first stop was at a mountain of papers with a desk underneath it. You'd have to assume it was made of wood; the desks next to it were, anyway.

'Madison, can I introduce you to Morag?' said Ruby.

'Just a sec, Rubes, I need to finish this email quickly,' said Madison, either typing or bashing her keyboard to death.

'Madison is *always* busy,' said Ruby.

'Wow,' I said.

'Sorry, Rubes, I know, right? These people have been waiting for an answer from me for absolute aaaaages, and Mr Mathews has just told me we can go ahead. Just firing off an email quickly. *Hugely* important. Bear with, bear with ... there, pinged! Sorry, say again?'

'Madison, this is Morag Williams, our new storytelling manager. Remember I told you she was joining us today?' said Ruby.

Madison looked blank. The sort of blank you look when someone's talking to you in another language.

'The new David,' said Ruby.

'Oh, right,' said Madison, looking blank again.

(When I first joined the charity, I was referred to as the "new David" for about six months. David was an Australian guy who'd been in the role before me. I knew my feet were properly under the desk when people started referring to David as the "old Morag". It's quite funny if you think about it, really.)

'Morag's from Zimbabwe,' said Ruby, her voice going up at the end of the word "Zimbabwe". She looked at me, and I shrugged.

'Yes. More recently South Africa, though, but either is true,' I said.

'Phew!' said Ruby. (This is how she pronounced phew: *few*.)

'So it's Morag's first day at The HAMP and her first job in London. Morag, this is Madison Porter. She's our Senior Marketing Officer, and she's going to be your pod-buddy – your desk is right next to hers, over there. I'm sure Madison will make you feel very welcome,' said Ruby.

'Hi! Oh, yay! Sorry, what was your name again?' said Madison, who'd completely stopped listening to Ruby after the word "so".

'Morag.'

'Oh, right, sorry. I'm *terrible* with names. So when did you join The HAMP?'

'This is my first day.'

'Of course. That's marvellous,' said Madison.

(I'm not being funny or anything but, if you ask me, I don't think for one minute Madison believed that was marvellous.)

'How long have you been in London?'

'About six months.'

At no point in this conversation was Madison listening.

'Oh, right. They say it takes about five years to settle in anywhere, so you must be feeling like a local now after six years. Where else have you worked since you've lived here?'

'We've only been in London for six months, so I still have a lot of settling in to do. This is my first ...' Madison had already turned back to her screen. She started pounding her keyboard again, mouthing and moaning words as she slammed out her message. Boy, I wouldn't want to be the person on the other side of that email, if you ask me.

Ruby felt bad for me. Madison glanced up again, even more distracted.

'Soz, guys, *huge* deadline looming, and I need to respond to this email urgently. *Really* sorry to be rude, but let's chat later. Let's do lunch sometime. Once things slow down. A-all right? Anyway, welcome ... sorry, what's your name again?'

'Morag,' I said, to the back of her keyboard-bashing, not-listening head.

Madison has never "done lunch" with me. Ever.

Next, Ruby introduced me to Ash.

'Hey Ash, this is Morag Williams, our new David, yeah?' said Ruby. 'Morag, this is Ash Thomas, our graphic designer.'

'Oh hey, Morag,' said Ash. 'Ruby told me you were starting today.'

'Hi there. Sorry, I didn't quite catch your name?' I said.

'Ah, no worries! My name's Aashish but, unless you're my mother, you can call me Ash. Yeah?'

'Okay, cool. I don't think I'm your mother, not as far as I know, anyway' I said, laughing. Oh my goodness, what an idiotic thing to say.

Ash breathed in and breathed out the word, 'Yeah.'

'Nice to meet you, Ash,' I said.

'Likewise, yeah. How's your first day going, Morag?'

'It's great, thanks.'

'Information overload, right?'

'Oh yes, for sure, hey.' I mimed that my head was exploding and immediately regretted doing such a stupid thing again.

'Ha, sorry about that, Morag!' said Ruby. 'So like I said earlier, you and Ash will work together on pretty much everything. The words-and-pictures team, right?'

Ash smiled and rolled his eyes.

'I guess. Whatever you say, boss,' said Ash.

'Lol! So you guys have an induction meeting, right?' said Ruby.

'Yeah,' said Ash, again drawing the word out like a deep exhale. 'So Morag, I thought today might be a bit full-on for you, yeah, so I've booked some time in your diary for tomorrow. I'll also tell you about stuff coming up – some of it's slated for super soon. Yeah?'

'Sounds good.'

I gave Ash a double thumbs-up. No clue why I did that, but Ash smiled sweetly back at me, probably wondering how the hell he was going to work with such a loser. Maybe he didn't think that, but I worried for the rest of the day that he did. That stupid voice in my head and everything.

Ruby told me the rest of the comms team was in a meeting, so she walked me around the rest of the office. We popped into Mr Mathews' office and he didn't notice us at first – he was slouching in his chair, engrossed in looking at something on his phone. His brow was furrowed, and his tongue was lodged between his bottom lip and his teeth. He looked so funny, I wanted to laugh; Ruby squeezed my arm. She was struggling not to laugh too. She cleared her throat and Mr Mathews stood up.

'Sorry, chaps, just catching up on some social media chatter. The traffic's heavy there today, isn't it? Come in, come in,' he said, waving us into his office.

'Ah, not to worry, Mr Mathews, we don't want to take up any of your time. It's Morag's first day and we just wanted to say hello,' said Ruby.

(When Ruby said, 'We don't want to take up any of your time', this is what she meant: *'We don't want you to take up any of our time'.*)

'Indeed, it is your first day, Morag. Welcome,' he said.

'Hello and thank you,' I said, waving. (How stupid was that? I felt awkward and everything around him, but that was just *stupid* stupid.)

Mr Mathews waved back at me. Not sure if he was waving hello or goodbye but Ruby pulled me out of his office. He looked a little sad, like he'd wanted to share another meaningless fact or something. At a safe distance away from his office, Ruby bent over and laughed so hard she could barely breathe.

'Sorry, Morag, that's so unprofessional of me. It's just that when he makes that face when he's concentrating, I'm just, I don't know, *finished*! Every time!'

I didn't know whether to laugh with Ruby or to stand up for Mr Mathews. I know which I wanted to do, but Ruby could have been testing my professionalism on day one. I'll never know, really, but I decided to keep quiet.

'Also, when I joined the charity, someone told me Mr Mathews slouches like that because he's got no sodding backbone! It kills me to think about it.'

Ruby was laughing so much she snorted. I smiled at her and the only thing I could think of to do next was pretend to cough. Ruby composed herself and stood up straight, smoothing her skirt and taking a few deep breaths.

'Sorry, my love. As we were. I think I can breathe again now. Phew! So I also need to tell you Mr Mathews has retired from The HAMP, and he's got three weeks to go before he finishes here. And then we'll have an *awesome* CEO. She's this amazing Austrian woman who seems to be super well-respected in the charity world, and seems to be a popular leader and quite innovative in her thinking. That's what I got from her LinkedIn profile and her social media and stuff, anyway,' she said.

So Mr Mathews must have been waving goodbye. Ruby's news kind of perked me up a bit, I have to say. I was excited about the job and had absolutely no right to be picky or anything, but I'd been dreading having to work anywhere near Mr Mathews. Mostly because we could have ended up being the only ones in the kitchen at the same time, or we could have bumped into each other at the front door or something, and I don't know how I'd have coped with his trick questions.

I don't want to be mean or anything, but if my dad were still alive, this is how he'd describe Mr Mathews: a bore.

We carried on walking through the office. Some people Ruby introduced me to told me about their jobs in about two sentences, and others took *ages* and told me every single detail of their job, as if they were doing actual presentations.

When we got to Kevin Wells, the HR Manager, he quickly closed the windows on his PC and stood up. He and I had talked on the phone but hadn't met yet. Ruby asked him to tell me what he did and he clasped his hands together in front of his waist and recited a few clearly rehearsed lines about his job. He looked towards the far right corner of the ceiling and tilted his head to the right as he spoke. It was interesting, if gratuitous, that he mentioned how much he loved *Strictly Come Dancing.*

'We chatted on the phone a few weeks ago, hey?' I said to him.

'Yes. You're South African. And Zimbabwean. I wasn't expecting a whi– …'

'Kevin, you and Morag need to do some admin today, right?' said Ruby, rescuing Kevin from himself.

'Yes, that's right. Yes. I've booked a meeting with you for later today, in that small meeting room over there,' he said, pointing to but not looking at a door in the far corner of the office.

'Oh, right,' I said.

'Good,' he said. 'Do you like my new shoes, Ruby? I thought I'd try and break them in today, even though they're weekend shoes.'

'Those are great shoes, Kevin, yeah,' said Ruby.

'And do *you* like them, Morag?'

'Yes, they're super. Even on a Monday.' I just couldn't stop myself being such an idiot and everything, again.

'Good.' Kevin sat down, and opened the windows on his PC again.

Next Ruby introduced me to Tracy White from the fundraising team. She couldn't have been more different from Kevin if she'd tried.

'All right, Morag? You poor little fucker, working with Ruby and all!' she said, grabbing my arm and laughing.

Tracy's laugh sounded like a train riding over granite chunks. Harsh when you hear it from the other side of the office, and infectious when you're with her. A bit like her language and, as I've got to know her, a lot like Tracy in general.

I didn't take in much else on that first day, to be honest. By mid-morning, my other comms colleagues had finished their meeting and were back at their desks. Ruby introduced me to:

1. Wendy Coles-Davis, the direct marketing officer.

2. Mason O, the digital lead. (Mason told me his full surname, but said having grown up with people mispronouncing his Nigerian surname, he found "O" the easier option.)
3. Gennypha Coleman, the media and celebrity liaison officer.

They all seemed very nice.

'Oh, and by the way, if you're wondering what that is, it's your intro to the charity, Morag!' said Ash, pointing to a huge pile of papers on my desk. Not as huge as the one on Madison's desk or anything, obviously, but still pretty humongous.

'Oh, right. That's great,' I said.

'Yeah. It's the fundraising guide. Version thirteen. David said he'd scream if he had to look at it again, so we waited for you to proofread it. No pressure, though, but if you can go ahead and do it by Thursday, that'll be brilliant. It's going to print at COP on Friday. All right, Morag?'

'COP?'

'Close of play, Morag. Soz, we say that a lot here.'

'Oh, right. No worries,' I said, picking up a red pen. 'I'll start on this for you now now.'

'Now now?' said Ash.

'Sorry, hey,' I said. 'As in straightaway. I say that a lot too.'

Ash exhaled another "yeah". How could I be so embarrassing and still breathe?

'But now now can also mean a few minutes ago, or in a few minutes' time, or literally any time now or in the recent past or future. It makes no sense, sorry!'

'Right!' said Ash. 'David was also Australian but I never heard him say that!'

'I'm from Zimbabwe and South Africa, Ash, but no worries, hey – it's an easy mistake to make.'

(To be honest, it's really annoying and everything when people think you're from Australia or New Zealand when you're from Zimbabwe or South Africa, and vice versa. It's like calling a Scottish person English – ask Gennypha about that.)

'Ash, would you mind sending me the link to our style guide, please?' I said. 'Ruby said something about it earlier, and said it would be helpful when I have to proofread and everything.'

'Sure, I'll send it now now,' said Ash.

'Nice,' I said, and laughed.

That was quite sweet of Ash, if you think about it and everything. It was only when I laughed that Madison looked up. She'd already forgotten who I was and that I was going to sit next to her. She moved a small mound of her papers off the edge of my desk.

Here are three things to know about Madison and her desk:

1. It was, and still is, the messiest desk I've ever seen in my whole life. It's like a junk shop. It's full of papers, nail polish, notebooks, chocolate wrappers, tampons, lipsticks, newspapers, eyeliners and tea bags and everything. Madison never tidies it but sometimes she'll move a pile of stuff if she's looking for a coffee mug or something. And under her desk is just as bad. Once, when she had to unplug her PC, she climbed under her desk and moved broken brollies, odd shoes, Amazon delivery boxes, pizza boxes and box files out of the way to get to the plug. There was a big knocking sound as she came back out again, and Madison emerged rubbing her head but holding a top she thought she'd lost.

2. She never tidies up one thing on her desk or anywhere. Not one single thing, ever.

3. When Madison arrives at work, she throws her bag on to the floor and undoes her coat. She shrugs it off her shoulders and,

as it falls on her chair, she sits on it. And at the end of the day, she does all of that in reverse and leaves the building.

'Soz! Since David left, I've got quite used to having two desks to spread all my stuff all over. I should probably clear some of this away,' Madison said, as if she had to point out to me the state of her desk.

'No worries, Madison,' I lied.

Three other things to know about me:

1. When I say, 'No worries' rather than, 'No shit, Sherlock' or something like that, I'm just trying to avoid conflict. I have to feel really *really* riled to speak out and, when I do, my voice shakes. I really don't want people not to like me. I know it's weak and everything, but I've always been like that.
2. It really irritates me when the person I work next to has a messy desk, especially if their stuff spills over on to my desk and everything. I don't know why, really, it just does.
3. I love lists.

Mason made a trumpet sound with his mouth, jumped up and said, 'Right, who wants a drink?'

I know it always takes a while to get used to the culture of a new organisation and working in a new country, but I found it super shocking and everything when he asked that. I'd heard that people who worked in charities enjoyed a drink as much as the next person, but did they really start drinking this early in the morning, on a Monday, and while they were *actually* still working?

I waited to see who was going to have what but if anyone else wanted a glass of wine, I'd be down for one too.

'Ooh, basically I'd love a tea, cheers Mase!' said Gennypha.

'Me too,' chirped Wendy.

'Coffee, please. Cheers, Masey-Mase!' added Ruby.

So *that's* what it means when you offer someone a drink here. In southern Africa, mostly you'll say, 'Can I make you a cup of tea or coffee?' You'd say, 'Would you like a drink?' if you were offering an alcoholic drink.

'Morag? Can I get you a drink?'

'Yes please, Mason. I'd love a cup of coffee, if that's okay?'

'Sure thing. Milk, sugar?'

'Milk, no sugar, thanks hey.'

'Cool, NW!'

I'm so glad I waited before answering Mason; if I'd asked for a glass of wine, I'd have been super embarrassed and everything. Also, day one is way too early to plead South African-ness.

'Oh Madiso-on – anything for you?'

'You're very kind, Mason, thank you. But I'm all right thanks, my love. Peaked a bit early with my brews today.'

'I hate it when that happens,' said Gennypha.

'K. Lmk if you change your mind, yeah? That everyone?' said Mason, doing a full 360.

As he's The HAMP's digital lead, this is how he sometimes speaks: in acronyms. Some of them you'll know because you've seen them on social media and everything, but others he just makes up. He's quite funny, really. And he uses them ironically. I think.

And that's pretty much how I learnt how the tea rounds went in our pod. Everyone takes turns, although I've discovered Madison usually says, 'Ooh, I was just about to offer – I'll do the next round,' or, 'I must be in so much tea-round debt by now,' but then hardly ever settles it. And, well, you'll hear soon enough what Storm's like when it comes to tea rounds.

So that's the whole long story of how I got this job. My first day at The HAMP now feels so long ago.

Chapter 4

'Come on guys, we *have* to evacuate the building! This is *not* a drill!'

Storm Macleod, our now head of comms, gets bossier than ever when she puts on her high-vis vest. (Storm joined The HAMP about four years ago, when Ruby left to work at a bigger charity.)

'We have to get out of the building,' Storm says, licking the grease off her fingers from her late-morning bag of crisps. (This is what I call a bag of crisps: *a packet of chips*.)

'Not *again*,' everyone groans.

The alarm drones on.

'That's so stupid. Why do we have to evacuate the building when we're all so rammed?' Madison's in the online queue for tickets for some festival or other, and sneezes like a cat vomiting.

'Grief, Madison, your sneezes always give me a fright. Anyway, it's a long story. Come, come, guys, let's go, let's go!' bosses Storm, clapping her hands, crisp crumbs falling out of her mouth.

Kevin's flustered and looks at his phone. This is the exact time he needs to take his sandwich out of the fridge for lunch. He hates it when his plans go awry. (This is how I used to think you pronounced awry: *oary*.) He puts a post-it note on his screen to remind him to do that as soon as he's back at his desk. He does a few twirls behind his chair before heading for the fire escape. Everyone else is whingeing and tutting and rolling their eyes.

Warren Rankin is always doing stupid things. He was chewing his pen lid while he was making tea, and it caught on his lip. So, for fun and because that's what he's like, he tried levering it off with the gravy baster. (I have no clue why we have a gravy baster in our kitchen.) He hooked the pointy end of the baster into the pen lid and levered it with such force the pen lid hit the window on the far side of the room, and almost pulled his bottom lip off. But when the baster levered back, it got caught in the hem of Warren's jumper. (This is what I call a jumper: *a jersey*. In southern Africa, anything woollen is a jersey, and it's often the only thing you need to keep you warm through winter.)

Anyway, the baster got *really* caught in his jumper. And because he'd hurt his lip and given himself a fright and everything, he leapt around the kitchen trying to pull his jumper off over his head. He bumped into the toaster and switched it on with his elbow. The toaster is old and dodgy and often sets off the smoke alarm anyway, but because it's also full of crumbs, this time it caught alight.

Talk about a ridiculous sequence of events. You couldn't make it up, I don't think. Well, you could but no one would believe you.

I'm just standing at the kitchen door instead of evacuating the building, watching Warren; he's still jumping around, and smoke is still coming out of the toaster. It's not clear if Warren's trying to jump towards the fire escape to leave with everyone and can't see where he's going because his head is still inside his jumper, or if he's still trying to get the baster out of it. Or if he's trying to stop the smoke by flapping his arms and everything. Anyway, whatever he's shouting, it sounds quite sweary.

Storm pushes past me, picks up the fire extinguisher and blasts it like a bazooka, soaking the toaster and Warren in one go. She grabs a yoghurt from the fridge and yells at Warren, who probably can't hear her through his now-soaked jumper. But at least the alarm has now stopped.

'You *have* to leave the fucking building, Warren! You've triggered the alarm and it's all about health and safety. Everybody else is leaving, and we need to go too. Come on, come *on!*'

Storm shoves me around and flounces past me to stand guard at the door and eat her yoghurt. She hardly looks up as we walk past to assemble at the meeting point outside.

When Warren joins us outside, he's still wearing his soaked jumper but his head's sticking out of it now. His hair is dripping, and his lip is *really* swollen and bleeding a bit.

'So that'll teach me to do something stupid ...' Warren lisps. 'I know what you're all thinking: something *really* stupid. Yeah? But not in a bad way.'

Ash, who's the other fire marshal, blows a whistle to get our attention. Mason is standing beside him.

'Guys, give me your names so I can tick all your names *orf* the register, yeah? Hey Morag, you hear that? *Orf!*' he says.

'Yep, that sounds good to me, hey,' I say, mock-applauding Ash.

(This is how I pronounce off: *orf*. You'll probably join my colleagues and tease me about it too.)

'I'm being my authentic self, Ash. Thanks for showing your humanity and everything.'

'Whatevs, Morag. Thanks for going all *values* on me,' says Ash, doing one jazz hand. 'Now come on, guys, I've got to submit this register to HR. Come on, come on!'

I'm not sure who the blond guy is who walked out ahead of Wendy, but Ash takes his name down anyway. Behind him, Jasper Vaughan, the intern on reception, gives Ash his name, leaning to one side as he speaks.

'Yeah, I know you're Jasper, cheers,' says Ash.

'Really?' says Jasper, pushing his fringe back as his eyes dart between Ash and Mason. He swaggers off, with a backward glance at them both and then a bonus one at Mason.

Storm scrapes the last of the yoghurt out of her tub, licks her fingers and gives Ash a thumbs-up.

'Yeah, got you, boss,' says Ash.

Storm looks around and asks if anyone else is hungry. Loads of people say they fancy a sandwich from that new pop-up down the road.

'Ah, bollocks, don't have any dosh with me,' says Binny Bradley from fundraising.

'Not to worry, guys, I don't mind ordering and paying for us all and then you can just pay me back if you like. Today, though. Is that okay?' says Madison. No idea why she's speaking in a Lancashire accent.

Madison takes our orders on her phone and says she'll email us her bank details so we can pay her back as soon as.

'Soz, guys, still paying off my student loan. Not a lot of spare sausage and mash, yeah,' she says, now in a terrible cockney accent.

The blond guy offers to go and fetch the sandwiches but Madison turns him down in her annoying, patronising way. (I'm surprised she was listening, though, to be honest.)

'Ah, bless you, my love. Thank you, that's *so* kind of you to offer. But not to worry, though, I've asked them to deliver to us here at our tree. They should be here any minute. Aa-all right? Tha-anks. *Really* kind of you to offer.'

He says, 'No worries,' and looks at Storm.

'Is it okay if I leave now, Storm, or is there anything else you need me to do?' he says.

Storm also answers him in her annoying, patronising way.

'Ah, Tom, yes, of course you can. Sorry I was about to tell you you could leave. If you can go ahead and send me some examples of your work as soon as you can, that'll be *super* helpful. All right?'

'I think I sent you a few examples the other day, Storm. Remember

I mentioned them at the beginning of the interview today? You said you weren't sure if you got my email?' he says.

'I know, I do remember that, Tom, but this will just be easier. A-all right? Send it as soon as you can, and put "urgent" in the subject line, so I won't miss it. Is that okay? Super. Have a lovely day, and thanks again for coming. It was *super* helpful chatting to you and *really* lovely to meet you.'

'Yeah, lovely to meet you too, Storm,' says Tom, smiling.

'Cool. Okay, so I'll touch base with you again next week or the following one, all right? As soon as we make a decision, yeah? All right? Super. Thanks, Tom, tha-anks, bye. By-y-e.'

'Sounds good. I look forward to that, Storm. That's exciting. See you!' he says, with a little wave, and a skip in his step.

'I was in the middle of interviewing him for a freelance role when this whole thing kicked off. But no fucking *way* he's coming to freelance for us,' says Storm, studying her yoghurt tub for final scrapings. 'He's got no shitting *clue* about how the media works. Complete waste of my time.'

Here are two things to know about Storm:

1. She can be quite hypocritical.
2. She never reads emails.

Ash tells us we can go back to the office but most of us still have to wait for our sandwiches.

Chapter 5

Warren's the Executive Assistant to our now CEO, Pauli Gerber. She joined The HAMP not long after I did, and she's literally turned the charity around. This is what we call her: Coach.

Warren and I met each other in the kitchen soon after I'd joined the charity. Although he can often be quite awkward and everything, he's super friendly and seemed to want to help me feel at home at The HAMP straightaway. I've never forgotten how kind he was to me.

He told me about the best lunch spots near the office, showed me how to book meeting rooms, and invited me to join the office quiz team (he's the captain). I didn't, because I'm pretty useless at quizzes and everything, but he said that was okay.

Here are three things to know about Warren:

1. He's really popular – *everyone* likes him. Not only because he's friendly and everything, but because he's genuine, and an all round good guy. He doesn't talk about other people, he doesn't say one thing to you and mean another, and if you need someone to help you run some letters through the franking machine because you don't know how it works and you're a bit scared of breaking it or something like that, he'll always help. Not everyone at The HAMP is like that, trust me.

2. He's quite easily distracted. He often watches cricket on his PC,

or does those online quizzes and stuff, when Coach has asked him to prepare the meeting room for the Trustees meeting or something. And sometimes he'll make it super obvious because he'll look up from his PC and share some random fact like, 'Did you know it's considered animal abuse to own a guinea pig in Switzerland?' when he's 'in the middle of writing up the minutes from the Trustees meeting'.

3. He has a huge crush on Karo Adams, from IT. He thinks it's a secret, but everyone knows except Karo. She's quite often in her own little world or something too, so she doesn't really notice much. They're sort of made for each other, really, if you think about it. Karo just doesn't know it yet.

We're The HAMP charity. It's quite funny when Coach says the name of our charity, with her Austrian accent; this is what it sounds like: *The HUMP*. It's kind of appropriate, if you think about it and everything, but to be honest, it's also *super* inappropriate and offensive.

Here are some things to know about our charity:

1. We counsel people and help them manage their anger effectively. We're here as their first port of call, and the National Health Service, or NHS, might refer people to us too.

2. We want people to know it's okay to feel angry; it's a healthy emotion and a valid and appropriate response and everything. But when anger spirals out of control and becomes rage, then it's a problem. We're here to help people recognise the difference. (Coach says when you repress your anger, you're paving the way for passive aggressive behaviour, anxiety, antisocial or even criminal behaviour, or something. She'll be pleased I didn't waste this opportunity to tell you, too.)

3. We have a huge team of volunteers who counsel people online

or over the phone, run support groups, and offer face-to-face counselling.

4. We campaign to raise awareness about anger because there's a kind of stigma around anger, and it gets bad press and everything. We've developed a toolkit for the media, who often trivialise or belittle anger management issues.

(We don't like to use the word "we" too much in our content, because our work isn't about us but about the people we help. So the list I've just written isn't on charity brand or anything. It's on message, though. *Big* difference.)

Soon after Coach joined the charity, she ran workshops to develop new values because she felt the ones we had weren't "fit for any purpose". We emerged from the workshops with these new values:

1. Authenticity.
2. Honesty.
3. Accountability.
4. Humanity.

We called the outcome our "AHAH" moment, which is quite funny and clever if you think about it and everything. Coach briefed Ash and me to put together some materials so we could display our values where everyone would see them. We now have posters on all the bathroom mirrors, as backgrounds on our PCs, on the kitchen walls, on our office windows. Coach also has a chalkboard outside her office, where she notes an "AHAH-er of the month" (a stand-out example of someone demonstrating one of our values in their work).

We're all getting a bit sick of seeing these values everywhere, if I'm honest, but one thing's for sure: if you ask anyone at The HAMP what our values are, they'll be able to tell you straightaway. And we do strive to live to those values too. That's the point, I guess.

People often say it must be so amazing to work at a charity that does such great work. They say we all must manage our anger well and must all have good communications skills and tools for conflict resolution and everything. I usually say either of these things:

1. Are you kidding me?
2. Nope.

When you work at The HAMP, you have access to all the services on offer and a set of values to guide your behaviour. Coach encourages you to do the volunteer training because she believes it gives you a good grounding and understanding of what our work is about. She says it makes you a better fundraiser and communicator, a better colleague and a better person and everything.

I respect what Coach says but that's an astonishing stretch of the imagination, to be honest. The values and training are good, and they help you when you have to talk about the work of the charity and everything. But six years on, I know this to be true:

1. Even "AHAH" values can't cure arseholes.

Chapter 6

Simon Bindford, The HAMP's chair of trustees, is coming in to the office today. He has two meetings: one with Madison, so she can show him our conference photos, and one with Storm and Chester Proudfoot, our finance director. Simon arrives at the front desk and tells Jasper, the intern, that he's here to see Madison. Jasper stands up and tugs at the cuffs of his floral shirt.

'Good morning, Mr Bindford. I'll call Madison for you.' Jasper looks like he's about to curtsey.

'Not to worry, young man, I can see she's at her desk. I'll go and surprise her, yeah?' says Simon.

'Oh goodie! That'll be *so* much fun,' says Jasper, clasping his hands to his chest and leaning to one side as Simon walks off.

Simon's one of those people who walks with his whole body: his chin, his head, both arms and hands, both legs from top to bottom, and the entire length of each foot. It sounds weird, but I'm sure you know what I mean. Some people walk with just the top half of their bodies, with their shoulders and heads hoping to get to their destination first, and their legs going along for the ride. Simon's way of walking looks tiring, if you ask me.

'Sorry to crash in on you,' he says as he arrives at Madison's desk, darting his eyes around the office.

'No probs, Simon! We *love* seeing you! Don't we, Morag?' says

Madison, in her best posh English accent.

'And I you,' Simon says, winking and doing a weird click with his teeth.

I look up and smile, sort of. (This amazes me: Madison has noticed I'm here.)

Here are a few other things to know about Madison:

1. She will often recruit you into her opinion, which can be super awkward and embarrassing and everything. Especially if you don't really agree with her opinion about the person standing at her desk.

2. Most times, the minute you start talking to her, she stops listening. Her face goes into a kind of screensaver mode, and you may as well talk to the wall. If Simon or anyone else important is talking to her, or if she's waiting to ask you for something, *then* she'll listen. Or she'll *look* like she's listening. Or point 3 comes into play.

3. When she needs to have you on her side, she'll pretend to listen and make boring stuff you tell her sound like the most interesting thing she's ever heard in her whole life. Like she's really interested when she isn't at all interested, or even really listening. (She'll say, 'Marvellous', even if you've told her your dog's just died.) Or if she needs something from you, she'll say, 'Ah, you're someone who's good at this, can I pick your brain?' (Come to think of it, that's quite a strength, really, especially when you work in marketing.)

Madison chats to Simon for *ages*. She can be good at adding words to conversations about any topic. She'll do anything for her career, even if it means forcing herself to listen. Classic Madison, if you ask me. Simon makes the corniest jokes ever and Madison bursts out laughing, throwing her head back. She's added some extra hair-flicking today and has given herself a bit of whiplash – she winces and rubs her neck.

Talking of rubbing, here are three things to know about Simon:

1. When he's talking to you, he rubs his hands together like he's putting on hand cream.
2. He shifts from foot to foot until his feet are just wide enough apart to look awkward; it takes him a few goes to get it right. It's a bit weird and everything, but there's something quite endearing about a guy standing at ease, with his legs awkwardly akimbo, and then deciding they need to be just that one small step further apart.
3. Every time there's a trustees' meeting, he invites us to have sarnies (this is what I call sarnies: *sarmies*) with them at lunchtime. He doesn't want there to be a divide between governance and action, or words to that effect. A bit patronising, but it's also quite kind, really, if you think about it and everything.

While he's chatting to Madison, Simon leans forward and touches her shoulder as he looks at her screen. He looks around the office, hoping people are watching him.

'Right, let's have a look at these conference photos, then,' he says in his loudest voice, glancing around again. (This is how he pronounces conference: *comference*.)

'Here we go, Mr Bindford, sir. Ready for your close-up?' says Madison, this time in a Scottish accent.

Madison often changes accents, depending on who she's speaking to. Sometimes she'll go all jolly and cockney, and throw a whole lot of terrible rhyming slang into her conversation. Other times she goes for posh, or Cornish, sometimes Welsh. She's okay at accents, but it's weird and a bit offensive to try and suck up to someone by changing your accent, if you ask me.

'Hmmm, I wonder who *that* bloke is in shirtsleeves in the background there. Hmm?' he says too loudly again. 'That one over there?'

He points at the screen and looks around but still no one's looking or saying anything. Madison over-chortles.

'Oh, I don't know. Maybe he's only the *chair of trustees,* hmm?' says Simon.

Madison slaps her thigh.

'Good one, Simon!' she says, laughing as if that were an actual joke. Everyone else carries on staring at their screens.

Another thing about Simon, which is a little sad really, is that he can look smug and disappointed at the same time. You kind of feel sorry for him when he looks like that. I often wish he were as funny as he wishes he were.

He pulls himself up straight and asks Madison to show him some more photos. Madison gives him a double thumbs-up.

'Gotcha, Mr Bindford, sir! Job's a good'un,' she says, this time in a Cornish accent, and rubs her neck again.

Chester's on his way to our pod. You can usually hear him before you see him; he walks like he's measuring the room. (Ash once counted and there were eleven Chester-strides between his office and our pod. He also once conned Chester into walking from one end of the kitchen wall to the other, because he needed an estimate to get a quote for a mural of our values on the wall, and it saved him measuring it out properly.)

When he gets to our pod, Chester looks so happy he's about to burst. He and Simon haven't seen each other since our conference. When they see each other, they jump up and down, clap their hands and swing each other around and everything. That's what they do in their minds, probably, but in reality, they high-five each other. It's kind of the same thing.

Chester stops in front of Simon for the high-five. He's too far away and loses his balance, stumbling forward a bit. He rights himself and stands stiff-legged and awkward, planting his hands on the back of his hips. Chester probably has magnets on his palms and the back of his hips and, when he stops striding or he stands up from a chair, the magnets draw together.

'You aren't here by any chance to discuss the big cover-up with the finance director, are you?' he says, swinging his body around to look in the direction of his office. 'I'll see if he's available, shall I?'

'If, by that, you mean the annual report cover story, then I believe I am. It's the only show in town, I hear,' says Simon. 'I came in early to have a look through the conference pics with Ms Porter here, and I'll join you in your parlour at my allotted time, oh finance director, my finance director.'

'I thought you were a bit keen, getting here so early. Can't get enough of this,' Chester says, pointing at his whole self.

The two of them laugh like drains and high-five each other again. This time they only just make contact. They look at each other like they're both waiting for something else, so Chester swings his right arm forward in a rallying kind of way and says, 'Let's crack onwards,' before his hands land on his hips again.

Chester's catchphrase of 'let's crack onwards' doesn't really make sense and it's super annoying and everything, but it's also his kind of full-stop. Whenever he leaves an awkward conversation he's started and can't sustain, or he's just high-fived someone and doesn't know what to do next, he flings his right arm forward and says, 'Let's crack onwards'. And when he wants to close a meeting and he feels awkward and doesn't know what to do and everything, he says that and claps until everyone leaves the room.

When Chester starts walking back to his office, he tries a bit too hard to saunter. He spins round, as if he's forgotten something, and catches my eye. He strides back to my desk, and goes straight in for the high-five with *me*! My worst. It's so awkward and everything, and impossible to avoid. I have to stretch to make our hands connect.

'Pppwwooogghhh!' He shows all his teeth in an unnerving grin. His lips don't seem wide enough for his mouth, so when he smiles it looks like his teeth are crowning.

'What's the high-five for, Chester?' I ask.

'Morag, Morag, Morag. Someone's been out of the loop, haven't they? We've only gone and filled another recycling bin in three days. *Three days!* See what happens when someone like me drives things like this? This Charity Recycling Award Prize work is gaining traction and we're in touching distance of winning,' he says, straightening his tie and looking to see if anyone in our pod is impressed.

'And nowhere near touching distance for the high-five.'

I immediately regret saying that.

'What was that?' says Chester, looking back at me.

'I was saying we're in touching distance of the high prize, for the Cash for CRAP scheme, hey?'

'Exactly! Isn't that something?' he says, looking around for anyone else to high-five, but everyone's avoiding eye contact.

Here are three things to know about Chester:

1. He has a healthy, perhaps over-developed, sense of his own importance.
2. If he's not interested in what you're saying, he fiddles with his tie and looks at his watch and fingernails.
3. When he's trying to make a point, he does this weird thing with his hands that looks like he's folding linen.

He saunters back to his office, basking in the glow of his awesomeness.

Ash and I have a briefing meeting in the Tight-head Nook today, with Ronda Brown from events. She's bringing her new assistant, Shaquille Josephson, too.

'Oh hey, guys,' says Ronda. 'You know my colleague, Shaquille, yeah? He's my new assistant.'

'Hi Shaquille, welcome to The HAMP,' I say.

'Thanks,' he says, and turns bright red.

'Where did you work before?' says Ash.

'At Boots in St Albans. I live there.'

'In Boo–' Ash stops himself.

Shaquille gives us both a fleeting grin and returns to his blank expression. If ever anyone didn't look like his name, or look like he's up for any banter, it's this shy, young, blond-haired chap from St Albans.

'Well, thanks for meeting with us today, guys. I know you're super busy with one thing and another, but Shaquille has a killer idea that has *huge* potential,' says Ronda, splaying her hands. 'Honestly, it'll blow you away when you hear it. It totally blew me away, you know. When me and him had our blue sky session yesterday, it was amazing. We was just riffing, bouncing ideas around and stuff, as you do, and he came up with this idea. I was like – why have we never thought of this before, you know?'

Poor Shaquille looks terrified and embarrassed. He keeps staring at the table.

'Isn't that right, Shaquille?' says Ronda.

'Yes,' says Shaquille, swallowing hard.

'Okay, then, take it away!' says Ronda, swinging both arms towards the timid young man who'd rather do anything else in the whole wide world than take it away.

'Okay. So. You know how everyone always finds it hard to sell charity places at the London marathon?'

'Well, I'm not sure that's really the c–' says Ash.

'Hear him out, Ash!' says Ronda. 'Carry on, Shaq.'

'Okay. So. You know how everyone loves giving everyone else presents? I've done some research.' He darts a look up at each of us. 'The research says when you give someone a gift you feel seventy-one percent better than you did before.'

'And quids down for days, yeah?' says Ash.

'Ash! Shaquille, you pitched the idea so brilliantly to me yesterday. Just keep going and try to ignore these guys, yeah,' says Ronda.

'Okay. So. You know how The HAMP tries to make people feel better, right? So I thought we could ask people to buy marathon places to give to their friends as gifts. And then everyone will make everyone feel better.'

'Seventy-one percent better.' I can't help myself.

'Thanks, Morag. And then? Remember the last part, Shaquille?' says Ronda.

'Right. Okay. So. Then everyone makes more money and we meet our targets.'

'Stick to the script, Shaquille, remember?' says Ronda.

'Oh right,' he says, paging through his notebook. 'I think I've forgotten the last part. Oh, here we are. When everyone makes more money, we …'

Shaquille reads from his notes and says the last few words in unison with Ronda.

'… can help more people manage their anger!'

Ronda claps.

'Isn't that genius, guys?' says Ronda. 'I can't believe we've never done that before. Can you?'

Ash and I are fresh out of words.

'So, we'll just need you guys to go ahead and package this for us, write the key messages and all the copy and stuff, and badge it up.

Then once we have all the content in place, we can share the assets and tweet about it. We'll have to make sure we have the resources to deal with the uptick in responses.'

Ash puts his hand up like he's stopping traffic.

'Okay, guys, I have a question or two for you.'

Ronda glares at Ash as if he's just helped himself to her pencil case.

'Sorry, I'd just like us to take a few steps back, first?' adds Ash.

'Okay, sure, sure, sure,' says Ronda. 'That's a good place to go, I guess.'

'Yeah,' Ash exhales. 'You're so right. Okay, so forgive me if I've misunderstood, but we're asking people to buy a gift for a friend that will mean they will have to train for about six months to run twenty-six miles or whatever it is in a marathon, yeah?'

'Yes! It ticks *all* our strategic boxes as a charity. Mental well-being, physical well-being through sport, committing to a long-term goal and achieving it. It still blows my mind that Shaq came up with this idea,' says Ronda.

'Okay,' says Ash, wiping his mouth with his hand. 'So they have a charity place – now we're asking them to fundraise what is it, like £1,200, while they're training?'

'Yes! Bonus! Well, it's more like £2,000, but isn't that amazing? They'll get our free fundraising pack. Soz, but we'll need that too, yeah? So they have loads of options. Isn't it just the best idea you've ever heard?'

Ronda pats Shaquille on the shoulder.

'Well, you were the one who said th–' says Shaquille.

'Thank you, Shaquille,' says Ronda, putting her hand up.

Right now, I'm pretty sure I'm way more embarrassed than Shaquille is. I have no clue how to respond to this idea, and Ash isn't saying anything else either, so he must feel the same. We stare, silent and incredulous, at the two people across the table from us.

'It's a lot to take in, I know,' says Ronda, taking a noisy breath in through her back teeth. 'Hope that's enough of a briefing for you guys. So soz, but we'll need to send this out by the end of the week. This one has a tight deadline.'

As if Ronda's ever given us anything but tight deadlines.

'You're going to have so much fun with this, guys! Go forth and be creative, lol. Any more questions?'

Ash and I don't say a word.

'Can't wait to see how you bring Shaq's idea to life. Thanks, guys!'

Ronda and Shaquille get up from the table.

'Before you go,' I say, 'do you know how many places you'll need to sell this way?'

'*That's* a very good question, Morag,' says Ronda, looking me up and down. She sits down and makes a note in her book. 'I'll have to check that and get back to you. Nice!'

'Guys, another quick question, yeah?' says Ash. 'Has Coach signed this idea off?'

'Another very good question. You guys are good, you know! I'll chat to Coach, but she'll love it, absolutely love it!' says Ronda.

Shaquille tries to fold his arms but his notebook gets in the way.

'So should we wait to hear from you guys first, before we do anything?' I say.

Ronda nods. 'I guess so, guys. She'll love it, though.'

Ash and I look at each other and then watch as Ronda follows Shaquille out of the meeting room. Ash drops his head into his hands, and I lean back on my chair. When Ash lifts his head, he takes a deep breath.

'That's the shittest idea I've ever heard,' he says.

'Mmhmm,' I say.

'Yeah,' Ash exhales. 'We'll never hear another word about that idea again, I can tell you. Never.'

Here are a few things to take away from that pointless briefing:

1. That's half an hour Ash and I will never get back, ever.
2. I'm sure you're not even allowed to buy a marathon place for someone else. But if you were, there isn't a single person in the whole world I would give a gift like that to. Not only would I be about £50 down, but the other person would have to train for about six months, fundraise £2,000 and then run an actual marathon. I'm not a researcher or anything, but the person you give the gift to could well end up being seventy-one percent less happy, if you really think about it.
3. I might be wrong and everything, but I'm pretty sure Ronda and Shaquille didn't think this one through.

Chapter 7

'What a flipping waste of time,' Ash says as we get back to our desks. He mimes his head exploding; he always teases me about that since I did it to him on my first day, and felt such an idiot.

'I have no words–' I say.

'About what?' says Storm, as I put my notebook down.

'You don't want to know, Storm,' I say.

'Okay, good.'

Storm has a unique way of managing her team's morale: she doesn't give a shit.

'See you in there, Ms Macleod?' says Simon, who's appeared at our pod again.

'Yes, I'll be there in two ticks, Simon,' says Storm.

Simon and his whole body walk to Chester's office and when they get there, Chester steps out of his office to high-five him. As the two walk in, Chester taps the sign on his door that says *Chester Proudfoot – The Finance Director*. Storm rushes in after them.

According to Storm's outlook calendar, this meeting is to discuss "Annual report – strategic direction and celebs". This is what she means: talk crap and then choose an influencer whose picture we can plonk on the front cover.

It's strange to think Storm called a meeting with three senior people to decide on the cover story for the annual report, and didn't involve anyone who works on the report. Ash and I should be in the meeting too, but Storm told us we didn't need to be there because that would be overkill. *That* would be overkill?

We're going to decide on the rest of the content at the cross-charity think tank meeting next week too, to "generate organisation-wide buy-in and organic collaboration". But Storm says this is an important publication and it requires a *strategic and intentional* decision, upfront. Storm has to be involved in any conversation that involves *strategic and intentional* decisions about comms. It's a rule. Well, not an *actual* rule but this is what Storm calls it: a rule.

The thing is, in my experience, collaboration is good but *strategic and intentional* decisions from upstairs aren't always practical. Or even right. The higher-ups will often want montages of images for the cover "to show the breadth of our work". Our supporters' stories tell the story of our charity much better than a gallery of literal images crammed on the cover of one publication. Plus, Storm's brief for the annual report is to create a "strong, authentic, organic publication that has dynamic cut-through amongst the white noise of other charities' publications". Good flipping grief.

To be honest, Ash and I could come up with our own concepts for the whole report without using up anyone's time. Our supporters understand what we do; we don't need to bash them over the head with it. Nor do we need to serve it up to them in a series of images of celebrities or influencers, who either supported us once or whose backgrounds might "chime with our core work". But that might just be me.

Storm and Chester are both *mad* about celebrities and influencers. Obsessed. Chester's latest fixation is McKayla, the young Scottish influencer he's following on social media. A couple of years ago, she started filming herself thinking out loud and posting her videos online, and now she has millions of followers.

It seems Chester and her other followers can't wait to find out what she feels like for supper, how frustrated she gets when her mascara clumps, or how annoying her younger brother is. The self-styled "unboxing guru" even got a place on *Strictly* last year.

'Big up @McKaylaFluencer for your work on #strictly. You deserved to win; your a great dancer and a sheero to many. You go girl. #mckaylarobbed #glitterballformckayla.'

It can be quite embarrassing for The HAMP when Chester tweets like that from his work account. Not just because of his spelling or his cringey slang and everything, but also because he grovels over anyone *slightly* famous. He'll find some reason to tweet at them, hoping he can invite them to come to our conference or join "our tribe", as he says.

It's more so that *he* can meet them, but still. His tweets are mostly harmless and everything but, despite the "all tweets my own" caveat on his account, he's only one tweet away from making an idiot of himself. And of The HAMP.

As for Simon, he's kind of indifferent about celebrities and he has little experience in comms. He's in this meeting because he chairs the Trustee Sub-Committee for Celebrities, High Value Donors and VIP Engagement. (It's also called the CHVDVIPE Sub-Committee but no one can ever remember that acronym.) Also, his sister, Charlotte, is a journalist at one of the red tops and she can sometimes be a good contact for celebrities.

Charlotte is keen to help and everything, but to be honest it's a bit of a stretch to call the people she tells us about "celebrities". You usually have to Google their names because either you've never heard of them before or you're not sure they're still alive. But, as Storm says, we're not exactly one of the big charities that everyone's heard of, so we take who we can get. Actually this is how Storm usually puts it: beggars can't be choosers.

Two minutes into their meeting, Storm opens Chester's office door and whistles across the office. She points at Ash and me and we look at each other and behind us.

'No, *you* guys. Come, come, come! You're supposed to be in this meeting!'

'It's not in our calend–' says Ash.

'What*ever*, Ash. Move it!'

We grab our notepads and move it.

Chester has a small meeting table in his office, with four chairs around it. Ash wheels his office chair in while I look around for the spare chair. Storm has settled into her chair, with her A4 notepad, *Hello Kitty* pencil case and a tub of curry in front of her. She pushes her chair in for me to get past to sit next to her. As Ash sits down between Storm and Chester, Simon stands up, squeezes past me and Storm, and walks out of the office.

It's an awkward five minutes of silence until Simon returns, carrying three mugs of tea.

'You two were late so unfortunately you missed Simon's tea round,' says Storm, with not one ounce of irony.

Here are three more things to know about Storm:

1. She says she *never* has time to take a lunch break because she's *so so so* busy, so she always eats her lunch in meetings. (In what world is she *so so so* busy, I wonder? It's a fair question, to be honest.)

2. Her real name is Susan. She says someone at uni gave her the nickname Storm, and she likes to go by it because she really likes it. She thinks it's ahead of its time, and maybe it was before it wasn't. She says it's because her surname is Macleod, and Storm Macleod sounds like 'storm-a-cloud'. (It could also be because she's loud and scary and can potentially ruin your day with one

of her outbursts, but I've never asked her that. Obviously.)

3. Storm never does tea rounds. Ever. If you skip her out of a tea round, she'll always shout, 'Ooh, can you make one for me too? That would be super helpful; I'm absolutely rammed – I have to finish this board report. Thanks, lovey. *Really* strong with not too much milk. No sugar. Super. Tha-anks.' So you can't really *not* make her tea. Ever. It's so annoying.

Storm claps her hands. Not the palms or anything, just the ends of her fingers. This is what I call it: a storm-clap.

'Right, guys, I'm *so* excited! Aren't you? This could be *huge* for our charity, moving forward. *Huge!*' says Storm.

(Storm calls *everyone* guys. If she met the Queen, she'd probably say, 'Thanks, guys, milk and no sugar for me, please,' or something like that.)

Storm opens her curry and points to it.

'Hope you don't mind, guys?' she says, not waiting for an answer before starting to shovel it into her mouth.

Chester steeples his fingers, and nods and winks at Storm, Ash and me before looking at Simon. Like he knows something we don't, or he's about to be told he's getting an OBE for recycling or something. (This is what his whole life's ambition is: to get an OBE.)

'Right, guys, I don't have a *huge* amount of bandwidth today, so shall we get on with it?' says Storm, with her mouth full. 'We've got a lot of ground to cover as you know, and it seems Chester has made a contact…'

'Sorry, Storm – may I?' Chester interrupts, folding a small tea towel with his hands. 'Sorry, but I think it'll be better if the finance director opens his kimono here. The one with actual skin in the game, okay? Given that this is the annual report, hmmm? Sorry, would you mind?'

'Go ahead, Chester. Sorry.' Storm salutes Chester with her fork.

'So as Storm was starting to say ... I was with a group of other finance directors at a high-end work function last week in Kensington. You see where I'm going with this? Yeah?'

None of us has a clue where Chester's going with this.

'Well, I met someone there who I think will be a top guy for our cover image. I met Johnny Cheetham!' says Chester. 'He's a perfect fit.'

'Oh, wow,' says Storm, to either Chester or her curry.

'Oh, right,' says Simon. 'Remind me where I know that name from?'

'People, people, people! Don't you remember? Or am I the only one who's brought his brains to the meeting today? Hmmm?' Chester steeples his hands, presses them to his lips and taps his fingers together.

'He's the guy who came third in *Britain's Got Talent* the year that dog won, yeah?' says Ash.

'Yes, Ash, you win this round. He's an amateur contortionist. Cheetham is, not Ash – lol!' says Chester, laughing and snorting. 'Do you remember him? He folded himself into a wheelie case – not one of those big ones, but one of those ones you take on board with you. So funny and clever,' says Chester, now folding the teeniest-tiniest cloth.

'That's a useful talent,' says Simon, smiling.

'And I think he spoke about having mental problems too,' Chester says, looking to Storm for approval.

'Chester! We don't *ever* use that language. Good grief!' Storm points at him with her fork but still doesn't look up from her curry.

'Sorry. I'll bow to your superior knowledge, shall I, Storm? He *struggled with anger*,' he says, using air quotes. 'Is that better?'

Storm nods.

'Anyway, he was amazing! Don't tell me you're going to disappoint us all and not remember him? This is *your* field, isn't it, Storm? And you people's?' Chester points at Ash and me.

'Or am I wrong? I thought *you* were the comms team, yeah? Surely *you* remember him. Isn't it *your* job to deep-dive into lists of celebrities whose stories chime with ours?' Chester's now folding a whole bunch of hand towels.

'I know hi–'

'It's all right, Ash,' Storm interrupts. 'I've got this. Er, Chester, of *course* I know who he is. Duh.'

'Oh, I remember him too, now I think about it. It was a while back but if I remember right, I voted for him, actually,' says Simon.

'Good, that's very interesting, Simon,' says Storm. 'But guys, I'm sorry to have to be a Debbie-downer here, but I need to nip this discussion in the bud. That ship has sailed. Moving forward, we're not going to go ahead and link ourselves with Johnny Cheetham.'

She continues. 'In the abstract, his story might jibe with ours but I don't know if you remember, he said something after the final that caused a huge uproar on social media. He said he was just trying to be funny, but it was super creepy and inappropriate; offensive, even. We just can't go ahead and link ourselves with him. He's just not *us*, you know. And, of course, it wouldn't do our rep any good.'

Storm always over-pronounces the word "rep". And say what you like about Storm, but when it comes to "rep" stuff for our charity, she's *on* it.

'Oh yes, at the risk of mission creep, I was just about to say I didn't really think he was the right fit for us, either. You know me – ever the disrupter!' says Chester, shrugging his shoulders and darting his eyes between all of us. 'Just throwing this into the mix. Keeping you on your toes. Controversial, I know. But at the end of the day, what do I know? I'm only the finance director.'

'Yes,' says Storm.

'Oh right, Storm,' I add. 'I kind of remember the Twitter-storm now.

He lost a *lot* of followers, didn't he?'

'What was it he said?' says Chester.

'You don't want to know, to be honest,' says Ash.

'Ash is right, we can't repeat what he said,' says Storm.

'Can't, or won't?' says Chester.

'Won't,' says Storm. You just *know* she's going to tell him later anyway.

'Okay, any other ideas on anyone else's radar?' says Simon. 'Chester, you'll have other ideas – you're always telling me you're not a one-trick pony.'

'That I am not indeed, Simon. You're on point. Let me think,' says Chester, tapping his chin. 'Unle-ess ... would we consider approaching McKayla? You see where I'm going with this?' Chester's voice goes up when he says these words: "McKayla" and "this".

Storm pats his hand.

'Chester, Chester, Chester. She's got her own charity. Remember, we talked about this the other day. She's now an ambassador for the hen charity. I thought you'd read about that – it was all over social media.'

Storm can be super condescending if you give her time.

'Just for info, all over *what* media, Storm?' says Simon.

'It was everywhere, Simon. All over ... erm ... her Insta, I think,' says Storm.

'Oh right, fair enough. Bad suggestion. Bad finance director. I told you – what do I know?' says Chester, fiddling with his tie and looking at his watch and fingernails.

'Let's focus on other options, and don't forget this needs to be about our actual work,' says Storm, focusing on her curry.

'If I may, who's going to pick up a publication with a picture of angry people on the cover?' says Chester.

'Chester! Language!' Storm wags her fork at Chester. 'But let me teach you guys something today. Ash, Morag, you may want to take notes: it's a comms principle that we tell our story best when we use *authentic* images of how we help transform people's lives. We support people who have anger management issues, right? We can't and won't try and disguise that. Yeah?'

'Fair enough. Consider me taught, and put in my place,' Chester says, saluting Storm.

'Breaking news, to be fair,' says Ash, not even disguising his sarcasm.

'Anyway, while we're all thinking, anyone want to hear a joke?' says Chester, who has zero skill in reading the room. 'I have only good ones; you won't be sorry. Hmm? Yes?'

Simon looks to Storm for approval. Her forefinger says no.

Here's another thing to tell you about Chester: he *loves* telling jokes. I don't understand his sense of humour or his jokes one single bit, to be honest, and my heart sinks when he asks me if I want to hear a joke, because I know I'm going to hear one anyway. No matter what you say, *all* he'll hear is "yes".

Those moments fill me with dread because I know I won't laugh or understand it or even *know* when the punchline is or anything. The punchline is usually when he looks at you and waits for you to laugh, but I'm usually looking at my feet because I can't bear feeling so awkward and everything.

The worst example was in my first or second month at the charity, when Chester caught me at my desk as I was about to go out for lunch. I'd just stood up.

'Before you go, Morag, do you want to hear a joke from the finance director? Hmm?' he said, looking around our pod.

'Who's the finance director?' I said, not even trying to be funny.

'Nice one! You're only looking at him,' said Chester, poking himself in the chest.

'Oh, right. Of course! Well, I'm about to go out for lu–'

'Thought you'd say yes. All my friends say to me, ooh Chester, you must be such a fun boss, right? Always telling jokes, always having a laugh, yeah,' he said, his eyes looking down each time he said the word "always".

'You have fr–' said Ash, but Mason put his hand up to stop him.

I just couldn't bear the risk of not understanding his joke, so I fell back down on to my chair. I told him I felt like I was about to faint and needed to put my head between my knees. He said he'd wait for me to sit up because I'd love the joke. I waved my hand up at him and said – from between my knees – that I needed fresh air.

He still didn't go so I stood up and ran out of the door, and I heard him offer to tell the others the joke. There was a chorus of voices saying they had to take phone calls, go to meetings, finish emails and everything.

It was pretty stupid of me to do that but it was the only thing I could think of to avoid hearing his joke.

'Sorry, Chester, I don't mean to cut you off, but let's circle back to the issue at hand here, shall we? Yeah?' Storm circles her hand with the fork in it. 'We're drifting across the field and we need to ladder back to the agenda point, yeah? I have a hard stop at 2.30, back-to-back meetings this afternoon. Let's make what time we have left count, yeah?'

'Right you are. Of course,' says Simon, looking disappointed. He's one of the few, no he's the only person I know who says he enjoys Chester's jokes. Chester will make sure Simon stays afterwards to hear this new one.

'So, guys, can we think of anyone else?' says Storm, closing her eyes to think. 'We need to find an image that really fits into our vibe here. An image that's really *us*, so our supporters will *get* us, you know?' She opens her eyes again to make sure her next forkful of curry reaches her mouth.

'Umm, what about that Northern Irish folk-singer who opened up about his anger issues on national TV?' Simon adds. 'He and his wife spoke openly about it; his anger was so bad, she left him. He was rock-bottom, realised he needed help, went for serious therapy, wife came back? Fab singer.'

'Got you, Simon! Gosh, that's a *lot* of detail. Great, yay!' Storm does a mini storm-clap.

'I think he's okay now and back in the recording studio. It could be a win-win if we reach out to him: he could be that perfect fit,' says Simon, holding his hands together and saying "perfect fit" out of the corner of his mouth.

'It could be good for his career restart to be connected with a good cause like us, and good for us if his career takes off again.' Chester's now folding a fitted sheet.

'Simon, is it Quinn you're thinking of? A singer-songwriter?' I say.

'Quinn. Of course. Yes, that's the one, Morag,' says Simon, poking his finger at me. 'He's brilliant. Love his covers too.'

'He's a bit of a grumpy old git, though, isn't he?' says Chester.

'Yeah, can be. You never know what to expect from his gigs. But he's a brilliant songwriter, though, and that *voice* …' says Simon, kissing his fingertips.

'He's a *bit* before my time, yeah,' says Storm. 'But then, a huge proportion of our TM is geria–, um, older adults.'

'TM?' says Simon.

'Sorry, Simon. I forget we're not all comms professionals. Another teachable moment: TM means target market. The people who support us, those we want to reach when –'

'Yes, Storm, I know what a target market is, thank you. I'd just never heard that acronym.' Simon sounds defensive.

'Nothing to be ashamed of, Simon,' says Storm, condescending from an impressive height. 'Okay, you know what, guys? We don't need to reinvent the wheel, yeah? He's probably worth trying to onboard, yeah? I'll get my guys to do some digging to see if he's a good match and there's nothing dodgy in his background, and then maybe Charlotte could reach out to his people, yeah, Simon?'

'I think so, Storm,' says Simon. 'Probably. She's been to Belfast and knows *so* many celebs, as you know. I tell you what, leave it with me.'

'Yes, I was going to say why don't you leave it with Simon,' adds Chester.

(Jeepers, this meeting is bloody exhausting. Strategic and intentional? A strategic, intentional and monumental waste of time, if you ask me.)

'Super! That'll be *super* helpful, Simon, thanks,' says Storm, licking curry sauce off her fingers. 'Let's shoot that one up the flagpole and see if it flies, yeah? Tell Charlotte I know a few paps over there who've worked with shlebs, yeah? And then, shall we touch base soon, so Simon can bring us up to speed? Yeah?'

Simon and Chester look at each other, shrug their shoulders and do those "why not?" expressions with their mouths.

'Okay, super. Just ping me when you know more, Simon. Will that be okay?'

Simon smiles and gives Storm a thumbs-up.

'Yep, I was about to say the same, Simon. Can you loop us both in, please?' says Chester. 'You know, when I suggested McKayla, I knew she wasn't the right fit. I was just getting you people talking, yeah? Getting your *creative juices* flowing. Not bad for a finance director, eh? After working with Storm and the gang all these years, the creativity has just seeped into me. I'm literally seeped in innovative ideas.'

'Thank you, Chester. Yes, not bad at all,' says Storm. 'Okay, guys, so action points moving forward: Simon is going to reach out to his contacts, including Charlotte, to see if any of them knows Quinn, and then he'll let Chester and me know. I'll keep you guys posted; we need to keep this higher up the food chain for now, yeah?' Storm points at Ash and me with her fork.

'Then I'll get Gennypha to look into him, to see if he fits our *crite*, and then we can catch up again. Hopefully we'll hit the road running and get the ball rolling to see if he'll be prepared to be featured in our annual report. Have I covered everything?'

'Thanks, Storm. A quick devil's advocate question from me, though, if that's okay?' says Simon. 'Why would Quinn want to feature in our annual report? What's in it for him? And, I mean, have we ever actually supported him or had anything to do with him? How would his story *jibe* with ours, as you say?'

'I knew someone would ask that. I'm way ahead of you, guys,' says Storm, tapping the side of her forehead. 'If we haven't supported him yet, I'm sure we can do *something* for him before the annual report comes out. And that'll give us a killer quote from him too, yeah?'

'Wouldn't that be a tadge disingenuous?' says Simon. 'Not being funny or anything?'

'No one's actually going to check, Simon. No one's going to ask him if we supported him before or after the fu–, the *actual* photo shoot and interview, are they?'

'Soooo, by *authentic*, we mean ...?

'Authentic. That's one of our AHAH values,' says Chester.

'Thank you, Chester, I think we all know that,' says Storm. 'And Simon, for goodness sake, we don't have time for this. We only have to *look* authentic.'

Storm pauses for a minute before continuing.

'Sorry, Simon. You do make a good point, though. But it's not a hundred percent relevant in this situation, yeah? *Authentic*,' she says, doing air quotes, 'is when our supporters say what we want them to say but in their own words. We can easily swing that in a pic and quote. You know what I mean?'

'Oh right, I see what you mean. Fair enough, Storm. *You're* the expert,' says Simon.

'You're right, thank you. Here at The HAMP we work best when we're all in our own lanes. Yeah?'

'In our own box...' adds Ash.

'Thank you, yes, that's very true. So are we clear on next steps, guys? Have I covered everything?' says Storm.

'More than adequately, as you *always* do, Storm,' says Chester. Sometimes it's hard to tell if he's being sarcastic or not.

'Okay, cool, super,' says Storm, storm-clapping again. 'Thanks, guys, for such an awesome meeting. It's been *so* much fun. Don't you just love being *out there*? Being *creative*? I think I've really taught you a whole bunch of new stuff today. It's been a sacred space, guys.'

(Not being funny, but sacred is the last word I would use to describe this meeting.)

'Absolutely, yes,' says Simon.

'So I'm just going to go ahead and excuse myself, guys, if that's okay? You guys can go,' Storm says, standing up and shooing Ash and me away. 'Off to my next meeting. Absolute 'mare of a day, back-to-back meetings, you know. *Never* ends.'

Storm rolls her eyes, licks her fingers again and chucks her curry tub in the bin.

'Think that could be recycled, Storm?' says Chester, pointing at the bin.

'Of course, silly me!' says Storm, retrieving the tub from the bin. Ash and I still can't get past her to the door.

'Thanks, team comms. I'm just going to stay on here, if that's okay – me and Chester have a few more things to discuss,' says Simon.

'Super! That'll be super,' says Storm. 'See you soon, guys. Okay thanks, guys, *really* good meeting. Thank you. Take care, tha-anks.'

Chester stands up.

'Let's crack onwards,' he says, swinging his forearm forward as Ash and I follow Storm out of the door. As Chester closes the door behind us, I hear him say to Simon, 'So this Zimbabwean arrives at Heathrow ...'

Back at our pod, Storm throws her notebook and pencil case down and grabs her bag before rushing out of the office for her "next meeting".

Ash and I look at each other and this time we both mime our heads exploding. Wouldn't it be great if drinks at work really *did* mean alcohol?

Chester *loves* Zimbabwe and talks about it whenever he gets the chance. He doesn't understand irony so he thinks telling jokes about Zimbabwe is still being supportive of everything Zimbabwean. (He doesn't understand racism or hypocrisy either, I don't think.)

When Chester found out I came from Zimbabwe and still had friends and cousins living there, he was so excited he nearly fainted. He high-fived me twice. He told me how much he loved the country and told me about all the places he'd visited when his love affair with Zimbabwe started. After two weeks in Harare in 1997, visiting a friend who was on contract there, Chester now considers himself an expert on anything to do with Zimbabwe. It's so jolly annoying.

'My friend introduced me to a fellow he knew, who was, you know, a *black Zimbabwean*, and he'd won a scholarship to study at *Oxford*,' he said, miming the words "black Zimbabwean" and "Oxford".

Chester looked at me as if this were the most amazing thing anyone had ever done in the history of anything, ever. Or because he'd met someone who'd done what he thought was the most amazing thing anyone had ever done in the history of anything, ever.

Zimbabwe is *full* of amazing, awesome, brilliant people, and it's not rare for a Zimbabwean to get a scholarship to study at a major institution anywhere in the world. Not that every Zimbabwean gets a scholarship or anything, but you couldn't go up to someone in Zimbabwe, for example, and say, 'Do you know that guy who got that scholarship to Oxford?' People would be like, 'Which one?'

Also, there are so many Zimbabweans who have done amazing and impressive things, it's hard to know who to be the most impressed by. Chester also doesn't realise how racist it is to be impressed by someone doing something amazing just because they're black. Or just because they're Zimbabwean. I suspect Chester now wants a Pride of Britain award because he once met a black Zimbabwean.

But other than a Pride of Britain award, Chester's biggest dream is to get an OBE, which he wants more than anything else in the whole wide world. He comments on other people who've got honours from the Queen, especially some of our funders and VIPs and celebrity supporters and everything, and he just can't disguise his envy.

'Ooh, they've got an OBE. Big deal. Big fat hairy deal. I wouldn't wear a suit like that to Buckingham Palace, would you? I'd make more of an effort, wouldn't you?'

He's probably already bought a morning suit ready for the occasion.

He's always putting us forward for recycling awards, in the hopes that will make him eligible for honours. His latest quest is for us to win the Cash for CRAP and, as he did when he told Storm to recycle her porridge tub and when he told me about filling the recycling bin in three days, he bangs on about it *all* the time.

He can be *so* annoying about recycling. He says he's concerned about the environment and everything, but it's more about getting some kind of recognition for himself because he's the recycling lead for The HAMP. He even once told us in a team meeting that we should always buy food wrapped in plastic so we can have more stuff to recycle. It seems a bit counter-productive to me, to be honest, but Chester thinks that'll help us win.

'When the finance director says we're CRAP winners of the future, he means it,' he always says.

Chester would stand more chance by entering us into the Charity Finance Team of the Year awards, but he says recycling is more on-trend and "sexier".

Whenever Chester says anything about his team, like, 'The finance team has only gone and done it again – we've got all our ducks in a row for the audit,' you know that by "finance team" and "we", he means Robyn Rownes, his finance manager and champion team member.

Chester is very clever, for sure. He knows what he's doing, there's no doubt about that. But because he's focused on so many other things, like recycling, trying to get an OBE, McKayla, being on-trend and everything, it sometimes looks like he's not on top of stuff. I'm not saying he doesn't have a clue or anything, but you do sometimes wonder.

It's quite funny, if you think about it, that his wing-person is called Robyn. In the story of The HAMP, would he cast himself as Batman, do you think? When you're a legend in your own lunchtime, you probably *would* cast yourself as the superhero, wouldn't you? In *my* story of The HAMP, though, Coach is the actual superhero.

Chapter 8

Pauli, our CEO, likes us to call her 'Coach' because she *really* loves sport and she says she sees us as a team rather than a charity. If anyone else asked to be called Coach, it would seem a bit cheesy and everything, but because Coach is Coach – and an awesome leader – we've always just gone with it.

Soon after Coach joined the charity, she told us there were loads of parallels between sport, and running a charity. Because rugby is her favourite sport, here are some of the principles she's asked us to embrace at The HAMP:

1. Rugby is a game of strategy, and so is running a charity; while you can't win a match without having and executing a game plan, your charity will go nowhere if you have no idea where you're going. Or, as Coach says, 'If you fail to plan, you plan absolutely to fail.'

2. If you want to succeed in rugby, you need to get out in front of the competition, be aware of your environment, train, play as a team, and have the resources you need for the full ninety minutes; the same applies to succeeding as a charity (apart from the ninety minutes).

3. Don't play in your own half. (I've never really understood how that one applies to a charity, to be honest.)

Coach has a reputation in the charity world not only for her original style of leadership, but also for her team-building skills. People haven't wanted to leave The HAMP since she became CEO, so that says something, doesn't it?

Coach says she learnt the value of teamwork from her years of playing rugby when she was at school and at uni, in her home country of Austria. The game is so important to her that she often speaks to us in rugby and team language and metaphors. It's the same as calling her Coach; if anyone else used that language and those metaphors in our office it would seem super-corny and everything, but it's Coach, so it's fine. And the funny thing is that it rubs off; we all often do the same too.

She's also renamed all of our meeting rooms, so Meeting Room A became the Scrum Room and Meeting Room B, the Tight-head Nook.

She used to work as a sports development manager for an international NGO, so she *really* understands and feels strongly about the value of sport in all other areas of life. She says it's the best way to manage our anger and take care of our mental well-being.

Here are three things to know about Coach:

1. She moved to the UK after she graduated because she hadn't yet come out to her parents and she wanted "to sow her wild oaks", as she says. When she did come out to her parents, they told her they'd always known.
2. Her long-time partner recently ran off with a colleague. Coach was gutted. She's never afraid to show her true, vulnerable self – being authentic is one of our values, as she says. Sometimes she wears a tough exterior like a scrum cap, but you can see it's just temporary protection for a gentleness underneath.
3. She is, hands down, the best boss I've ever had.

So Coach's big concern at the moment is that we plan well for next year's annual report. We've just had this year's one published and it's okay but, to be honest, it ended up being kind of pulled together at the last minute. And probably because no one was sure who was wearing the captain's armband. That's what Coach said, anyway.

It's super frustrating working like this. Ash and I do most of the work, but it becomes something of a vanity project for others. Storm wants us to put the report forward to win an award (this is what Storm loves the most, and wants as much as Chester wants an OBE: awards), and the development team wants us to create something compelling that focuses on our fundraising successes for our current and future donors.

I'm a fan of the latter approach, to be honest, but it often becomes a bit of a tug of war. Last year we thought Storm was leading on it, but she said she thought Chester was, and Chester thought Tracy was. So a lot of the details fell through the cracks. Or got kicked into touch, as Coach would say.

This year, Coach has kind of taken the lead on it. She's asked Storm to find a strong feature story and cover image (that pointless meeting), and she says she'll keep a few other potential leads on the bench until the planning is in full swing. Then she'll hand over the captain's armband.

She's arranged a cross-charity think tank meeting today. (This is what Coach calls a cross-charity think tank meeting: a *cross-fit think tank meeting*. This is what she also called it once: a *tank top meeting*.)

Another thing about Coach is that she often gets English words and expressions wrong. She finds it funny and laughs a lot when you tell her she's got something wrong, so you don't have to worry about offending her or anything. She's good like that. She also says she'd like to see us try and speak German, and who'd be laughing then? That's quite a powerful come-back, if you ask me.

Coach wants us to have a first-class game plan for the annual report. 'Prepare and don't piss on your performance,' she says. We know what she means, if she means preparation will prevent a piss-poor performance. You hope all the right people are listening, but when you know you're the one who'll be doing most of the work, you know you need to be the one with your ears the most open.

Today's think tank meeting is going to be a long one. I grab my coffee and run to the Scrum Room. You don't ever want to be late for Coach. She says it's disrespectful of other people's time to be late or not to start your meeting on time.

'Time is not a renewable resource; waste not, why not,' she says.

We know what she means.

On the dot of 9.30, Coach closes the Scrum Room door.

'Good morning, team! I can see you've put on your game faces today, which is excellent. Now, up on your toes,' she says.

Coach starts all of our think tank meetings with a stretching and exercise session. She says if we stretch and exercise our bodies, it opens up our minds and makes us more productive and creative. To be honest, she also just wants to wake us all up. Ash hasn't made it into the meeting yet, and nor has Storm.

There's a scraping of chairs on the floor as everyone stands up. Wendy yawns, Madison spills her coffee on her new suit and Chester's hands fly on to the back of his hips.

'Right, team, let's start by closing our eyes and doing some deep breathing, ja? In: one, two, three, four; hold: one, two, three, four, and out: one, two, three, four. Again, ja?'

Coach blows her whistle and gets us to stretch our necks and shoulders, and then to run on the spot. Wendy groans as she stretches her arms in the air, and there are more groans and moans as we start jogging on the spot.

'Come on, team, we need to keep it tight around the fringes!' Coach shouts, clapping her hands. Storm opens the door and comes in, porridge tub in hand.

'So sorry I'm late, guys. Trains. Such a 'mare.' (That's a bit of a weird excuse, even for Storm. This is how she gets to work: she walks.)

'Come in, Storm. Put your things down and join immediately us. You owe me two minutes of jogging on the dot,' Coach says, tapping her watch.

Storm does as she's told but looks super reluctant. Coach tells us to "wobble out" our arms and legs again before we sit down.

Coach has invited one of our volunteers to facilitate today's meeting. She loves working with volunteers and consultants. She says that even though she's our Coach, she likes the support of specialists to "home" our skills in other areas. She says they're like "conditioner" coaches.

'I'd like to welcome Alex Andersen, one of our volunteer trainers and our guest coach for the day, ja. Alex, this is my team. Team, please give Alex your full-time attention; we're playing for the full ninety minutes today. Alex, please do step up to the place,' says Coach.

As Alex gets to the front, Ash opens the door and sneaks in. He must have been in a rush this morning as he's not wearing a button-up shirt as he usually does. He's wearing a T-shirt with *No, I will not fix your computer* on the front.

He stage-tiptoes around to a spare chair next to Chester. Coach catches his eye and signals five; that's how many minutes he'll have to jog on the spot for, for being late. Coach never misses a thing.

Alex introduces herself. She's from Zimbabwe, and came to London five years ago to do her master's at King's College and decided to stay in the UK in the short term. (Bet you anything you like, Chester will ask her if she knows that guy he met.) She tells us she used our services when she was studying.

'It was so helpful to speak to someone on your helpline. That woman really talked me down off the ledge, hey. Not literally, but you know what I mean. It was tough being away from home, and in a world that's so different from mine – the weather, the food, even the jokes. I was near breaking point and everything was making me feel angry and irrational. I went from nought to a hundred percent angry, just like that. I didn't know why.

'My mom always says it's a sign of strength to ask for help. So I did, hey, and the person on The HAMP helpline was amazing. And non-judgmental. She gave me techniques to help me when I feel I'm beginning to spiral. Guys, I hope you know what a difference The HAMP makes, in ways you might never know or hear about, hey.

'I really wanted to give something back, so when I finished studying I did your volunteer training. I met Coach, and offered my help as a management consultant too. So, here I am, and that's my story. The short version, hey!' (This might make a good story for our annual report.)

'So now it's your turn to introduce yourselves. Please say your name and job title, how you came to work at The HAMP, and what you hope to get out of the meeting today. And then your top wish for the annual report.'

There's a lot of eye-rolling in the room. Most of my colleagues *hate* talking about themselves, but at the same time *some* of my colleagues bloody love talking about themselves. So one by one we stand up and do what Alex has asked us to do. Madison asks someone to remind her what the questions were, and then speaks for way longer than two minutes. This time she speaks in her own accent. As I've said, some of my colleagues bloody love talking about themselves.

When it's Warren's turn, he drags himself slowly out of his chair. In a lazy and coy and reluctant way, he kind of shuffles across the room. He *hates* being the centre of attention and probably imagines people won't look at him if he doesn't lift his feet off the floor when he walks.

He stands next to Alex, and we all look at him.

'So, my name's Warren, I'm the senior admin officer at The HAMP. I've been working here for seven years – the longest I've ever worked anywhere, to be hon–'

'Because you never *worked* anywhere else! Don't look like you do much here either, to be fair,' says Tracy.

'Nice one, Tracy. Cheers.' Warren blushes. The truth can sometimes do that to you. He laughs and looks at his feet.

There are sniggers around the room, and Alex raises her hand.

'Carry on, Warren. You were about to tell us how you came to work here,' she says.

'Right. Okay, yes. So, I was working at another charity and we used to do these pub quizzes against The HAMP team, right, and everyone always seemed so happy and got on so well. And you always beat us. So when I saw this job advertised, right, I spoke to some of you guys about it and off the back of that, I did some research on your website, and applied. And I got the job. That's me!'

Warren bites his lip and raises his eyebrows and nods a few times.

'Oh, and I'm hoping today we can plan well for the annual report to be a huge success. So everyone who gets it reads it, right, supports us, and tells their friends and families and colleagues about us. Yeah,' – he looks to the ceiling – 'now that's me!'

He rocks forward on his toes, raises his eyebrows, opens his mouth into a weird grin and nods again. Alex thanks him and tells him he can sit down.

'We almost don't need to carry on, hey? That was a great summary, Warren, thank you,' says Alex.

Warren blushes again.

Chester stands up, and his hands cling to his hips.

'My turn, yeah? I was about to say the same as Warren, actually.'

'Your name's also Warren, hey?' says Alex, with a smile.

'Haha, excellent, Alex! So my name is Chester, the finance director. I've *often* facilitated meetings like this myself and I find it quite a funny experience to be on the other side of the room today, which might account for the confusion.' While Chester speaks, he folds a few small cushion covers.

Alex folds her arms and nods.

'Thank you, Chester the Finance Director. No worries, hey. Go ahead and introduce yourself, and relax. Lucky for you, there's only one guest coach here today, hey.'

Chester rambles through his intro, then fiddles with his tie and looks at his watch, fingernails and around the room. Alex thanks him and invites him to sit down.

'Is that everyone?' says Alex, after Wendy sits down after two minutes of exaggerated self-promotion.

'I haven't gone yet,' I say.

'Okay, cool, go for it – I think you're the last,' says Alex.

'Last man standing,' I say, wiping my sweaty palms on my skirt. 'So my name's Morag Williams, and I'm the storytelling manager. I came to work at The HAMP by bus.'

Jeepers, what an absolute loser. Why would you say something so stupid in front of everyone? Some people do laugh, though, to be fair.

'Nice one, Morag!' says Tracy.

'Sorry, that was just silly. I've been at The HAMP for six years – well, apart from going home every night.'

There's literally no stopping this flow of stupid from me today. Oh my goodness, I'm the worst.

'So my hope for the annual report is that it tells our supporters' stories in a way that makes more people want to fund our work and more people make use of our services and everything. A simple story, well told, can do that. So that's my hope. That's me. That's all I have to s–.'

70

'Thanks, Morag, that's brilliant.'

Thank goodness Alex stopped me from myself, my all-time poorest performance, which I've saved for this whole group of people and everything. What an unmitigated disaster. I'm *such* a loser.

'Is that a Zimbo accent I hear?'

I nod, and Chester shouts out a "yes" too.

'Such Zim humour too. I love it!' Alex steps back into centre-stage. 'Okay, thanks, everyone, that was super helpful. Right, now please get up, and get yourselves into four groups. Try not to sit with your team – let's mix it up a bit, hey? We're more creative when we're out of our comfort zones,' she says.

Everyone stands up and moves around without getting anywhere near making four groups. Chester says he'll lead a group. There's a lot of tentative group-making, a ton of "sorrys", and a few of us walk around in circles or into each other before Alex stops us. She gives us each a number between one and four and tells us where each group will sit.

Chester adds, 'As the finance director, I was about to suggest that too, Alex. These people can *never* get into groups.'

He's dying to be on Alex's side of the room; approximately seven Chester strides away.

'So you're from Zimbabwe, eh?' Chester literally can't wait to tell Alex about the other black Zimbabwean he's met, like we've all heard a hundred times before. Coach stops him.

'Yes, that's right, Chester, although I don't think that's relevant right now, ja? Let's get into our groups, ja?'

'Of course,' he says. 'I was about to say the same thing. How long does it take to get into groups, eh?'

His hands fly back on to his hips as he measures the room in search of the other number twos.

Coach calls out, 'Shall we give our groups names, Alex? Or no?'

Alex says we don't have to think of names for our groups. Thank the Lord. That would have been absolute torture.

Wendy and I are in the same group and, to be honest, it can be exhausting being in any group with her. Wendy means well and everything, but she's really an over-faffer.

She stands up and gathers the small household of stuff she carries with her everywhere. She shoves all of her loose pieces of paper into her notebook, grabs her mug of rooibos tea and, with the same hand, tries to pick up her diary and the extra jumper she's draped over the back of her chair.

'Wendy, love, you've knocked the chair over, yeah?' says Madison, looking up briefly from her screensaver.

'Oh dear, that's what happens when you try to be too clever,' says Wendy, dropping all of her papers and unhooking her jumper. She spills tea on her shoes as she bends down to pick up her papers and the chair at the same time.

'Sorry, sorry, I'm almost there with you,' she says, from way down next to her shoes. 'The curse of the perfectionist. I was trying to do too many things at the same time.'

I'm not being unfair or anything but I'm not sure who Wendy sees when she looks in the mirror; it can't be Wendy. She probably sees a reflection of the person she'd like to be, and believes that's who she is. She calls herself a perfectionist and a details person and everything, and she *really* tries hard to be. But, to be honest, every one of her direct marketing projects I've worked on with her has been chaotic from start to finish.

Here are three things to know about Wendy:

1. When I first met her, I thought she knew everything. She talked like she did. But I soon realised that she'd only ever *heard* of

everything. *Big* difference.

2. Like Madison, she's also not a great listener. She has a huge imagination and a poor memory, and she loves a story. So when those elements converge, she'll tell you stories that aren't even walking distance from the truth. For example, you can tell her what life's like in South Africa, and she'll remember one or two details from your story, embellish them a bit and then incorporate them into a story of her own about living in Wigan. I don't think she got our values memo.

3. It sounds to me like she and her husband, Lance, believe they're much higher up in the world or, as Storm would say, up the food chain, than they are.

Alex has asked us to draw pictures on post-it notes of the elements that make an ideal annual report. Wendy says she'll do the drawings for our group because she did art at school.

'I don't get to draw much in direct marketing, but let's all play to our strengths,' she says.

I've never been much good at leading groups or anything, and anyway I worry my mediocrity will rub off on everyone else in the group. It's always better for someone else other than me to take charge. Madison puts her phone away and steps up.

'Okay, guys, so what I think we should do is this: let's think about all the elements that make a great annual report, and Wendy can draw pictures of them. Yeah?'

Literally what Alex has just asked us to do.

When Madison talks, she cups her hands like she's measuring and caressing a small coconut.

I suggest stories of people we've supported; Wendy draws a group of people. Madison suggests impact through media coverage; Wendy draws a megaphone. Mason suggests content you can repurpose throughout the year on social media; Wendy draws a mobile phone. Say what you like about Wendy, she's interpreting what we're saying with her drawings.

When Jasper suggests strong images, Madison says, 'There's no such thing as a stupid suggestion, guys.'

Alex walks over to our group to ask how things are going.

'We were just saying how much we're loving this exercise, Alex,' says Madison, completely forgetting that we weren't just saying that.

And so the cross-fit think tank meeting goes. We cover the walls of the Scrum Room with a whole lot of post-it notes, with drawings ranging from the out-there to the basic. In reflecting on them, Alex puts a pin in the less practical suggestions.

'So, guys, what do you notice about these drawings here?' Alex points at all the unpinned post-its.

'They're all on blue post-it notes, obviously,' says Tracy.

'Well, true, hey. But what's the common denominator? Morag?'

'Is it people?' I say.

'Yes! Guys, it's so simple, hey? The most important ingredient in your annual report – in fact in any external-facing content – is people. People you support. And those people have? Stories. The more authentic, the ...? Better. That's where you'll have ...? Impact.'

Coach walks to the front of the room.

'Thank you, Alex. You make actually a huge amount of sense, ja? We believe in people, don't we, team? Our people within The HAMP, our volunteers, our fundraisers, our donors, our supporters, those who rely on our services, and people who don't even know already about us. We believe in humanity, ja?

'So, Alex, you've given us grist for a meal. We'll find the right people and get their stories, and we'll make actually our best annual report yet. Ja? Storm, maybe we can win eventually that award that you're looking for, ja?'

Storm's eyes are on her phone, with that slack-mouthed look of someone who's supposed to be listening but you know they are:

1. Not listening.

I'm know I'm weird and everything, and look at the world a bit differently, but you can't pretend to make that face. I've tried and you absolutely can't.

Coach calls Storm's name again.

'Yes, Coach? How can I help?'

'Maybe we can win eventually that award for this year's annual report, ja?' says Coach.

A small storm-clap and Storm smiles at Coach.

'Gotcha! Yes, that's totally our direction of travel, yeah?'

'Okay, I thought so, Storm. Before we close, I want to ask if when you leave today, you'll put actually your thinking cups on for story ideas. If you have suggestions, send them to the comms team to discuss at their away-day, ja? And Morag, will you take the captain's armband on this, please?'

'Yes, sure, Coach. No worries,' I say.

This is the first time I've been given the captain's armband for this, and on a day when I've made such a fool of myself. I can't believe it. Coach is so awesome. I hope Storm will let me wear it.

'Good shout, Coach,' says Storm, swinging around to look at me. 'And Morag, I'm going to need you to go ahead and curate some really strong story ideas to share with me first, yeah?'

Coach responds to Storm's patronising two pennies' worth.

'Thank you, Storm, can you leave actually the armband to Morag, ja? She'll take it from here and she needs only your support.'

'Okey dokes. Understood, Coach,' says Storm.

Coach thanks Alex, and blows her full-time whistle. Warren takes down the post-it notes to give to Alex.

'Ah, thanks, but we've got what we needed, hey. Just pop them in the recycling, thanks.'

Chester will be thrilled.

I won't say the meeting's been a *total* waste of time, but Coach wasn't thinking straight when she brought sixteen people into a room for three hours for that. She sees the annual report as an important fundraising tool and everything, and she said she wanted to take a "braces and suspenders" approach. But I'm not being funny or anything; *nobody* cares that much about our annual report.

If Coach were to ask any of us in the comms team what makes a good annual report, we'd say people; our supporters and their stories. That's how you generate more support. It really isn't rocket-science. It's communications 101. Plain and simple.

It's like getting the entire Springbok rugby management team together to decide that if you want to win, you have to beat the opposition.

Chapter 9

After the cross-fit think tank meeting, Storm asks Madison to arrange a comms away-day. Madison sets up a WhatsApp group for the team.

Madison created "HAMP comms Away-Day Planning group"
Madison added you
Storm (the new Ruby): Guys, I asked Madison to start this group so we can share ideas for our away-day in early December.

Madison: Such a good idea, Storm. It's a great way to share ideas in a group like this. *Thumbs up emoji.*

Wendy New Phone: Meh+ *# toop., *snail emoji*

Mason: Ta, Madz. *thumbs up emoji.*

Morag: Thanks, Madison. *thumbs up emoji.*

Ash: Yeah, nice one, cheers Mazza.

Madison: Mazza? *laughy phase emoji* Let's get thinking, guys. *thinking emoji.*

Gennypha: Will do. *thinking emoji.*

Mason: Anything specif? AFF. Ta.

Storm (the new Ruby): Haha, Mase! AFF?

Mason: Soz. Asking for a friend.

Storm (the new Ruby): Ok. Agender to follow.

Morag: Did we decide a date?

Storm (the new Ruby): Next Tues the 4th. That same place near

Tower Bridge again. 9.30 start – don't be late.

Wendy New Phone: *poop emoji / //* nghsorry

Binny S: Hi comms-peeps, much as I'd love to join you, I think I might have been added to this group by mistake, so I'm just going to leave. K? So sorry, guys.

Madison: No worries!!! Soz, I meant to add Binny B from fundraising!!!

Binny S: No worries, happens all the time. #toomanybinnys

Madison: I'm sure!!! Must be so annoying!!! #wrongbinny

Binny S: *cryey laughy face emoji / cryey laughy face emoji / cryey laughy face emoji*

Binny S has left the group

Madison: *cryey laughy face emoji / laughy face emoji*

Madison added Binny B

Gennypha: *cryey laughy face emoji / face palm emoji /*

Binny B: Who dis?

Madison: Hi Binny!!! Sharing ideas for our comms away-day on the 4th.

Binny B: Smashing. Ta for add.

Madison: *thumbs up emoji*

Wendy New Phone: ~ ~# £

Ruby: Hi guys, I don't think I'll be joining this meeting from Italy! I probs shouldn't be in this group any more?

Madison: OMG, Rubes!!! I didn't know you were there this week!!! Have the best time!!! Not at all jealous!!!!!!! Soz, added you automatically – keep forgetting, even after all these years!!!!!!

Ruby: Great weather here, and the food is amaaaaazing. *tropical emoji / pizza emoji*

Wendy New Phone: No.

Ruby: Miss you guys!!! *kissing face emoji / kissing face emoji / waving emoji / waving emoji*

Ruby has left the group
Wendy New Phone has deleted this message
Wendy New Phone has deleted this message
Wendy New Phone: what
Wendy New Phone has left the group

It's our away-day today, and it's windy and pouring with rain when I leave home. They said on the breakfast news that the weather was going to be "disappointing" and "a little gusty" in London, so I run to the bus stop. The wind keeps turning my brolly (umbrella) inside out, making the spokes go wonky. (This is how I say wonky: *skwonk*.)

I get on the bus behind someone who's just sniffed her fingers and wrinkled her nose. I take a seat upstairs and try not to think too much about what that was about. Here are some things I've seen people do on the bus:

1. Pluck their eyebrows.
2. Cut their fingernails and toenails.
3. Pick their noses.
4. Dig wax out of their ears.
5. Other disgusting personal stuff.

As I get off the bus, it starts to pour again. My southern African instinct kicks in and, because the woman next to me doesn't have an umbrella, I ask her if she wants to share my skwonk one. She nods and we begin an awkward, yet intimate, four-block walk to her office. We should be chatting and everything, but we don't know one single thing about each other, even though we're walking almost arm-in-arm. It's such a relief for both of us when we get to her office.

I won't do that again; I'm such an idiot. It was so embarrassing and awkward and everything. And what's worse is that because her office was in a different direction from our away-day venue, I have to backtrack fast.

It's about twenty past nine by the time I get to our away-day venue. Mason's at the coffee counter in the downstairs deli. He nods at me as he stirs his coffee with a thin wooden stick, holding an unopened bag of Hula Hoops (*really* noisy crisps) in his teeth.

'Oh hey, all right? Have a good evening?' he says, taking the bag out of his mouth and putting the lid on his coffee.

'Not too bad, thanks. I did a bucket collection at Southwark tube station after work, and then an early night. You?' I say.

'Bucket collection at London Bridge. Made quite a few quid. Must be this,' he says, pointing to his face. 'Irresistible, cute me, lol.'

'Apart from those who pretend they can't see you when they walk past, hey?' I say.

'Obvs. Lol. Hardly slept a sodding wink last night, though, house mate's studying – always so bloody noisy. Crashing around the kitchen getting food every half hour. Might fall asleep in the meeting today.'

'Okay, I'll throw something at you if I hear you snoring! I hope it'll be a good away-day like last time. You can never tell with Storm, though, hey?'

'Oh God, don't,' he says, lifting his hand like he's stopping traffic. 'A riddle, that one. Confusing AF. Never tell what mood you'll find her in. Stairs?' He opens the door as I finish putting a lid on my coffee and follow him.

Storm's already in the room, putting flip-chart paper, post-it notes and Sharpies (this is what I call Sharpies: *neos*) on the tables. Her porridge tub is unopened. She looks up at the clock as we walk in. It's twenty-five past and no one else has arrived.

'Oh hey, Storm. All right?' says Mason.

'Not too bad,' she says, looking at the big screen. 'Would be better if people did what they said they were going to do.'

'Oh right,' says Mason. 'Madison said she'd be here early to set up the room, yeah?'

Storm nods.

'Yikes, someone's going to be in trouble.' Mason whistles.

'Can I help, Storm?' I ask.

'No, I'm just about done, thanks.'

Storm is *really* cross. When you're that cross, you won't accept help when people offer it, even though you really want someone else to do the crappy work you don't feel like doing. It's a bit pointless and counter-productive and everything really, but anger can make you childish, can't it?

'K. Sit anywhere?' says Mason, throwing his bag of Hula Hoops on a table.

'Wherever you like. Take your pick. Hardly a rush on seats,' Storm says, as she looks at the clock again.

The door opens and Gennypha walks in with Binny Bradley from fundraising.

'I normally just get a shower in the evening. But I was that uncomfortable after the night I had, I got one this morning too,' says Binny.

As Gennypha is about to close the door, Madison, Ash and Wendy walk in behind her. It's just after half-past nine.

'Storm, I didn't think you'd–' says Madison, wearing a stretched, wrinkled sweatshirt. Sometimes she comes to work like this, looking like she forgot to get dressed.

'Didn't think I'd what? Start at 9.30? With stuff to prepare?'

When Storm's really *really* cross and, okay, also when she's feeling sanctimonious and everything, she speaks quietly. It's quite unnerving, really. It's like the calm before the storm.

'Guys, guys, take your seats quickly please so we can get started?

Madison, you're doing the ice-breaker, and I'm *hoping* you've prepared for that at least, yeah? But there's something I need to do before we start. All right?' says Storm.

(She definitely won't be starting with Coach-style stretching and exercise, I can tell you that for free.)

We move around the room to grab seats as quickly as we can. It's like our version of musical chairs, when you all have to sit before Storm loses her shit. Madison's eyes dart around the room as Storm pulls herself slowly up out of her chair.

'Now guys. Please. I expect more from you. You're all adults, *senior* members of my team. When I say the away-day is starting at 9.30, it damn-well starts at 9.30, yeah? Not 9.35, or 9.40, yeah? As Coach says, we need to respect each other's time and not waste it. We have a lot of ground to cover today, and I have to say I'm *super* disappointed in all of you,' she says.

'Weren't *all* late, tbf,' says Mason, plucking a Hula Hoop out of the bag.

'Let's not get clever, Mason, yeah? I'm not in the mood for it,' says Storm.

Mason puts his hands up in surrender. And starts putting Hula Hoops on the end of each finger.

Storm sits down and opens her tub of porridge.

'Sorry, Storm, it won't happen again,' says Madison. 'It is my fault. I should have got here sooner and set up the room. Soz. The bus took a lot longer than I expected, but I probs should have left home earlier.'

Say what you like about Madison, when she's actually listening she knows what to say and she's not afraid to take responsibility for something she's done wrong. She demonstrates our accountability value; it's surprising and quite admirable, really.

Binny's hand goes up.

'Yes, Binny?' says Storm.

'Storm, not being funny or anything, but who are the *junior* members of your team?'

'Nobody likes a clever clogs, Binny,' says Storm, with a mouthful of porridge.

Madison introduces her ice-breaker and it's the one where you have to write on a piece of paper something no one else knows about you. You fold up your paper and put it on a pile on the table at the front, and then you each choose one and read it out. Everyone has to guess whose it is.

It's really funny, especially when we learn that Storm was a street-dancing champion when she was a teenager. No one guesses it was Ash who once went to a dress-up party as Madonna.

'Whaaat? Thought I was the only fan of Madge around here,' says Mason, striking a pose.

Wendy baffles us all when she says her best friend at school was Jamie Oliver. (We all know Jamie Oliver didn't go to school in Wigan, to be fair. Wendy must have claimed the story as her own when she read about his actual best friend at school.)

I lead the session on content planning for the annual report, and Storm says we should include a feature on that Northern Irish folk-singer Quinn, but no one's really heard of him. Binny says she thinks the public, and her fundraisers, respond better to stories of ordinary people, rather than celebs.

'But the strategic and intentional imperative for the report is to use a celeb, yeah? An influencer. That's what upstairs wants,' says Storm. It looks like she's going to try and snatch the captain's armband from me at some point.

'Is that a directive, Storm, or can we consider other options?' I ask.

'Whatever.' Storm picks up her phone.

'Okay, well basically, in my experience in fundraising, right, if we want to reach people who don't know about The HAMP, we need to show them the work we do *on the ground*, yeah?' says Binny. She speaks quickly until she gets towards the end of the sentence. Then she slows down and her voice goes up as she says each of the last three or four words as separate, staccato sentences.

'Look, I'm from Yorkshire, right, and they wouldn't see themselves in a story about Quinn or any other celeb using our services. But they would, if I told them a story about an *ordinary* person, right. Your average Joe who lives down the road, you know what I mean? Someone like Morag, for example, yeah?' Binny gestures towards me with upturned hands.

I do get what she's trying to say and everything, but I should also probably try to be better. Just generally. At everything. And not just be your average Joe. Or your flipping mediocre Morag.

'Thanks, Binny. That's a good point,' I say.

'Y'er all right, Morag.' Binny nods at me.

'Any other suggestions, guys?' I say.

'What about Alex? You know that Zimbabwean person from our cross-charity workshop? She said The HAMP helped her, didn't she?' says Madison, peering above her screensaver.

Two things surprise me about this:

1. When I first heard Alex's story at the workshop, I thought it would be a good one for the report. This must be the first time Madison and I have ever agreed on anything.
2. Madison had been listening.

'Is she *average* enough, though, Binny?' I say, immediately regretting my lack of grace.

'Haha, yeah!' says Binny. 'Too right. Didn't mean to offend, Morag!'

'I know, I know,' I say, laughing a bit too falsely.

'Basically, what I think Binny means is that anger management problems can affect anyone,' says Gennypha. 'We know that. But we need to focus on folk who really need our services, rather than people with huge resources, who would go private for help anyway. Is that what you meant?'

'Too right, Gennypha,' says Binny, biting her nails.

'I agree with you, Gennz and Binny,' I say. 'And with you, Madison. When Alex shared her story at the beginning of that workshop, I also thought she'd be a brilliant person to feature. And you're right, we need to find the right balance and everything, if we want to reach the right people. We don't want to put people off, hey.'

'Orf,' says Mason under his breath as Madison looks up briefly. I reach deeply again for some grace, and force a smile.

'Okay, guys, what I'm hearing here is all good,' says Storm. 'Some ideas we just need to kick down the road, yeah? But I still want us to reach out to Quinn, and get him into our annual report this year, yeah? Gennypha, can I get you to do some digging to see if there are any skeletons in his closet? Check there isn't anything that might not jibe with our story, yeah?'

Storm puts down her phone and makes a slicing movement with her hand as she says "jibe".

'Sure. No worries, Storm,' says Gennypha, in her broad Glaswegian accent. It's my favourite pronunciation ever.

'Any other ideas, guys, before Morag closes this session?' says Storm, taking over again.

'Boss, how about that insurance company that had a bake sale for us last summer? The ones that have our logo on their website?' says Binny, studying her fingers to choose which nail to bite next. 'They're well under the radar, no silly business, and we want to apply to be their CoTY. This might get them on board, yeah?'

(It took me a while to get used to the acronyms and jargon my colleagues use. CoTY stands for Charity of the Year. "eom" stands for end of message.

And when Tracy emailed me and put her whole message in the subject line and put eom at the end of it, I learnt two things: what eom means, and that it takes way longer to read a whole email in the subject line, especially if it's a few paragraphs long.)

'Umm, say more, Binny,' I say. 'What would the story be? A bake sale?'

'Brilliant. Yeah,' says Binny, crunching her nail bits.

'We could do a whole *spread* on bake sales,' I say.

'Nice one, Morag,' says Mason. 'You could do a whole *report* on bake sales, judging by the number of posts we get about it on social media.'

'It would be like a HAMPer,' I say, again feeling stupid for making such silly puns. 'That would really take the biscuit and everything.'

I just can't stop myself. As subtle as a sledgehammer. I'm such an idiot.

'Storm, what do you think?' I ask, trying to divert attention.

'Huh?' Storm looks up briefly from her phone. 'Sorry, guys, just keeping an eye on, um, on Twitter, in case someone's asking us something, yeah? Talk amongst yourselves.'

She's doing a *lot* of swiping left and right on Twitter, to be honest, and seems to have lost interest in what we're doing.

The conversation continues, with suggestions flying in for stories that aren't really stories for our audiences. By the end of the session, we've generated this many useful ideas for the annual report:

1. One.

We end our away-day on time, despite Storm's threats to end later as a punishment for starting later. The plan is to go to a pub in Angel for supper and karaoke. It should be fun. While we're waiting for our ubers, Storm's phone pings. She reads a message.

'Shit! Shit! Shitting shit shit shit! Seriously? What a shitting arsehole!' Storm shouts.

She tells us Coach has just text her (this is what the past tense of text is: *text*) and Chester has just tweeted that tweet. That one tweet he was away from making an idiot of himself and the charity.

All the colour's drained from Storm's face. She's fuming grey clouds.

'Chester's totally compromised our rep, guys. We need to act fast to get out in front of this to control the narrative. Aaaaaarrrrrgggghhhh! I have to speak to Coach,' Storm screams into the air as she dials Coach's number.

I wonder why she didn't pick that up when she spent all that time "on Twitter" at the end of our workshop? She walks to the end of the block and back, holding her phone to her ear and goose-stepping as she speaks to Coach. She ends her call and walks back to us.

'Guys, we're going to have to go ahead and cancel our karaoke evening,' she says, putting her phone in her pocket.

'Goes without staying, Stormzy-Stormz, we've cancelled the ubers,' says Madison, pointing at Binny, who winks and gives her a double thumbs-up.

'Thanks, guys. Morag, Mason, Gennypha – I'm going to need you to go ahead and come back to the office with me, okay? Ash, it's up to you if you want to stay or go. Madz and Binz, you're both free to go home, if you like? Wendy too – this won't need any direct marketing.'

'That's what you say now, Storm,' says Wendy, with an annoying wag of her finger. Her laugh is even more annoying as she adds, 'Just winding you up, as always, Storm.'

'Oh, is that what you're doing? Lol. Okay, thanks Wendy. And thanks for everything today, my lovelies, see you tomorrow, yeah?' says Storm.

'Smashing, cheers,' says Binny.

'You sure you don't need me, Stormz?' says Madison.

Storm shakes her head and turns to Gennypha, Mason and me. The others wave and walk away, looking both disappointed and relieved.

'Right, guys, we're in injury time for real. We need to have a proper game plan before we lose everything. Chester's *really* landed us in the shit this time. This is what I need you all to do: Gennypha,' says Storm, pointing at her, 'I'm going to need you to go ahead and reach out to Quinn's people as soon as, yeah? Coach wants to speak to him.'

'Quinn? What exactly did Chester do, Stormz?' says Gennypha.

'Coach will tell you all about it back at the office. Mason, I'm going to need you to put out a holding tweet right now, yeah?'

'Sure,' says Mason, getting his phone out. 'Shit's getting real.'

'It is indeed. Morag and Gennz, you can go back to the office now. Coach wants a quick scrum about this, yeah. Mase and I will join you shortly. Okay, this is what I need you to say, Mase,' Storm says, shooing us away.

'Wow, hectic stuff, hey?' I say.

'Yeah. Hey ho,' says Gennypha.

I find it quite funny that regardless of whether you're feeling wildly or slightly disappointed, devastated, hopeless, frustrated, thwarted, fearful, angry, miffed, or your plans are in ruin, this is what you would choose to say: hey ho.

When we get to the office, we go straight into the emergency scrum in the Tight-head Nook. Coach and our chair, Simon, are waiting for us there, looking ashen and anxious and everything. Coach has told Chester to go home, but he's still at the office.

'I've told him to go home, so I'm not sure why he's still here with a face like a spanked arsehole,' says Coach. 'Sorry, guys, I know that's not very professional but I'm feeling so angry with him, I'm not sure I can control my lips.'

Storm and Mason walk in.

'Right, team, thanks for coming in,' says Coach. 'No warm-ups today. We need quick, clean ball here, ja. I have no clues why, but Chester has gone absolutely hammer and screws at Quinn.'

'That's such strange timing, Coach. The other day, we were all discussing possibly getting in touch with him for our annual report, and we also talked about him at our away-day today,' I say.

'Yes, but that's irrelevant now, Morag. Let Coach speak,' says Storm. I sink a little lower in my chair, with my neck wound in.

'So our supporters are up and arms, slating The HAMP and standing, of course, by Quinn. We must put quickly out a statement and I need the collected wisdom of this group to help stitch up our messages, ja?' Coach's tone scares me, almost as much as her mixed metaphors.

As Coach speaks, Mason switches on the big screen on the wall and faffs around with the keyboard in front of him.

'For anyone who doesn't know, Chester got into a Twitter-spit – is that how you say? – with Quinn today. He tweets from his HAMP account, and today it went from bad to worst,' says Coach. 'Storm, you'll read now out the tweets, ja?'

'Coach, I told Mase to put out a holding tweet until we come up with a proper statement. He's just pulling up our Twitter feed on the big screen now, yeah. How're you getting on, Mase?' says Storm.

'Connecting ... talk amongst yourselves,' he says.

'Team, we need to dig deep to grind out the win here, ja? We have to imitate this,' says Coach.

'Mitigate, Coach. Mitigate. Don't stress, Coach, we've got this,' says Storm. 'We'll fix this. We'll do this, together. You've got the top team here, and we've got your back. Yeah?'

One thing that often surprises me about Storm is that she's actually *really* good in a crisis. She kind of loses her shit and everything at the beginning, and she can be super bitchy along the way, but she does calm down in a storm. When it really counts, she can keep her head. And she doesn't even eat through a crisis. You have to be impressed all round. Maybe *that's* why she has the nickname Storm.

'Voilà! Read it, and weep,' says Mason, as the tweets and replies thread from The HAMP timeline appears on the big screen:

- *@Quinn: So so proud to get this new gig, bringing #dance and #diy together. #BallroomBlitz @Channel80 you rock*
- *@HAMPChester: @Quinn @Channel80 wow u got the gig? Not McKayla? #disappointed #mckayla4ballroomblitz #youth*
- *@Quinn: @HAMPChester @Channel80 thanks 4 ur encouragement. Cheers. Thumbs up emoji*
- *@HAMPChester: @Quinn no worries. U must be so proud of urself, stealing from a young rising star. #irrelevant #hasbeen #loser*
- *@Quinn: @HAMPChester What's ur problem?*
- *@HAMPChester: @Quinn me? No problem. Don't get ur Guinness in a froth. I'm not the one pretending to still be relevant #irrelevant #loser #angerrehab*
- *@Quinn: @HAMPChester What? Ur relevant how? #troll #loser #weak #spineless*
- *@HAMPChester: @Quinn WTF? Will reconsider asking u to support my charity moving forward. No wonder yr wife left u. #domestic #lowlife*
- *@Quinn: @HAMPChester Whoa!*
- *@McKaylaFluencer: @Quinn @HAMPChester smh*
- *@LondonDick: @McKaylaFluencer @HAMPChester @Quinn Whoa! Wicked burn, mate!*

'Whoa!' goes everyone in the Tight-head Nook.

'Why don't you tell us what you really think, Chester?' says Gennypha.

'Exactly! And in case you're wondering, London Dick is Richard, the building's security guy downstairs,' says Mason, rolling his eyes.

'No idea why he felt he had to weigh in. Do you want to see all the responses, Coach?'

'Thanks, no. It'll resemble watching a car crashing, ja? You get the picture, team?' says Coach. 'And Storm, you said you and Mason have put out already a holding tweet, ja?'

'That's right, Coach,' says Storm.

'Yes, exactly. That's good, yes. But what I don't understand is why Chester said all that? It's not *his* charity,' says Simon.

'I know, Simon, but I don't think that's really the point. Let's keep our eyes on the ball here,' says Storm. 'What we need to do, and quickly, is shut this down. The fall-out obviously is immense, although it's slowed down since we posted our holding tweet.

'Drilling down,' Storm continues, 'I see that our supporters, especially our Northern Ireland supporters, are taking Quinn's side and most are threatening to pull their support from us altogether. I don't blame them, to be honest. They say if we're an anger management charity, and our finance director can't manage his anger, we must be doing a crap job. That's a perception we need to change, ASAP.'

'Yes, I understand,' says Coach. 'But let's not lose eyesight of the ball, ja? This is not about whether we do actually a good or a bad job. This is about one of our team shooting us already in the feet and giving this celebrity absolutely the hump with The HAMP, ja?'

(Maybe this is what Coach means when she says, 'Don't play in your own half.')

'Exactly. Basically a fan going rogue. But in *our* name. What the *actual*!' says Gennypha.

'Why did Chester have to get involved at all? He's mad about McKayla obviously, but he's not exactly her agent, is he?' says Simon. 'What made him think he could speak on her behalf? He just can't keep his mouth shut, can he? He's implicated us from every direction here. The fall-out from this is going to be huge. *Huge*.' Simon's eyes dart around the room.

Simon might not be as mad about Chester as I thought he was.

'You're right, Simon. Okay, team, we need to get quickly out the ball here from the scrum. Cut this off at the knees,' says Coach.

'Gotcha, Coach. I think we need to distance ourselves from Chester, to be honest. Surely this is a dismissible offence, Coach?' says Storm.

'Ja, but we need to deal separately with that. We need to reinforce what we stand exactly for, ja, with positive messages of honesty and authenticity. Use our values, and get out in front of this, ja? Isn't that what you tell always me, Storm?' says Coach.

Storm nods and winks at Coach.

'And for accountability, we need also our Twitter people to know we're taking action, but we can't say already more than that. Kevin's preparing Chester's red car–, excuse me, all the HR documents for tomorrow,' says Coach. 'Chester has turned actually our AHAH values into ha-ha values.'

'Good one, Coach!' says Mason, with a thumbs-up.

We all over-laugh. Ten out of ten to Coach for relieving the tension in the room.

It's weird being part of a discussion dealing with something so intense and personal, especially involving such a senior colleague. It's a first for me, and I feel a bit embarrassed and out of my depth and everything, to be honest.

'It goes without saying obviously that everything we're discussing now is confidential, right?' offers Simon.

'Completely so, Simon. Nothing leaves this room, ja? But we have to act quickly – we have a small window of time before our holding tweet runs out of steam. Isn't that what you told me too, Storm?' says Coach.

'Yep, Coach, spot on. Let me be clear: we need to get out in front of this and deconstruct the narrative Chester has created out there. Then we need to set out a road map of where we need to go and plan our journey there.' Storm's doing a deep-dive into her lexicon of jargon.

'Good. Ja. This is a sensitive issue and we can't let it end The HAMP's game. We all have a role to play in putting it right, and I'm depending on all of you for the strengths you bring, ja?' says Coach, looking at all of us.

Now we're in *Invictus* and Coach is Nelson Mandela. And Storm is Francois Pienaar. Well, maybe that's all too much of a stretch, but I sit a bit taller in my chair, taking on the burden of shared responsibility with pride.

'So what I think we need to do is this,' says Storm, steepling her fingers. 'Go to our profile, Mase. Shall we say Chester's from *another* charity called The HAMP?'

Everyone stares at Storm, incredulous.

'Well, not ano–' says Simon.

'Sorry, guys, I was joking!' Storm interrupts. 'Just trying to lighten the room a bit – it's been getting a bit heavy. So maybe what we need to say is this. Mase, won't you do me a favour and write this: "We regret & apologise without reserve for the tweets from at-Chester, which we in no way endorse. We apologise to at-Quinn for any hurt caused. We're distancing ourself from at-Chester."' Storm taps her chin.

'If that's too long for one tweet, it'll need to be a thread of tweets, yeah? What do you reckon, Coach? Simon?'

'Excellent, Storm. But I don't like actually the bit about distancing ourselves. Rather say we're dealing internally with the matter, ja?' says Coach.

Simon nods.

'Sure, sure. That makes sense, Coach. Mase?' says Storm, in a low, calm voice.

Mason tweaks the tweets.

'Any other thoughts from the bench?' says Coach.

'Coach, if we apologise, aren't we implying we're guilty?' asks Simon.

'Perhaps in a legal sense, but not here, Simon. We can't afford actually one bit to be defensive, ja?' Coach points at Simon as she speaks. 'We have to be swift and decisive and humane, and we need straightaway to show remorse, and accountability. Those are our values, and that's what our followers want. And that's how we win in the long run our supporters back, ja?'

Simon nods and makes a kind of "fair enough" expression with his mouth, which is sort of shaped like a warship: long and thin, and goes up at sharp angles at either end.

'That makes sense, Coach. I think our response sounds authentic,' I say. 'Like our AHAH values. It sounds like we actually mean it and everything.'

'Authentic is good; yay for our values!' says Storm, with a little storm-clap. 'And, of course, we need to speak to Quinn directly, yeah? We'll reach out to his people, right Gennypha?'

Gennypha nods.

'No luck today yet, guys, but I'll try again tomorrow. I left a message so basically his people will know we're trying to reach him, yeah?' says Gennypha.

'Well played,' says Coach. 'Mason, are you happy also this approach will work on Twitter?'

'Does the job, yeah,' says Mason.

'Don't we need to say this isn't actually Chester's charity?' says Simon, darting his eyes between Coach and Storm.

'Simon, our followers know that. Sometimes we do need to hit them over the head with the facts, but not this time, yeah? So, everyone, we go with this?' says Storm, looking around the room. Everyone nods. 'Okay, Mase, go for it. Post it and pin it, yeah?'

'Done!' Mason bashes the return key with a flourish.

'Okay, cool. So guys, we're going to need to go ahead and have a bigger plan of action moving forward here.' Storm's reverting to her bossy self. 'Let's get together with the fundraising team tomorrow to talk about how we turn this crisis around and, with the helpline team and our volunteers, draw up some lines to take, yeah? Mase, if anyone tweets at us tonight, our holding response is that we'll post a further statement tomorrow. Keep an eye on our feed, but don't get into the weeds with anyone and don't get defensive with anyone, yeah? Keep me posted, and I'll keep an eye on it too, yeah? And let's discuss tomorrow how to deal with this, moving forward. Yeah?'

Mason nods and cracks his knuckles.

'And Morag, lovey, I'll need you to go ahead and draft an all-database email to go out tomorrow from Coach, yeah? Get some quotes from Coach too.'

'Okay, sure, Storm. I'll do that,' I say.

'And Mase, we'll also need a website story, which you can draft from Morag's email.' Storm is on a roll now. 'I'll handle the press, obvs, along with Gennypha and hopefully Quinn's team. But we'll talk about that tomorrow, yeah? We'll need to work hard tomorrow.' (This is how Storm pronounces you: *we*.)

'And run *everything* by me to sign off, okay team?'

You can feel *fat chance* shuddering around the room. This is how many pieces of work Storm has signed off since I've been at The HAMP:

1. Three.

And this is how many pieces of work waiting for Storm to sign off:

1. About five hundred.

'I just love it when a plan comes together and we can pivot and work things out in-the-round as a team. Don't you, guys?' Storm digs in her handbag for loose crisps, so she must be moving out of crisis mode. 'It's *amaaaaaazing*. Really gets the adrenaline flowing, yeah? Coach, should we enter this campaign for a charity award?'

'Hold your houses, Storm, we have first a battle to win, ja?' says Coach. 'The full-time whistle hasn't even gone yet, ja?'

'Fair enough, Coach,' says Storm, pulling her hand out from the depths of her bag. she licks her fingers and gives Coach a gross, greasy-fingered thumbs-up.

'Right, team, *that's* what you call crisis comms. And *ace* teamwork,' says Storm, bits of crisp around her mouth. 'I was looking forward to our karaoke evening but I guess crisis comms rips the power ballads out of you, yeah?'

'Maybe you can still go, with Richard downstairs?' says Mason. 'He owes you one after that "burn" tweet.'

Storm punches Mason in the arm.

Chapter 10

Our team and the fundraising team have to go into the Scrum Room this morning, as agreed last night, for the next round of action plans. Storm and her tub of porridge arrive a few minutes late.

'Morning, guys. Thanks for coming in early for this. Everyone here?' she says.

Everyone shrugs and nods.

'Right, shall we get going, guys?' Storm says, opening her tub of porridge.

'Ja,' says Coach, 'it's big stuffs we're dealing with here. Our finance director tweeted without thinking yesterday, and he offended really Quinn. If you haven't seen, look at our feeder and you'll see our pinned tweet with our positioning on it.'

'Who's Quinn again? Name's kind of familiar,' says Binny.

'So Quinn is that Northern Irish singer-songwriter we talked about in our away-day yesterday, yeah?' says Storm, her mouth full of porridge. 'From the early '70s. Yeah? I don't know his music either, but he was big news back in the day. He played at one of the early Glastonbury festivals, according to Wikipedia.'

'I also found out he used to tour a lot and do gigs all over the shop. He's a bit of a grumpy and unpredictable old sod, to be honest, but he has a massive following, and the media love him. He used to be in the red tops all the time, mostly because of his temper and his outbursts at gigs,' says Gennypha.

'When I Googled him, I found an article in a rock magazine where he opened up to a rock magazine about his alcoholism and anger issues and everything,' I add. 'He said his wife left him, so he checked into rehab and started to try getting his life back on track. It took a few years, but then his wife came back to him, and he started to write new music.'

'Thanks, Gennz and Morag,' says Storm. 'So he's also just got the role to host that new Channel 80 series, *Ballroom Blitz*: the one like *Project DIY* except it's about bringing characterful concert venues back to life, or something like that. He's a devoted countryman, so he's already been working with classic Northern Irish gig-spots to fundraise for their restoration. Guess that's why he got the Channel 80 gig. But he really got riled by Chester yesterday.'

'He's such a bellend,' says Ash.

'Who – Quinn?' says Mason.

'Sorry, did I just say that out loud? I meant Chester, obvs,' says Ash, laughing.

'I'm even not surprised Quinn got riled by Chester,' says Coach.

'True, Coach,' agrees Storm. 'Chester hit a nerve and Quinn lost it on social media. We hadn't even got to ask him about our annual report yet – basically his story chimes really sweetly with ours – but we obviously can't do that any more. Such a pity. With all he's gone through, he could be a real role model for our audience.'

'Or an eidolon,' I add, for absolutely no reason. Now I feel such an idiot again, and Storm's looking at me sideways, thinking *WTF* as she spoons more porridge into her mouth.

'Right. So as you can imagine, we're literally *haemorrhaging* support, especially from NI.' (This is how Storm pronounces literally: *litchly*.) 'We need to get out in front of this, which is why I've brought you all here today. We need to go ahead and develop a game plan to get back on track with our supporters, yeah?'

'We need to act quickly, and put actually action behind our tweets, ja? On Twitter, the ball moves faster than we do, so we need to get it going through the hands fast,' says Coach. 'But right now, our charity is only as strong as its weakest link, and Chester has weakened significantly us. We're dealing with this with HR but we need to keep it out of the public dominion as much as possible. We also need to get quickly Quinn into the office, ja?' she adds, clapping.

'Got you, Coach,' says Storm, now licking the porridge off her fingers. 'Gennypha's all over that. We'll need to see into the whites of his eyes to let him know how *genuinely* sorry we are for all of this, yeah? We need to go ahead and find the positives here, and rebuild our reps, moving forward.' Storm pauses as usual on the word "reps". She leans back to throw her porridge tub into the bin.

'Right, action plans.' Storm stands up and walks over to the flip chart, wiping her hands on her dress.

'Okay, I'll leave actually you guys to it, ja? I have now to go and meet with Simon and Kevin,' says Coach, as she walks to the door. 'Good luck and thank you, to each and all of you. I'll be back.'

Coach loves saying that, to make us laugh.

How must Coach be feeling? And how will she face Chester and talk to him and everything? It's hard to tell how well they got on, really. But I'm guessing he's going to have to fling his hands on to his hips and measure the rooms in some other workplace. Maybe he'll find another Zimbabwean to bore and others to try and impress with his stories and jokes and everything.

It'll be weird not having Chester at The HAMP any more, though – not that I'll *actually* miss him or anything, but without him I'm worried that the office might be that tiny little bit less interesting.

Probably not, now that I really think about it and everything.

Today's been a long day of Chester crisis comms with loads of extra, unexpected work to do. It means I've had to stay late to catch up on everything else on my to-do list. It'll be quicker to go home on the tube rather than the bus this evening.

I pack up my stuff and walk around the office. When I get to Chester's office, he walks through the door and we both jump.

'Chester! You gave me a fright! I was checking to see if I was the last one here,' I say.

'Ah, Morag, me too. I'm glad everyone's gone home, I must say,' Chester says, as his hands find their way safely to his hips. A screwdriver falls out of his hands.

'Well, not exactly everyone. I'm still here,' I say. 'Hey, you dropped something, Chester.'

'I did?' he says, bending down to pick up the screwdriver. 'I wonder where that came from?' he says, tossing it from hand to hand with a bit too much casual.

'Okay, well, I'm leaving now now, Chester, and I'll need to lock up. Unless you're planning to do that?' I say.

'Morag, I had to han–, I don't have a key. Will you give the finance, I mean the *former* finance director, a few minutes to finish up here before you lock up?' he says, gesturing to his office.

'Sure, no worries. Hope you're okay, Chester?'

'Oh, I'm just fine, Morag. All good. Yes, all good. I've outgrown this place in a lot of ways, you know, Morag. People say to me, ooh Chester, you're too big for The HAMP. You're such a disrupter. And I say, yes, that's all true. But there is, *somewhere* out there, a place that *is* big enough for me. A place that has, I don't know, the *balls* for a maverick like me, who can take them places they hadn't even realised they wanted to be. The HAMP's loss, though. Time for me to find a new challenge, a new tribe.'

And some new jokes, while you're at it, but I don't say that out loud.

'Thinking of not big enough, shall I get you another waster-paper basket? It looks like yours is overflowing.'

I go and fetch the bin from next to my desk, and put it down in front of him.

'You know, Morag, when you work at my level,' he says, indicating somewhere way above my head, 'your job involves so much important, high-level, confidential stuff. There's a lot to take care of,' he says, nodding to his almost-empty office.

By the looks of things, he's cleared his desk and shredded every single thing that came off it. He's also filled a cardboard box with his framed certificates and a dying cactus.

'Okay, Chester. Well, I need to go to the bathroom and then we can leave together after that. Or do you need a bit more time?'

'No, that's fine. Excellent. I'll crack onwards, yeah?' he says, doing his arm swing as he steps back into his office.

In the bathroom, I look up at the HAMP's AHAH values poster beside the mirror and wonder how often Chester has looked at those values. At first I would say he never has, but in some ways, you could say he's always lived by them: if you think about it and everything, he really is a double AH.

When I go back into the office, I see that Chester's door is closed. I knock and open the door, but he's not there. His office is blanketed in shredder dust, there are piles of reports and magazines next to his overflowing waste-paper bins, and his wall has a few dusty, certificate-shaped outlines on them.

I was dreading an awkward and cringey farewell but I do feel a little disappointed that he cracked onwards out of the office, without saying goodbye.

As I close his office door. I notice four little screw-holes where the *Chester Proudfoot – The Finance Director* sign used to be. He must have thrown the sign into his cardboard box, along with his dream of winning the CRAP award, and his hopes of getting an OBE and everything.

He'll be finding it difficult to saunter, carrying a box so heavy with disappointment.

Chapter 11

December is a crazy month in London. It's the month of office Christmas parties and tubes filled with sad Santas, and dishevelled elves, almost every day. It's very different from Christmas in the southern hemisphere, but I now rather love the charm of the mid-afternoon darkness, and the magic of the dark, clear, freezing, twinkly nights. Jamie and I love going to the Christmas markets next to the Thames with their festive lights, and the smell of mulled wine and roasting chestnuts everywhere.

It's the day of our office Christmas party and, from murmurs I've heard, the party team has planned something special for this year. It'll be good to let our hair down after Chester-gate, that's for sure. Our office parties never lack drama, although they always lack alcohol. The actual party bit, anyway; the after-party's another story.

Ash and I walk together to the party so we can talk about the materials we're working on for the new year events Tracy from fundraising has briefed us on.

'I don't think Tracy liked it when I told her she *wasn't* a designer, when she started to give me notes about my design!' says Ash.

'I think she needed to hear it, though,' I say. 'She looked a bit shocked, but I think the penny dropped, don't you? I mean, imagine if we tried to tell her how to run an event and everything?'

'Things would properly kick off, yeah. Imagine if we told her she'd be better off having the event at a less busy time of year or thinking of another event. How would that go down, do you think? Haha!'

'That would be hilarious, Ash! It's so funny when you think about all the things people say to us and the things they ask us to do. We could write a book, hey?'

'We could, but no one would believe us,' says Ash, shaking his head.

The party room's decorated with tinsel and streamers and, once we've put on our reindeer antlers, put our secret Santa gifts into the black bin-bag near the door, moo'd, whinnied, oink-oinked and trumpeted our way into our animal teams, we have the now-traditional quiz. It starts out as fun, but ends up being super competitive and everything, with the elephant group winning the out-of-date box of energy bars (donated by the events team). The small plastic floating trophy is theirs until next year's party.

Binny from training (the other Binny) dresses up as Santa, and is a very merry, ho-ho-ho-ing giver-out of secret-Santa gifts. In normal times, most of us hate being in the spotlight, but with the chance of a gift worth a fiver, we all run up to the front like we're collecting an academy award.

Kevin loves the red and white Santa socks I got him, and moves from person to person saying, 'Did *you* get me my Santa socks? Did *you* get me my Santa socks? Did *you* get me my Santa socks?'

When he gets to me and I say yes, he gives me the biggest hug ever and tells me he's *always* wanted Santa socks. It's an unexpectedly over-the-top reaction. But he tells me they'll go perfectly with the new weekend shoes he's got for his choir's Christmas concert.

My gift – and I still don't know who it came from – is a South African flag face-cloth, and I *love* it. (Last year I got a small, slightly squashed tube of hand cream.) Warren gets a set of teeny-tiny corn cob holders. It's quite random, if you think about it and everything.

Storm's gift is a thin book called *How to be Better Organised.* She looks at it, turns it over to read what it's about and says, 'Ah, brilliant. I've always wanted to get some practical tips to pass on to my team. Thanks, whoever gave this to me. *Super* useful.'

Sometimes Storm's thick skin comes in handy.

Coach taps her Shloer bottle with a plastic fork. It makes no noise, so she blows her whistle.

'Team, after all the drama of Chester-gate, I'd like to thank you all for your hard work throughout this past year. All credit to you all, each and everybody, you've left it all out on the field for The HAMP and you've helped our supporters manage their anger. When I called, you answered, and you made me a very proud Coach indeed. You've made us the better team on the day, given our community the support and help they deserve and, if I'm honest, there would be no HAMP without you all.' Coach is moving herself to tears.

'So without any further *adieu*, I'd like very much to wish you all a merry Christmas and a happy new year. If you're going away for the holidays or even if you're not, keep safe and enjoy the break. But first, I have actually a small surprise for you, ja?

'I know I'm always banging on about tight budgets and so, but the Board has approved a small Christmas gift for each of you. We want to thank sincerely each of you for your loyalty and for making always a difference. So, tomorrow, you'll each find seventy-five pounds in your bank accounts. It's a small but sincere token of thanks. Now, enjoy the party!'

Warren shouts, 'Coach, you beauty!' and stands up, clapping like we've just won The Ashes. He takes a sip from his "water bottle" and waves his arms around.

'Standing O for the Coach, yeah? Say what you like about charities, guys. We've got the flipping greatest boss around. She's phenomenal!'

(This is how Warren pronounces phenomenal: *phenonemal.*)

'This is the best night of my life,' says Warren, his lip trembling. He must have brought tons of "water bottles" with him. And the after-party hasn't even started yet.

Very few of us make it into the office on time the next morning. The after-party was epic, and super boozy, as always.

Madison feels her way to her desk, nursing what looks like a worse head than mine and still wearing the same red dress she wore last night. She got all weird with Gennypha at the after-party. She'd had *way* too many shots and was struggling to stand when she leant on Gennypha's shoulder and said to her, 'If I was a boy, Gennz, you'd be my girlfriend. I'm not just saying that because I'm drunk, I really *really* mean it, you know.'

Gennypha said, 'Well, Madison, basically I'm super glad you're *not* a boy,' and lifted Madison's arm off her shoulder.

Ash got pretty intense and emotional with me too. When I asked about his little son, who's three, he pointed at me and shouted, 'Morag, he's a piece of me, yeah? He's a proper friggin' piece of *me*, yeah? I can't believe how much I love him. I love everyone, you know. Everyone except that knobhead, Chester. But *all* these beautiful people here. Mate, I get to work with all you beautiful people every day, yeah? Every day. Bring it in, Morag, come, come, bring it in.' Tears were rolling down his face.

I took that as my cue to disappear, quickly, and Ash didn't even notice. He might still be waiting for that hug; he's not in the office yet, that's for sure.

Last night, when I got outside, I found Warren and Karo in the middle of a loud argument. All I could make out was Warren had told Karo she was "shit at quizzing", and Karo had told Warren he was "terrible" at his job. Everything else was just shouty. They both turned to me to explain.

'Stop yelling in my face, you guys!' I said. 'You're both angry, and shouting doesn't help. You don't want to say something in anger you'll regret tomorrow, hey. What do you think Coach would say?'

That was so corny and goody-two-shoes of me and everything, but I was desperate, and it worked. They looked at each other, mouths wide open, and fell on to each other's shoulders. I couldn't hear what they shouted into each other's ears, but they both stood back and started to jog on the spot.

The office today is full of empty desks, glasses of water, boxes of aspirin, bacon sandwiches, bottles of Lucozade, throbbing heads, mugs full of embarrassment, and the pungent whiff of shame. 'Tis the season and everything.

Chapter 12

Jamie and I often go travelling in search of some sun during our Christmas break. People at work think we're a bit weird to do that, but it makes us feel a little less homesick and lonely. Christmas is one of the worst times to be away from your family, especially when everyone around you is spending time with their families and everything.

We've managed to have one Christmas at home in Cape Town since we've been in the UK. We had such an awesome time, under those expansive and improbably blue skies. It was also wonderful to see Jamie's family and our friends, although it did feel different; most of our friends had moved on without us. It made us feel a bit sad, but I guess we've done the same too, really.

This year Jamie and I are going to Valencia. Because I don't have a settlement visa yet, I have to get a Schengen visa to travel into Europe. It's quite expensive and the process of getting one is straightforward and everything, but it's still quite annoying. I hate getting to the boarding gate and feeling like a fugitive.

Today is no different; the ground crew radio their colleagues, saying, 'Single-entry Schengen visa at departure gate,' which sounds to me like 'Foreigner alert! Foreigner alert!' I'm suddenly in that drama movie where the border police haul me into a small room. I start to cry and reach out for Jamie as he fades into the distance and I wonder if I'll ever see him again.

Jamie grabs my arm and leads me through the departure gate.

'Rags! Didn't you hear what the guy said to you at the gate?' he says.

'The one taking me away?'

'What? Taking you where, Rags?'

'Never mind,' I say, back in reality.

'When you handed the guy your passport, he said you'd love Valencia. It's his favourite place. He looked a bit bleak that you didn't answer him,' says Jamie.

Sometimes my stupid imagination takes me places I don't even want to go.

Our hotel's in the centre of Valencia and it's easy to walk everywhere from here. We walk everywhere in London too, but we walk much further in Valencia and see things we haven't planned on seeing because we're brilliant at getting lost.

We do all the touristy things and it's really fun. We go on an open-top bus tour, ride bikes along the Turia River bed, shop in the Old City, eat delicious food and drink good wine, and relax in the winter sunshine on the beautiful, white beaches.

We celebrate New Year in the Plaza del Ayuntamiento, joining thousands in a Spanish tradition at midnight, when you welcome the New Year in by drinking bubbly and eating a dozen grapes: the twelve grapes of luck. If you can eat them all before the clock strikes twelve, tradition suggests you'll have a year of prosperity. We probably should have bought smaller grapes but we manage to eat them all in time, without choking or anything.

Our little holiday in Valencia really refreshes us, and the distraction helps us not to miss our friends and family too much. And with a dozen grapes under our belts, it feels like we're starting the new year on the right footing. It's a great feeling, I have to say.

Chapter 13

It's the first working day of January and everyone's back in the office, complaining about eating too much cheese over Christmas. Having grown up in southern Africa, cheese was never a thing at Christmas, or ever, really. I'd never even *heard* of a cheese hangover before moving to London.

Coach has booked an all-staff meeting this morning to discuss an idea she has to win back support after what we now call *Chestergate*. Our supporters seem pleased to know Chester has "decided to leave the charity to pursue other interests". Overall, we suffered a loss of about 50 supporters, mostly Quinn fans from Northern Ireland. But when you work in a charity, losing one supporter is one supporter too many. That's what Coach always says, anyway.

I want to get to the Scrum Room early to get a seat. As I stand up, Kevin walks past my desk and I say *hi* and join him. He says *hello* without looking up from the floor, and a few paces later, he says, 'Oh traveller from an arcane land,' for no apparent reason. He's still looking at his feet, and I'm not sure what I'm supposed to say to that, to be honest. I smile and go and grab a seat.

Karo is having trouble logging on to the big screen. *Everyone* struggles to log on to that big screen, to be honest. You'd think Karo wouldn't, being our IT person and everything, but every single meeting we have in that meeting room starts the same way.

Also, if you ever have to play a video on that big screen for a meeting or anything, the volume is always wrong. This is what usually happens:

1. You can't hear anything at all, so you pause the video and try to increase the volume from the keyboard and then remember you have to do that from the remote for the big screen.
2. When you restart the video, the volume is so loud – Hyde Park concert loud – that it almost blows the big screen speakers. Every single time point 2 happens, Wendy gets a massive fright and jumps out of her chair. And then she laughs her huge backward-screeching laugh.

Warren likes it when point 2 happens; he sometimes waits for Wendy to sit down and then he sets the volume at industrial levels just to get that reaction from her. He can be mischievous like that, if you think about it and everything.

At eleven, Coach closes the meeting room door. She gets us to stand up and do some warm-up stretching and jogging on the spot before she blows the whistle for the kick-off – the sign for us to sit down.

'*Guten morgen*, team, and welcome back after the festive break. I hope you all had a good time and if you're anything like me, you'll have eaten your bodily function in turkey and chocolate.'

(Sometimes Coach's mistakes with English kind of make sense.)

'And cheese,' says Mason, opening a bag of Wotsits.

'Exactly, Mason! Well, team, it's time to get back in the game for the new year. It's going to be a good year for The HAMP, ja? I have three things I want already to discuss with you all today. First,' Coach grabs her left pinkie finger, 'I want to let you know, now that Chester has left to persuade other interests, I have promoted Robyn to the role of finance director.

'As most of you know, she has been in the finance squad for four years and has equipped already herself well to take over as director. Full disclosure: we would normally advertise this role, but in the circumstances and with the Trustees' blessings, I took an executive decision and short-circuited the process. Simon and I interviewed her, and Robyn interviewed actually brilliantly. It's a well-deserved promotion and I'd like you all to join now with me in congratulating already Robyn, ja?'

We applaud. Not only is Robyn good at her job and a good choice for finance director and everything, but she's also not Chester. Both points are worthy of loud applause.

'Nice one,' says Ash, giving Robyn a double thumbs-up.

'Which brings me to my second point, ja,' Coach grabs her middle finger. 'I'd like to introduce you to Barry Jones, who is joining us next week as the new finance manager. Simon, Robyn and I interviewed him just before the Christmas breaktime. He's joining us today for this meeting but he starts already next week full-time. Barry, stand up so everyone can see who you are, ja?'

Barry stands up and waves at the room. A few people shout, 'Hey, Barry!' and he makes a heart sign with his hands, which is a bit corny and everything, if you think about it. He's also wearing a HAMP T-shirt. Full marks for sucking up. (This is how we say sucking up in Zim: *slooshing*.)

'Thank you, Pauli, for the intro,' he says, in a thick Welsh accent. 'I'm pleased to be joining you at The HAMP, I am. I've wanted to move away from internal auditing and into the charity sector for some time, so this is very exciting for me. I'm looking forward to meeting you all, yeah?'

Coach smiles at Barry, and stands up again.

'And the third and final point,' Coach grabs her thumb. 'This is the one I'm most excited about. Not that I'm not excited about Robyn and Barry, ja, but you'll see what I mean. We're going to be on the second season of the reality TV show called *Britain Loves a Trier (It's the Sport that Counts)*. We applied for the first season, you may remember, but didn't get through. When we applied again for season two, we decided to keep that under wrapping because we didn't want to disappoint again everyone, ja?

'But Channel 53 got in touch with Tracy just before Christmas to tell us we're in. They choose only one charity, along with corporates, the civil service, and the NHS. So we're flying alone the flag for the charity sector. No pressure, ja?'

There are woohoos around the room.

'Exciting, ja? The timing is also perfect, ja, exactly when we need to rebuild support. I'll tell you more about that in a few minutes. We still need absolutely to keep this under our caps, so only within the charity, otherwise mum's the word, ja? Did anyone watch the programme last year?'

Mason licks some Wotsits spice off his fingers before raising his hand.

'The programme's *brilliant*, Coach. *Loved* it, tbh. It's a rugby challenge and teams compete against other *triers*. Bit of a pun – Morag, you'll love that – because you score *tries* in rugby, yeah?'

'You have *try-scorers* in rugby, rather than *triers*, to be fair,' says Binny, studying her nails.

'Yes, Binny, true. Nobody likes a show-off, yeah?' says Mason, smirking.

'Nice pun, anyway, Mase. But you can't win the maul.' I can't help myself. There aren't enough laughs to make it worth being such an idiot again.

'Right, cheers, Morag,' says Mason. 'Where was I? Rules a bit sketchy, but you have to start on a level playing field ...'

'Are some of them skew-whiff?' says Jasper, looking for his share of a laugh.

'Walked right into that, yeah?' says Mason. 'The teams need an equal mix of experienced and inexperienced players, yeah? So there's a points system; each player has a value in points, according to whether they've played before or not, and each team has to have the same number of points on the field at all times. Make sense?'

'Thanks, Mason, you're a real fan, ja? You've hit absolutely the nail in the coffin. Yes, that's how it works, ja,' says Coach.

'Cool. So last year that insurance company won, yeah? Props to them.' Mason turns to Gennypha. 'Bloody love reality TV, me.'

'Me too! Brilliant!' says Wendy. She's wearing a knitted hat that looks like a tea cosy.

'It's brilliant, ja? And the tournament happens at Cardiff Arms Park...' says Coach.

'Wow, that's huge, Coach!' says Warren.

'It's actually the smaller stadium next to the big one, ja? That one is, I can't remember actually how it's called now already.'

'Principality Stadium, boss. It was the Millennium Stadium until a few years ago,' says Binny to her nails.

'Of course, ja. Good. Okay. So our first challenge, team, is to create a HAMP rugby sevens squad. This programme ticks nicely a number of boxes for us, ja? The link between sport and anger management, about which, as you know, I feel passionately. And, if we field a strong team – and yes, we have absolutely the passion and drive to build a strong team and train hard – we have a chance to win the big prize. It's half a million pounds, which could pay for all of our volunteer training for a year. It would make actually a huge difference, ja? And all this in a Rugby World Cup year, ja? It all fits nicely together.'

Lots of *wows* around the room.

'And, even if we don't win actually, we get already ... Tracy?'

'Fifty thousand, Coach, obviously,' shouts Tracy from fundraising.

'Ja, that's just for taking part! Isn't that something, team? Channel

53's advertisers support the programme, ja, and they will screen the festival live,' says Coach.

'Between 2am and 7am on a Tuesday, yeah?' Ash laughs.

'No, Ash, you're quite wrong, ja? On a Saturday, prime-time,' says Coach.

'Prime-time, low-level channel,' says Madison.

'No, Madison. This is the semi-big league, ja? Last year they had – correct indeed me if I'm wrong, Tracy – over one million viewers, ja?'

More *wows*.

'That's right, Coach,' says Tracy, standing up. 'May I?'

Coach beckons her to the front.

'Cheers, Coach. So I just kind of like wanted to add, yeah, how it all works and that kind of thing. Channel 53 obviously promotes the series. It starts with a build-up: we each film our preparations, they share it on their social media, yeah, and their TV channel too – and then broadcast live from the festival obviously. That's when they pull in those huge viewer numbers, and the pounds.' She rubs her thumb and forefingers together. 'Ker-ching ker-ching! We're allowed to fundraise on the day too, obviously, as we're the only charity taking part, so we're like, I don't know, in the money for *days*, yeah!'

'Thanks, Tracy, we get nicely the picture,' says Coach. 'The last Rugby World Cup brought lots of new people to the game, and this programme is part of Channel 53's strategy to promote sport and healthy living, and to grow their rugby-supporting audience, ja? And this will flow nicely into their coverage of this year's Rugby World Cup too. The third box this ticks, ja, is the chance for us to build back support. We'll have a good platform to mend the fences. And we can reach even more new supporters by exposing ourselves at the festival. Any thoughts, team?'

'*Exposure*, Coach. We'll get *exposure*. We won't be exposing ourselves irl, will we?' says Mason, laughing. 'Not *that* desperate, yeah?'

'No, no, no! Sorry! My mind is boggling, Mason, but you're right. You know me and this English language, making always mistakes.' Coach hides her face in her hands. 'We'll get *exposure*.'

Storm stands up to throw her porridge tub in the bin.

'Coach,' she says, wiping her mouth with a tissue. 'It'll take a minute to process all of this. But can I just circle back to this central question, yeah?' Storm makes a circling motion with the tissue. Coach nods.

'There's a piece around whether this is going to distract us from our core business, moving forward. You see where I'm coming from, yeah? I'm going to have to go ahead and take questions and comments from the media. Once it gets *out there*, there'll be a huge uptick in media attention for us, and I'll need to understand our position clearly, so I can craft lines to take. We'll need to get cosy with those lines so we can speak off-script, on-message, yeah? We need to show we've thought this through. Are our motives fit-for-purpose? Does everything ladder back to our central mission?'

Storm always over-estimates the media's interest in our involvement in anything. In the world of network television, this is, well, really just a *small-potatoes* opportunity, and the spotlight will be on the programme rather than on us.

'Storm, we can talk about this offline, ja, but no need to worry. This won't take our eye off our balls. We'll treat it like any other fundraising sports event, ja? Our training will be out of office hours, and the details will come into the light soon enough. I'll get a cross-fit group together to flash out all the details, ja?'

'Gotcha, Coach,' says Storm, with a mini storm-clap. 'Although it's not the same as our mass pax events, to be fair.'

'Storm, now you're being actually infantile, ja?'

'I think you mean petty, but point taken. Sorry, Coach.'

'Who can be in the team, Coach? Anyone?' asks Karo.

'Yes, Karo, absolutely anyone. And–'

'Cool. So mixed teams?' Karo interrupts.

'Um, what do you think?' says Coach, laughing. 'I'm being actually flippant, Karo, but absolutely yes. They're trying actually to create a level playing field, so there have to be men and women in each team and on the field at any time, ja? I've never played actually like this, so it will be interesting to see really how it works. And, I wanted to a–'

'*All* of my best friends are sevens players. Can they join in?' Wendy probably knows a friend of a friend who watches rugby sevens. She's now taken off her tea-cosy beanie and her fringe has gone curly like a corkscrew, and it's sticking out at right-angles.

'I have to say unfortunately no,' says Coach. 'We have to field an in-house team, but what we *are* allowed actually is one celebrity in our team to draw in more viewers. *And,* I almost forgot to tell you the most important part of this challenge: as Mason said just now, our total squad of twelve has to include those who haven't played before rugby.'

'Coach, I'm not sure this is for us? Not in a bad way, but I mean, a charity, and actually putting a rugby team together from scratch – do they *really* go together?' says Warren, pushing his hands together.

'Warren, Warren, oh you of literal faith. A charity is a team, no? As I tell always all of you, the same principles of sports teamwork apply also to running a charity. Planning, selection, training, resources, communication, mutual respect, quick reactions, and supporting each other to play absolutely to our strengths.' Coach claps for each principle.

'Oh, okay, that makes sense, Coach,' says Warren, nodding.

'And we're learning always on the job, ja? Since I join The HAMP, ja, those are the principles I'm leading by.'

Coach walks around the room.

'And don't forget, everything we do, we do for our community, ja? We'll raise already funds, and a whole new audience will learn about

The HAMP. Ja? If we can dream it, we can achieve it, ja? We can't start by thinking of the negatives, Warren, and Storm; we must *think* like winners. When we do, we *act* like winners, and we all know what winners do, ja? They *win*. We have to give this hundred and ten percent, straight off the fence.' Coach claps again.

I don't know if it's just me, but I'm kind of expecting an altar call. Coach is super keyed-up and everything.

'For our community, our supporters, and for ourselves.' Coach is whipping herself into a frenzy. 'Who's in? Who's with me?'

The room erupts.

'Let's do it for The HAMP, ja!' shouts Coach.

'HAMP! HAMP! HAMP!' rings out from across the room.

'Yeah, HAMP!' I shout, as the room falls silent. I kind of regret jumping up and punching the air – I thought everyone was going to do that. What an idiot.

'Thank you, Morag. And thank you, Team HAMP! That's actually the spirit, ja? I like it. But that's all for now, and I'll keep you posted. For now, it's back to your desks, ja? And thank you, everyone, for all you do.'

Coach blows her full-time whistle, and draws a line across the room with an outstretched arm to close the meeting. I slink out of the door, trying to look invisible, but I'm as amped as anything. This is going to be *awesome*.

It was surprising, to be honest, that Karo said anything at all in the all-staff meeting. She doesn't like speaking in front of big groups of people. And, because she daydreams and everything, it seems she doesn't have a clue what's going on in meetings most of the time.

Here are three things to know about Karo:

1. She absolutely loves cats. She has two, called Peas and Carrots, and she posts a lot of videos of them on Instagram. Even when

she's "at work".

2. Her tops are often pulled (by her cats), always wrinkled, and sprinkled with post-laundry tissue or post-breakfast porridge.

3. In the times between creating or making cat videos, she looks after our charity's IT needs. Bonkers, I know, but she does it pretty well too.

Karo comes over to speak to Madison. One leg of her trousers is tucked into her shoe and the other drags, unhemmed, on the floor.

'Madison, can I ask you question?'

Madison nods, without looking up from her screen.

'Give me a mo, my lovely, just need to fire off this email. My inbox has been rammed since I've been back. *Super*, super busy.' Today she's going for the Welsh accent.

I don't know if it's just me, but when people have to tell you all the time that they're busy, they can't be *that* busy. Especially if you can see they're shopping or buying tickets for a festival or something.

'Right, how can I help you?' Madison puts away her bank card. 'Are you looking for Ash's birthday card? I told Warren I couldn't find it.'

'No, no, it's not that,' says Karo.

'Oh okay, cool. Right, I'm all ears,' says Madison, with her all-ears face on.

'I know you know a lot about shopping online and bargains and stuff. Do you know the best place to get activewear?'

That's a word I wouldn't expect to hear Karo use, ever.

'*Moi*? Online shopping?' Madison mock-protests, throwing her head back and laughing. 'Just joking, my lovely. Yes, sure, I know a thing or two about the online shop.' She gives the word "shop" about fifteen Ps. 'Men's or women's?'

'It's actually for me, Madison. Don't laugh, but I need some decent kit if I'm going to play in the rugby sevens – even the trainers I have are falling apart,' says Karo, softly. 'I used to play rugby at school and uni, believe it or not. Please don't tell anyone; I know you all think I'm a bit of a loser, and I don't want to look like one on the rugby field too.'

Say what you like about Karo, she can really surprise you and everything.

Karo thinks she's talking just to Madison, but our whole pod just heard that. All leaning-forward-listening, to be honest.

'We don't all think that,' I say. Karo smiles and blushes. So do I. I've not only made it obvious I was eavesdropping, but I've also made her think *some* people think she's a loser. Oh my word, I'm such an idiot, but I'll only make more of an idiot of myself trying to correct what I've just said. I leave it there, and I know I'll play this over and over in my head for the rest of the day.

'Anything exciting to report, guys?'

Warren has suddenly appeared behind Karo, stuffing his hands into his pockets and lifting his shoulders. You know how Chester's hands and hips drew together like magnets? Well, Warren's shoulders and hands repel each other in the same sort of way.

This is how good Warren is at eavesdropping:

1. World champion.

And here's something to be aware of if you were ever thinking of working at The HAMP: if you want to have a confidential conversation on your phone or with someone in person, you have to go into a meeting room or get as far away from the office as you can without using public transport. We're an eavesdropping charity living in an open-plan office; it sounds like a song title but it's a kind of unspoken value or something, I think.

Warren takes it to a whole new level, though. You can be having a really interesting conversation at the other end of the office, and Warren will slouch-shuffle across to you, with practised nonchalance and his hands in his pockets. He'll pretend he was about to walk into that corner of the office anyway, even though there aren't any meeting rooms or bookshelves or doors or any other reason to be there or anything.

The truth is, he wants to join in your conversation. He'll always pretend he hasn't been eavesdropping but you'd have to be a bit dim to believe him, to be honest; sometimes he makes it super obvious and everything. Like sometimes he'll already know about something before you've even got around to telling him. When I told Wendy I'd just booked our tickets for Valencia and everything, I was really excited. In the kitchen two minutes later, Warren went, 'So when do you leave? I *love* Valencia.'

Karo shrugs and says, 'Cat talk,' and walks back to her desk.

Warren must feel a bit stupid. He spins around on his heels, his hands deep in his pockets and his shoulders high, and slouch-shuffles back to his desk. Sometimes I feel kind of sorry for him. It must be horrible when you really try to make an impression on someone you really fancy and everything, and they just fob you off.

Chapter 14

Storm's in early today and, while she's dishing up her porridge, she dishes out orders. She doesn't do emails, as you know; she prefers working out loud. She shouts things from her desk and demands a response, even when you have no idea who she's talking to or anything.

'Are there two Ns after the O in *definite*?'

'One N and no O. D-E-F-I-N-I-T-E,' says Mason.

'What?' Storm spells it out on her fingers. 'Then why do we say deffo, and not deffi?'

(Storm's spelling isn't great. She spells numb like this: *num*.)

'Gennypha! Where's that press release? I need it to go out today, yeah? And don't forget to pitch it to the *Daily Mail*, yeah?'

'Why is the Tight-Head Nook always booked? Hello? Anybody out there? Hello-o-o! Answers, guys, I need answers!'

'Morag! Send me that all-staff email before it goes out today, yeah?'

'Guys, give me a nine-letter word starting with haitch! Guys!'

(She's even more impatient when she's doing a crossword.)

'Mason! Why hasn't that tweet gone viral? I asked you to make it go viral.'

When Storm shouts and you don't answer straightaway, she'll just shout louder. And it's best to stand up to answer her, otherwise she won't hear you and things will escalate quickly and everything. Sometimes, when you're all standing up one-by-one to answer her, you feel like you're in a flash-mob.

'Guys! I can't find a free meeting room. Madz! I'm going to need you to go ahead and find us somewhere to meet – the whole team. We need to put together a comms plan for this *Britain Loves a Trier* programme, yeah? Coach wants it by the end of this week.

'Guys! Cancel your meetings this afternoon – *BLAT* needs to take priority. Are you listening to me, guys?' Her mouth's full of porridge.

Everyone, except Mason, stands up and says 'Yes'.

'Mason?' Storm scrapes out the last bits of porridge with a plastic spoon and chucks the tub into the bin. I've really come to hate the sound of plastic tubs and containers and wrappers landing in the bin. It makes me feel anxious and worried I'll be in trouble about something or someone's about to shout at me.

Mason makes a "toot-toot-toot" sound like a trumpet and gives Storm a thumbs-up over the desk partition. 'Soz, just needed to get an email off before nine.'

Here are three random things to know about Mason:

1. He makes funny noises at his desk – like a trumpet, or a ringtone, or a doorbell. It can surprise you or scare you at first, but mostly it's pretty funny and kind of breaks the ice.
2. He must surely be addicted to crisps or something. He eats them all the time. And for me, the crinkling of the packet and his open-mouthed crunching are the most excruciating, *annoying* sounds in the whole wide world. I can't *stand* it. When I can, I do literally *anything* to get away from that sound.
3. He has one of the kindest faces I've ever seen in my whole life.

Madison emails a meeting request for two o'clock at a small coffee shop down the road, because our meeting rooms are all booked. Ash and I have to reschedule the briefings we had with other teams, otherwise Storm will be furious and things will end badly. I hate having to do that, but my colleagues understand the reality of working with someone like Storm. When she says "jump", you don't want to tell her you have another meeting or anything. It doesn't work both ways, but then that's not how *Do as I say, not as I do* works, is it?

I ask Storm if we need to prepare anything for the meeting, and she promises to send an agenda before lunchtime.

When we get to the coffee shop, Storm isn't there and nor is the agenda. I could have told you that for free, to be honest. Madison texts her to check where she is.

'Oh, right. Guys, Storm says she'll be a bit late but we must go ahead and start without her.' Madison reads from her phone.

We follow Mason to a table in the corner, and wait. Storm rushes in at quarter past two.

'Soz, guys ...'

'No probs, just having a natter,' says Mason, opening his bag of cheese and onion crisps.

'I had to go to the post office and there was a queue almost out the door. I literally had to run to get here.'

She's not as out of breath as you'd expect if she'd been running from the post office. Her fingernails, on the other hand, are looking mint.

'Right, guys, I thought you would've started already but it doesn't sound like you have.' Storm digs around in her handbag, trying not to spoil her fingernails. She pulls out a chilli chicken wrap and a Diet Coke. 'Hope they won't mind if I eat this food here. Okay, so, guys?'

'We didn't know what the meeting was about, really, Storm,' says Gennypha.

'Didn't you get the agenda I emailed?' Storm scrolls through emails on her phone, using a little finger. 'Soz, guys, stuck in my outbox.'

(Sometimes Storm says "stuck in my outbox" instead of "I forgot". Or "I was late for the nail bar".)

'Okay, right, so what we need to do moving forward is put together a comms plan for *BLAT*. We need to think of a celebrity, and then get together a PR and media plan, internal comms, social media, the lot. Any ideas, guys?' Storm cracks open her Diet Coke and chews on a giant mouthful of wrap.

'Do we have the green light to go public with news that we're on the programme yet?' says Mason.

'Yes, I thought you might ask that. It's a bit of a no-brainer, right?' Storm's mouth is full as she scrolls through her phone with a little finger. 'The festival's at the end of June, so the programme will start a month before that, so probably a couple of months before that, yeah? We're going to need to go ahead and put the plan together anyway – we need one, moving forward.'

Mason has some great ideas for curating video content from now until after the festival, to share with our supporters afterwards. He also says he'll schedule all the social media and website stuff. Gennypha wants to profile some key team members, and sell their stories into sports titles and trade publications, and I say we could run some great features on the whole team in our HAMP magazine. In a surprise move, Madison reminds Storm to keep the HAMP staff team involved throughout, too.

Storm gnaws her way through her wrap, holding it with her newly-painted fingernails, licking her fingers and lips, gulping down her Diet Coke, and talking with her mouth full. She storm-claps with her wrists to suggestions she likes. When Gennypha suggests we should invite Cali Shannon to join the team, Storm storm-claps a *lot*.

'Cali Shannon?' says Madison.

'Great shout, Gennz. What can you tell the team about her?' says Storm, bits of chicken flying out of her mouth.

'Okay, so I thought about her when Coach said something about a celebrity, because I remembered reading about her. But I stalked her on social media and found out some more stuff. Basically, she used to play rugby for Wales and was a bit wild but a gifted member of the Welsh women's rugby team. The media loved her. She retired from rugby in the early 2000s, became a presenter on that TV dance show, and then basically the red tops and gossip magazines were all over her.'

'Ooh, soapie-land. Love it,' says Mason.

'Right? But basically, she has quite a temper,' says Gennypha. 'So cue Soho in the early hours of a Sunday morning after a night of heavy drinking. She must have been on something too probz, but basically got in a tiff and punched a woman in the face. The pic appeared in the press, and the woman threatened to press charges if Cali didn't sort herself out. So she went into rehab for her anger and addictions.

'It's been a few years, but her life seems to be back on track. She's been on *Loose Women* and even *Woman's Hour*, and is looking for a new gig. Basically, put The HAMP and Cali together, mix in a bit of *BLAT* and boom! Synergy!' says Gennypha, miming an explosion.

'Sounds like *someone's* been around me a bit too long, using my kind of language,' says Storm, through a very small, very full mouth. 'But let's not get too carried away, yeah? It's a *big* ask. I'm not saying it's *impossible*. You're pushing the envelope, yeah, but it might just be actionable. Let's put a pin in it for now, and circle back to it once I've chewed on it, yeah?' She takes another big bite of her wrap and wipes her mouth with the back of her hand.

'This has been an *amaaaaaazing* meeting!' says Storm. 'There isn't another group of people I'd rather be on this journey with than you, and I'm so proud of you all. To think of where each of you were when I met you, I can't believe I've trained you all up to be such superstar comms whizzes. You were low-hanging fruit, but still. Wow!' She storm-claps so fast you can hardly even see her newly-painted fingernails.

There's something about being damned with faint praise: it can take you in but then, about a minute later, make you feel really angry and everything.

'So okay, guys, action points moving forward: I'm going to go ahead and send you the bare bones of a comms plan with our overarching strategic intent, which you can all flesh out with your own action points and timelines, yeah?' says Storm.

'Sounds like we need skeleton staff for this,' I say. Oh boy, my stupid attempt at a pun gets this many laughs:

1. Zero.

'When do you think you'll be able to tell us when the programmes are going to air, Storm?' I ask. It helps to change the subject, sort of.

'Morag, lovey, don't you worry about the detail, all right? You can leave that to me, yeah? As I said, I'll let you all know as soon as I know. Bottom line: what I need you to do, is go ahead and wait for my comms plan framework, and then fill in how much time you think you'll need for your bits. Yeah? Just focus on *your own* bits, yeah? Stick to *your* knitting,' says Storm.

'*Needles* to say, I *wool* go ahead and do that.' I'm not loving being patronised and everything, but I can't resist making puns.

'Nice one, Morag!' says Gennypha. 'Basically, love me a good pun!'

'Morag, that's *so* cheesy!' Storm wrinkles her nose and stares at me, her face in a huge, toothy grin. It's quite disarming and everything.

At least those puns got this many laughs:

1. Two.

'Okay, guys, okay, back to the business at hand, please,' says Storm. 'Let's meet once a week until I'm sure you've got everything right, and you're all on track. It'll be good to touch base and check in with each other, yeah? We need to hit the road running with this, so next time let's start doing some heavy lifting of the different elements, yeah? It's super important to us as a charity, and we need to do everything we can to make sure we win. Yeah? So, anything else, guys? I need to get back to my desk ASAP, so speak quickly if you have anything of value to add.'

'When's our next meeting, Storm?'

'Morag, I just said we'll meet every week, yeah? So this time next week. I don't have time for pointless questions, guys. Madison, you can sort out our meeting times, yeah?'

Madison nods.

'Shoulders to the wheel, guys; this programme has a lot of moving parts and we need to keep our fingers on the pulse. Guys, you're awesome. Great meeting. So glad I got you all together. Thanks again, guys, tha-anks.'

Storm leaves without paying for our drinks. That's more than a bit annoying, if you ask me.

Madison has now put in a weekly meeting on Wednesday afternoons at the same time, and she's booked a meeting room at the office so we don't need to go out, or buy our own drinks or anything.

Storm arrives late for the first one, a curry in her hand and a *huge* cloud over her head.

'Guys, let's get moving. This is going to be a really busy time moving forward, and we can't let the grass grow under our feet, yeah? We need to make the full ninety minutes count, yeah?' She opens her tub of curry.

'I'll need to leave early – didn't realise the meeting was going to be that long,' says Madison.

'Good grief, Madison. That's just a *rugby* analogy to get you into the groove.' Storm sighs. 'Come on, guys, who's going to start? Quick, quick!'

No one says anything.

'Guys, the comms plan? Someone, anyone? Now that it's in train, I'm going to need you to go ahead and run through your parts of the plan with me. *Guys-a!*'

When Storm starts to sound like she's twelve, you know things are going to get ugly.

'Errrr basically, Storm, we didn't get the framework of the plan with your strategic overview, did we?' says Gennypha, hesitating.

You *never* want to mess with Storm because nine times out of ten you'll come off second best. But when she's being unreasonable and everything, you also can't just say nothing.

'What's wrong with you guys, huh? Are you kids? Do I need to spoon-feed *everything* to you?' Storm's gone red in the face, and not just from the curry. 'Guys, I honestly expect more from you. Morag, *you're* an adult – why haven't *you* put the comms plan together? Where's the accountability, guys? Our values, remember?'

'You said you were going to …' I start.

'No excuses, Morag,' Storm's getting louder and louder. 'I need solutions, guys. What's going on with you? *Guys-a?*' She keeps looking at me. 'Morag, *what* is your plan for the internal comms? The emails? The magazine pieces?'

'I haven't –'

'*Guys-a!* This just isn't good enough. It's not fit-for-purpose. You're wasting my time here, and you *know* how precious my time is. You have *no* idea what it takes to lead this team, and if I can't count on you, well … guys, speak to me! Give me something to work with here! You guys – what's going *on-a?* Morag?'

Here's the thing about me and conflict: I hate it. It makes me shake. My default setting is to think everything is my fault and I'm not good enough. I'm conscientious and reliable and everything – a rule follower, if you like – and if you ask me to do something, I'll do it. You can count on it. But something else to know about me is that I'm not always a soft touch, even though when you look at me you might think I'm:

1. A pushover.

So, if you accuse me of something unfairly, I'll stand up for myself, even if it takes all the energy I have.

'Storm, it's not okay for you to speak to me like that. Especially not in front of my colleagues. What about our value of honesty? I don't think it's fair you're accusing me of not doing something you said you'd do, and I'm not going to stand for it. I'm really not.'

I'm shaking, and I just hope I don't start crying. Storm is unmoved.

'We were all in the same meeting last week, Storm. You said you'd send us notes from the meeting, and said you'd put together the comms plan framework for us to flesh out ...' My lips are trembling.

'I would have expected *you*, Morag, as a senior member of my team, to have taken that on. I'm disappointed in you,' says Storm.

'Storm, you didn't ask me to do that. That's not fair.'

I'm still shaking.

'Storm, Morag's right,' asserts Mason. 'It's unfair to expect her to have done what you said *you'd* do. Why Morag, anyway? Why not me? Or Madison, or Wendy, or Gennypha? We were all there. Any of us could have started the plan if you'd asked us to. But you didn't. I took notes, see?' Mason shows her his phone.

Storm waves it away. She looks a little powerless. Like when a bully gets a taste of what they dish out. She shovels the remaining curry into her mouth in huge forkfuls, her eyes darting around the room.

'Okay, guys, there's obviously been a misunderstanding, yeah? Let's give this some thought, yeah?'

Sometimes Storm says "let's" when she means "let me".

'So what I'm going to suggest, moving forward, is that we close this meeting. Let's take a minute, and regroup tomorrow with fresh minds. Yeah? Thanks, guys. I'll book another meeting in to talk about this.'

And sometimes Storm says "I'll" when she means "Madison will".

Chapter 15

Madison's booked the Tight-head Nook for our regroup meeting at midday today. She's called the meeting a "catch-up". Here, at The HAMP, you can call any meeting a "catch-up", really. These are the things it can mean:

1. A status update/project briefing/team meeting.
2. A 121 meeting/performance review.
3. A bollocking/disciplinary hearing.
4. A gossip.
5. Literally anything else.

I'm super anxious about the meeting. I've no idea what Storm is going to do next. She's *really* unpredictable. One day, she'll shout at you for something trivial and the next day she won't say anything about the exact same thing. When she's late for meetings and stuff, she's like, 'Ah, sorry guys, trains were late' and everything (even though she walks to the office). But when she's on time, or in a bad mood, and you come in late, she'll shout at you, regardless of your reason for being late.

And sometimes she'll be all interested in you, like, 'Ooh, Morag, how's your family in South Africa?' and that sort of thing, and other times you'll tell her something and she'll say, 'Sorry, Morag, I actually *don't* have time to chat about your personal life', making you feel stupid and everything.

An email pops into my inbox from Mason:

<no subject>

Hiya, heads-up b4 meeting with S. Told Kevin yesterday about the RG-BG, he was going to have words. Hope you don't mind.

M.

I give Mason a thumbs-up.

'What's an RG-BG?' I mouth.

'Soz, argy-bargy,' chuckles Mason, throwing mock-punches.

(I told you Mason liked making up acronyms and everything.)

Yikes, I don't know what to think about his email message, though. I'm chuffed he stood up for me and everything, but will Storm just think *I* went running to Kevin? And be even more unreasonable than ever with me?

We go into the Tight-head Nook and Storm comes in, smiling. These things surprise me right now:

1. She's on time.
2. She doesn't have one bit of food in her hand.
3. She's smiling.

'Hi guys, how're you all doing?'

No one says anything.

'Ooh, amazing dress, Madz.' Madison's wearing clothes that haven't come out of the bottom of her laundry basket.

'Thanks, Stormz. Warehouse sale.'

'Touch! Nice one,' says Storm. 'Okay, guys, let's not pussy-foot around the issue here, yeah? I've had a ... I've thought about our meeting yesterday, guys, and I realise I was a little unfair, especially to you, Morag. But I have a lot on my plate, guys, and when you're a real perfectionist like me, you get frustrated when others aren't. So, Morag, and the rest of you guys: I'm not proud of how I behaved yesterday, but please understand what it's like for me.'

I wonder if Storm's feeling dizzy all the way up there on the moral high ground.

'Storm, that's really big of you,' says Madison, on behalf of herself.

I don't want to say anything, really. I know it's a bit churlish and everything, but she was *awful* to me yesterday, and I feel I deserve a proper apology. Not a back-handed one.

'So basically, you're saying let's pretend yesterday didn't happen, Storm?' says Gennypha.

Sometimes Gennypha shakes her head when she talks. I find it quite sweet, I have to say. Either she's trying to shake loose the words she wants to say, or she's practising to be a TV newscaster.

'Thanks, Gennz, but no. Although I wish it hadn't happened, it had to, to be honest. But it is what it is. We need to go ahead and move forward, before we ruin the amazing teamwork we have. Yeah?'

Storm's working hard here, to be fair.

'Word.' Mason gives her a thumbs-up.

'I hear what you're saying, Storm,' says Gennypha, shrugging.

I still can't say anything. All of us in our team have had blowouts with Storm, well this is my first proper one, and this is the first time she's almost apologised to anyone. Is she changing? The optimist in me would love to think so, but I kind of doubt it. Kevin in HR must have had some harsh words with her, if you think about it and everything.

'All right, Morag?' Storm looks at me from under her eyebrows.

'No worries,' I say, even though I don't really mean it.

'Yay, sorted! Isn't that great, guys?' Storm looks around for affirmation, and Madison mime-claps.

'Okay, so back to work things: Gennz, please go ahead and test the waters with Cali's people to see if she's interested in joining our team for *BLAT*. We need to get in there quickly in case she says no and we have to find someone else, yeah?'

'No probs, Storm, that's cool,' says Gennypha, with an excited giggle. 'I'll go ahead and do that. I'm proper made-up, can't wait!'

'Okay, guys, let's get back to our desks, yeah? I'll send you the comms plan outline in the next hour or so, and let's discuss it next week at our *BLAT* catch-up, yeah?'

Surprise, surprise: the comms plan outline arrives in my inbox within the hour. So Storm *does* know how to send emails.

Gennypha is our media and celebrity liaison officer, and she works closely with Storm. Here are three things to know about her:

1. She has a ready and generous laugh that seems to gurgle up from way-down deep in her belly, and it draws everyone in. It's a wonderful attribute and the world would be a better place if more people could do the same.
2. She has big ambitions and once told me her dream job would be to handle PR for *Little Mix*, or for any celebrity, on any list, really.
3. Her favourite words are "basically", followed by "soz", "lolz" and "tomoz".

Gennypha's super excited about calling Cali's people, and gets to it straightaway. She limbers up for it with a few neck stretches.

The call goes like this:

- Hi, Vanessa? Cool, hi! All right? Cool. Cool. Yeah, me too. So my name's Gennypha Coleman and I'm calling from a charity called The HAMP.

- Yes, The HAMP. Basically, it stands for helping, H, you-deal-with-anger, A, management, M, problems, P. So, H, A, M, P, yeah?

- Yes, The HAMP. Yes, much easier, lolz.

- So, basically, why I am calling is, we're …. ooh, before I forget, can I just point out that, basically, this conversation needs to be confidential, yeah? Okay to keep this one on the down-low, yeah? Soz.

- Okay, cool. So, basically, we're wondering if your client – Cali …

- Yes, Cali.

- The one who used to play rugby for Wales? Yeah?

- Yes, that's the one. Cali Shannon. Soz – didn't realise you had two people called Cali on your books.

- Yes! Proper random. Lolz!

- Okay, so, basically, The HAMP has been chosen to be in a reality TV programme – you know that one called *Britain Loves a Trier*, where teams compete in a rugby sevens tournament, yeah?

- Yes, that's right, lolz! Tries; trier. Works well, yeah?

- Yes, they were great, weren't they? I know! Who'd have thought they could play so well! Lolz!

- Okay, so basically, what I want to ask is this: do you think Cali would be interested in playing in our rugby sevens team? We think her profile jives nicely with our charity – hand and glove, as they say. Does she still play rugby, do you know?

- Okay, cool.

- Cool. Yeah, yeah, yeah. Of course. You have to ask her.

- Yes, so, basically our challenge is to get a rugby sevens team together, train and practise together and then play in the tournament – it's a festival, basically – in the summer. I can't tell you much about the other teams, at the minute. But I can tell you the festival's in Cardiff, at the Cardiff Arms Park.

- No, the smaller one.

- Oh, right? No, I didn't know that. Wow, that's interesting.

- So, yes, Cali would be the only celebrity in the team. We're only allowed one, and we'd love it to be Cali. That'll knock the opposition into a cocked hat, yay!

- Sorry? ... Yes, absolutely. So, she won't be the only woman in the team. Basically, there'll be more women in the team than you could shake a stick at, to be fair. And a few people who've never even played rugby before, so they'll have to learn; that's the point of the programme, really.

- Okay, cool cool cool. Cool bananas. That'll be *amaa-aaaazing.* Thanks so much.

- Yeah, that'll be great. If you have any questions at all, basically, you can call me on this number – it came up, yeah? Oh, soz, can I have your email address? Is that okay? I'll ping you after this to follow up this convo, and to tell you about the programme, so you can touch base with Cali. And we can take it from there. Yeah?

- Yep. Yep. Yep. Mmhmm. Yep. Dot co dot uk, yeah? Gotcha.

- Brilliant! Thanks, Vanessa. Ace.

- Aye, great talking to you too. Cheers, bye, bye, bye. Nice one!'

Gennypha hangs up and bursts out laughing.

'Oh God, she sounded just like my mate Mia and I *nearly* said "love you"! Lolz, imagine?'

Someone behind our pod starts to clap.

'What?' Gennypha looks up and everyone across the office is standing up, clapping.

'Good call, Gennz! You go girl!' shouts Tracy.

'Yeah, top call. Brill!' says Binny, giving her a thumbs-up.

'Way to go, Gennypha!' says Karo.

'You friggin' beauty!' Ash points at Gennypha with way too much emotion.

One thing to say about working in an open-plan office is that even without eavesdropping or anything, *everybody* can hear *everything.* Just as well this conversation wasn't *really* meant to be confidential.

Chapter 16

Today I'm on annual leave to do my English and *Life in the UK* tests for my settlement visa, also known as 'indefinite leave to remain'. It's quite a faff, to be honest, but I'm not complaining. I appreciate the importance of the process and everything, and it'll also be amazing to have the right to live here indefinitely. But I do find it a bit weird and everything, that your indefinite leave to remain visa is only valid for five and a half years.

Anyway, once you've lived in the UK long enough to apply for your settlement visa, you have to:

1. Prove you can speak English.
2. Prove you know a large number of random historical and social facts about the UK.
3. Provide your biometrics (fingerprints and scans of your irises).
4. Hand over ridiculous amounts of money for all the above.

Having grown up in southern Africa, I speak English as my first language. I passed all my school English exams well, but the UK body doesn't recognise my qualifications. I can pay to have my qualifications verified but it's quicker and easier to do the test.

I arrive at the test venue nice and early, and meet a guy at the front door. He asks my name, crosses it off a list on his clipboard, and takes me to one side. He puts his clipboard down on a table, next to a small tray.

'Right, young lady, please empty your pockets and put everything into this tray.'

I do.

'Good, now pull your pockets out to show me they're empty.'

I do.

'Good. Now open your bag and show me what's in it.'

I do.

'Good. Now take out your passport and topic form and put your bag into the tray.'

I do.

'Good. Now, hair behind your ears, please.'

'Excuse me?'

'Hair behind the ears please, my love. May I have a look in your ears?'

I nod, and do what he says, but what the hell?

'Good. Thank you very much.'

'Checking for wax?'

'Nice one, lady! Nah. Checking for earphones, yeah?'

He seems disappointed he didn't find any. He picks up his clipboard and tells me to follow him into another room. We stand at the back and he puts a mic in front of my face and tells me to count from one to ten into it. He tells me to speak loudly. I feel a bit sheepish and everything, but I do it. He asks me to do it again, and to speak even more loudly. I'm now just short of yelling, and a few people turn around and stare at me and everything. This morning is taking a bit of a weird and unexpected turn, I have to say.

'Right, that's all done, lady. Please go and sit on that chair,' he says, pointing to a specific chair.

I have to climb over a few people to sit on that chair. A young woman climbs over those same people to ask me for my passport and my topic form. She takes them, climbs back over those people to make copies, and then climbs back over them again to give me my passport. She's satisfied with how I've written my topic on the form and everything, and tells me what to do next.

'Put the papers down, like this, when you're called to the front table.'

She climbs back over those people again. I don't know why they have to tell you exactly how to do *everything*. I feel like asking if I'm allowed to fold my arms while I'm sitting here, but don't think they'll find it funny.

When someone calls my name, I climb back over those same people to go to the front table, and put the papers down. It must be the right place because the person takes them. She takes out a pile of papers from a massive folder, and gives me a form to read and sign. She doesn't tell me how to sign it, or whether I should sign quickly or slowly or anything. She opens my passport at the photo page and holds it up at eye level.

She looks at me, at the photo, at me, at the photo, and then ticks another thing off her list. She gives me back my passport and some other pieces of paper and says, 'When you go into the exam room, put these documents on the table in front of you, like this.'

I wonder how many people put their documents in the wrong place, or upside down, or under the table by mistake? Or even refuse to let go of them and everything?

Another person tells me to *walk this way* down the corridor, just like that horrible HR person did at that interview years ago. I try, and realise my trouser pockets are still inside out. I tuck them back in and hope everyone hasn't noticed what an idiot I am and everything. The officer tells me to follow her into the exam room, to sit down (she doesn't say which chair I have to sit on or whether I have to face the table or the wall) and to put my papers down on the table in front of me *like this*. I follow her into the room, put my papers down; the examiner takes them, and clears and sets his stopwatch.

'Shall we get on with this, for what it's worth?'

No one's told me what to say, but 'yes' seems like a good option. We talk about:

1. My topic: my job as a storytelling manager at The HAMP.
2. His topic: entertainment.
3. A random extra topic: special occasions.

It's kind of awkward because I can speak English and everything, and I understand all the words he says, even when he ends the test and waves me out of the room, telling me to take my papers with me. He doesn't tell me which way to walk or which door to leave from, but there's only one.

Another person brings me an envelope and a complimentary pen, and is arms-stretched-out-in-front-of-her-excited to tell me I've passed the English test, with two distinctions and everything.

She tells me to like the exam centre on Facebook but to be honest, I don't think I will. I've had enough of every fucking person telling me what to do and how and when and everything, but they can't take away my distinctions now, can they?

This is also *really* testing my ability to keep my anger from spilling over. Well, maybe it has spilled over just a little bit. I really need to go outside and breathe in some fresh air. Maybe I'll jog around the park, or on the spot. (You can't really tell the difference between those two activities when I'm doing them, to be honest.) I need to be calm for my next helping of red tape: my *Life in the UK* test.

After a short walk, and a stretch and a jog in the park, I walk to the other test centre and join about twenty others in a small waiting room. The admin person there doesn't tell us where to sit or how to walk, but she does tell us to roll up the bottoms of our trousers so she can check our socks and shoes for hidden phones or other devices. After we do so, we put our belongings into a locker, and follow her into the exam room. She tells us to sit anywhere, and that makes me feel like a grown up again.

The test covers a predictable mix of questions about politics, history, how to be a good citizen and neighbour and everything, about the values the UK holds dear, and a whole lot of other random facts. Some facts reminded me of the ones Mr Mathews bored Ruby and me with in my job interview before I joined The HAMP. The relevance to your everyday life of both his and these facts ranges from about sixty-three percent to zero.

I pass the test, collect my certificate, swap my token for the stuff in my locker, and the admin person says I'm free to leave. I'm relieved to have passed both tests and everything, but I'm also exhausted by every single thing about today: the anxiety, the endless orders, the irony, the questions, the answers, the scrutiny, and having to climb over four million people and everything. When I get home, I'm going to put my coat wherever I want to, throw my handbag on to the floor, sit anywhere I like and I might just stuff my phone into my sock. Because I can, and because *no one else* is going to tell me what to do today.

Jamie had better have a magnum of white chilling.

Chapter 17

An all-staff email from Warren pings into my inbox, with a subject line: *BLAT – the players*. Coach wants everyone who's interested in playing in the festival to meet her in the Scrum Room at four o'clock. Warren reminds us this is open to everyone in the charity.

We have some chat in our pod to see who's up for playing rugby. It's funny but when you meet people at work and even when you work closely with them, you don't really get to know everything about them. Like you don't ever really talk about which school or uni you went to, or which sports you used to play or are interested in, unless you're still really involved in playing or watching them now and everything. So our conversation brings some surprises, really.

For example, I never imagined Storm had a sporty background, or that she'd be interested in playing. I didn't think Mason would be, either. I've learnt that he won trophies for sprinting and hurdles at school. He's *never* talked about sport before, so I never thought he'd put himself forward for the team. I've never played rugby either, but I've always watched and followed it and everything. My fitness is okay, plus I think it will be a fun thing to do.

'Wow, Morag, good for *you*,' says Madison, her screensaver briefly in repose.

That kind of comment jars with me, to be honest, but I decide not to react. I know I'm a little older than she is and everything (fair enough,

143

she's in her mid-twenties, so we're about twenty years apart). When Jamie and I go to concerts and stuff, Madison will often say, 'Oh God, old school. Is that band *still* going? I thought they'd all died.' Or 'Oh God, my parents bloody *love* that guy.' It's quite funny, really, but some people think throwaway ageism is okay.

Anyway, there's a real buzz right across the office. Everyone seems to be talking about *BLAT* and who's going to the meeting this afternoon. I can't wait to see who turns up.

It's making me feel super amped about this whole programme, and reminds me how much I love working here at The HAMP and everything. I love how Coach gets us involved in opportunities like this that focus us on the principle of team work and draw us all together. I guess that's the point.

Things like this put all the annoying things – like Madison's ageism, untidy desk and screensaver face, or Storm's unpredictable rantiness, or Mason's noisy crisps – into perspective. Or to get into the language of rugby, it kicks all of that into touch.

We troop into the Scrum Room at four, and Coach is already there, and talking to a visitor. When Coach goes to close the door to start the meeting, the visitor sits down. Coach walks over to the big screen at the front. Warren's trying to connect to the big screen and Karo's watching over his shoulder, whispering instructions.

'Hi, team!' says Coach. 'No warm-ups today, but while we wait for Warren and Karo to get the screen working, let me welcome you and thank you all for coming. This is a great turn-out, ja? It's at times like these when I see how dedicated you all are to The HAMP. When our backsides are against the wall, I know you'll step up to the place and help get us back on the tracks. Ja?'

The screen bursts into life and Warren gives Coach a thumbs-up. Karo pats him on the shoulder.

'Good, thanks Warren. Okay, team, so this is what the next few weeks and months are going to look like, ja?'

She points to the Excel spreadsheet on the screen. There's a hell of a lot of detail; it's quite hard to read, really. It must have taken Warren hours.

'It's going to be a busy time, ja? Once we've got a squad – and that's why we're all here today, ja? – we'll have to start training and having some practice matches,' Coach points to the screen. 'That's a schedule of all the dates for our training sessions and practice matches, ja? Two training sessions a week, sometimes three. It'll be intense, and I wanted you to have an idea of the time commitment you'll need to make.'

Coach pauses briefly for us to scan the spreadsheet and take in the info. I don't think anyone can actually read it, to be honest, but you kind of get the picture anyway.

'And I'm not sure if you know how this works, ja? We'll have a coach who will train us and teach us about the game because, for some of you, it will be the first time you're playing actually rugby, ja? There are other resources too, which I'll tell you about in a moment. All will help us to get super fit, learn quickly the rules, and get ready nicely for the festival in June. Any questions, before I move on?'

Jasper puts his hand up. 'Will we get rugby outfits?'

'Yes, Jasper, you will get rugby kit to wear on the day.'

'Get in!' Jasper jumps up and pumps his arms.

'I hope medium turquoise is your colour,' says Gennypha, laughing.

'I'll look *fab* in medium turquoise, obvs. So what do we wear to rehearsals?'

'You mean actually training, Jasper, ja?' says Coach.

'Absolutely. Yes, Coach.'

'Whatever you feel comfortable to train in is best,' says Coach. 'Binny, you have a question?'

'Brill. Boss, do we get time off in lieu for training? Asking for a friend.'

'Good question, Binny,' says Coach. 'This is an important point for all of you, ja. You need absolutely to volunteer your time for this, ja? So no time off in lieu, no.'

'Yeah, understood,' says Binny, chewing her thumb nail.

'Who will we be playing against?' says Mason.

'Not sure, yet, Mason. It's a round-robin tournament, ja, and they'll do closer to the festival the draw. Any other questions? No? Okay, so we move on, ja?' Coach rubs her hands together.

'As I said, Channel 53 has given us some resources to help those who have never played before to get up and speed. Warren will send you links to training videos. Whether you've played before or not, watch them before you come to the first practice, ja? Warren will also send a link to some sevens matches and festivals, which will be also helpful to watch, especially for those new to the game.'

'Amazing, Coach, cheers,' says Mason.

'Also, the producers have asked us to keep a video diary of the whole process, ja. They'll share some of it on their social media channels, but will put some of it on TV after the festival as part of their promotions for next year's tournament. And to get people more interested in the game too, ja. But they want us to film the video diary ourselves. It's the first time they're taking actually this approach. It's exciting to be part of something that breaks actually ground, ja?' Coach bends her knees as she says the word 'break'.

'And so, let me now introduce you to Pat Moore. Pat, will you stand actually up, so everyone can see properly who you are, ja? Channel 53 introduced us to Pat; she used to work for the BBC in the documentary-making team, and she's volunteered to do the filming for us, ja? Pat, do you want to say a few words?' says Coach, holding her arm out to the side.

(It's quite a silly thought and everything, but do you think all charities have a quota of Pats who volunteer for them?)

'Yeah, thanks Pauli, er, sorry, Coach,' says Pat, as she stands up. 'It's super to be here. *So* looking forward to being part of this exciting programme. Not so ground-breaking for me, though, because at the Beeb we used to do this kind of thing all the time.'

She over-enunciates the word *Beeb* and her eyes dart around the room to make sure none of us has missed which channel she used to worked for.

'So it'll be good to teach you chaps a thing or two; that's what I can bring to the table.' Pat closes her eyes as she talks. 'I'll bring you up to speed with what it means to do work for a TV channel, as I'm sure you won't have done anything like this before, right? Most charities I work with are the same, and it's a real privilege for me to empower folk like you with new knowledge.' She gestures to us folk with both arms.

'Because I know television, I know producers and I really *get* them. I know what they're looking for – that, that ... *secret sauce,* if you will,' she says, rubbing her fingers together and laughing that kind of laugh where you mostly inhale, audibly.

'If you have any questions, I'll be around after the meeting and will be happy to answer them. I'm going to use what I call *granular reality.* It's my *thang.* My wheelhouse, if you will.' She says "wheelhouse" out of the side of her mouth.

'I'll bring my *years* of experience, and together we'll nail this, yeah? Right, good, thanks, Coach. Back to you.'

Any other volunteer called Pat might have taken a humbler run-up to introducing herself. How will this Pat and Mason get along? As the digital lead and everything, he'll have to work with her, so there's a lot for him to take in all at once. He's holding his head in his hands, and that says it all, really. Mason's a lovely guy and everything, but he doesn't do well with people who are arrogant or clever-clogs straight out of the gate.

'Thanks, Pat,' says Coach. 'And ja, I feel also actually privileged to have someone with such experiences to volunteer here for us at The HAMP. I think you'll do a great job, Pat, and I know you'll enjoy working with my amazing team. Everything we do, we do to help people deal with their anger, don't we, team? And we couldn't do what we do without this brilliant bunch of people, ja? My superb team will make you feel welcome, Pat, and together we'll be the best side in the whole of *BLAT*, ja?'

And that right there is one of the reasons why Coach is the best boss I've ever had. She's gracious and secure enough in herself to give others credit for their achievements and expertise and everything. She doesn't let her emotions get in the way like I and, well, a lot of us do, really. But you can tell she feels things deeply. And she knows how to say the right thing, especially in moments like these.

Coach brings us back to what's important – why we do what we do – and reminds us that we're a team, that she's proud of us and that we're doing this together and everything. She's so amazing, and I hope I'm learning from her. Not sure I am, really, but I'll keep working on it.

Jasper puts his hand up again.

'Yes, Jasper,' says Coach.

'Will Pat be filming us at the practices?'

'Yes, Jasper, at most of them.'

'So will we be on telly on the day, and again next year?'

'Yes, Jasper,' says Coach.

Jasper jumps up again and shouts, 'Yes! Get in!'

'And in the papers?'

'Probably, yes, Jasper.'

'Yes! Get in!'

Jasper sits down again, looking super proud of himself.

'So, team, back to the team. We're allowed one celebrity player in our team and – Storm, am I allowed to tell everyone? Ja?'

Storms gives Coach a thumbs-up.

'Okay, so the comms team is asking actually Cali Shannon if she wants to play for our team. Cali used to play in the Welsh women's rugby team, ja? We're dotting our eyes and crossing our tees that she'll say yes,' says Coach, gesturing across her eyes and down her T-shirt, in an endearing, semi-Catholic, fully-mixed metaphor.

'Other than that, we're not allowed any other club or professional players in our team. I think we're okay there, ja?'

Mason raises his hand like he's stopping traffic.

'No friends and fam, yeah?'

'That's correct, Mason. Apart from the celebrity, who we hope will be Cali, the rest of the team has to be the charity's staff members, ja? Our own HAMP squad, ja? But by all ways and means invite your friends and family to come and watch the festival. The morer the merrier, ja?'

I raise my hand and Coach lifts her hand, palm-up, for me to stand.

'I've never played rugby, Coach,' I say, as I stand, 'but I grew up watching it with my dad and cousins and everything, so I know quite a bit about them. I mean the rules of rugby, not my dad and cousins. I know *them*, obviously. And I'm quite fit – not *that* kind of fit! I mean, I walk a lot and go to gym. So, I'm keen to play … rugby.'

I'm nervous and a bit embarrassed and, as always, making such an idiot of myself trying to be funny and then just fluffing it all up and everything. I've also just said too much. No one needs that amount of detail, right? I'm also worried I'm overselling myself here, and also, I'm sure someone's sniggering. Mason mime-applauds me and that makes me feel better. So does Karo, and Tracy winks at me and gives me a thumbs-up. Madison covers her mouth and looks away as I sit down. I guess she's the sniggerer.

'Okay, thanks, Morag. That's a good start, and I can hear clearly your passion. That's what we need in our team, ja? So who *has* played before?' says Coach.

Barry and Karo put their hands up.

'I once dated a rugby player, does that count?' says Tracy, guffawing.

'So did I!' says Mason.

Coach laughs her adorable, silent, closed-eye laugh.

'Coach, I played a bit at school. I was all right,' says Binny, choosing which nail to bite.

'Me too,' says Ash.

'Okay, great. So there are a four of you who've played before, ja, that's fantastic!' Coach holds up four fingers. 'Four of you plus Cali; that makes five experienced players so far, ja? That's if Cali says yes.' Coach crosses her fingers. 'Who else wants to play?'

Jasper, Storm, Tracy, Charlie, Robyn, Mason and I put our hands up.

'Brilliant, team, that's brilliant,' says Coach, counting us. 'Twelve players. We have a squad, team. We have a team!'

I'm super chuffed and a little nervous now, to be honest. It's getting real.

'Should I also email everyone else after the meeting, Coach? To see if anyone else is interested?' says Warren, sounding tentative.

'Ja, it's a good idea, Warren. Thanks.'

'Coach, my boyfriend plays too. I came to the meeting to tell you that, because he's super keen to be on TV– um, get involved, yeah?' says Madison.

'Er, Madz, didn't you hear what Coach said?' says Storm. 'That we can only have HAMP players and the one celeb?'

'Oh, right. Oh, okay.' Madison's screensaver glides back up.

'Thanks, Madison,' says Coach. 'And I've found already a coach who's happy to volunteer for us, so if you've put forward yourselves, you'll meet him at the first practice next week. And let's see what happens then, ja?'

'Shall we also wait and see what comes from the email?' says Warren. 'Maybe some people weren't able to come to the meeting today but would still like to play, yeah? Or maybe some people here might have said they want to play but when they think about it afterwards they might not be sure they still want to; not in a bad way, but you know what I mean? Or some people who are here might have another think and decide they want to play?'

'Okay, good call, Warren,' Coach gives Warren a thumbs-up. 'It sounds like you've thought of every possible permutation, ja? Keep me updated, ja, and we'll take it from there. I have to let soon the producers know who's in our team, but I think it's more than anything a formality, ja? They said we can pick our own squad. We just need to prove we're following their Ps and Qs, ja?'

'I think you mean Ts and Cs, Coach? But those too,' says Storm, laughing. Coach laughs too and gives her a thumbs-up.

As Coach looks around the room, her eyes light up.

'Oh my God, guys, what a great team you are. Each and every one of you, you make absolutely me proud. You do every day great work. Thank you for your commitments to The HAMP and for going out of the back and beyond for the charity.' Coach claps in the general direction of all of us.

'Let's go now back to our desks and keep doing good work, ja? Thank you, one and all of you,' says Coach, blowing her full-time whistle, and drawing the meeting to a close with an outstretched arm.

What a fucking legend.

Chapter 18

It's our first training session at a rugby club in Bermondsey in southeast London today. Coach lives in the area and sometimes volunteers here as a coach, at the weekends.

We're going to have our training sessions here after work, even though it'll be dark and everything, but Coach thought we should have our first session during the day. It's a cold Saturday today, the sky is dark grey and it's windy as all heck.

We gather outside the main clubhouse, Pat with her small hand-held camera at the ready. I'm jumping up and down and blowing into my hands; it's equally nerves and an effort to keep warm, and Pat's already filming us. It's quite hard to be oblivious to the filming, but you have to try and ignore the camera, don't you? Oh boy, I hope I don't make even more of an idiot of myself than normal, and have Pat capture it on film for the world to see and everything. I'm going to obsess about this a bit, I can feel it right now.

This is who's arrived today:

1. Karo.
2. Barry.
3. Ash.
4. Mason.
5. Tracy.

6. Binny.
7. Robyn.
8. Storm.
9. Charlie.
10. Jasper.
11. Me.

We haven't yet heard if Cali, our celebrity, will be joining us.

Richard, the security guy from our building reception, is here too. He's wearing his Spurs beanie and scarf, as he's going to a home game this afternoon. Not sure who told him about this practice, but he always seems to know everything that goes on in our office. He also *loves* reality TV, even though this one's nothing like *I'm a Celebrity Get Me Out of Here*.

Pat walks around filming us, as Coach gets us together to introduce us to our volunteer coach, Dave.

'Yeah, thanks Pauli, and hello everyone. My name's Dave Moody, and I'm proper chuffed and excited that Pauli invited me to coach you guys. It's a *huge* challenge she's given me and, full disclosure, I've never done anything like this before. But we're going to give this reality TV malarkey our best shot, yeah?' he says. 'Let me tell you a bit about myself, in case you're interested.'

'Oh yes please!' says Jasper.

'Well done, that was the right answer, yeah?' Dave laughs. 'So, like Pauli, your Coach, I also volunteer here every Sunday, and in my day-job I'm the head rugby coach at a public school in west London.'

Pat asks him to speak up a bit, as her microphone isn't picking his voice up as it should. Richard is standing right on Dave's shoulder staring into the camera, and Pat asks him to move away. He takes a few steps to the right, still staring into her camera.

'Yeah, this better?' says Dave, a bit louder. Pat nods. 'Okay, so I grew up right here in Bermondsey and played rugby at this club as a youngster, and came back to play here after uni. This community means a lot to me and my family – we've been living here for generations, and still do – so coaching here at the club is my way of giving back.'

'You're amazing,' says Jasper, who's easily starstruck.

'Cheers. Nice one. So you're an interesting-looking bunch, ain't ya? You'll frighten the life out of the other sides, just by the way you look, won't you?'

We all laugh. But he probably has a point, if you think about it and everything. Looking around, we're a bunch of ages, shapes and sizes, and we do look a bit scary and random. Not in a bad way, as Warren would say, but we don't really look like a sevens team. I'm wearing a scruffy old tracksuit and beanie, and pretty ancient trainers (this is what I call trainers: *takkies*), and I can't believe Jasper's arrived in full American football kit. Storm's wearing a bright pink velour tracksuit, shiny white trainers and a white bobble hat. She looks like a piece of coconut ice.

'But the most important thing, yeah, is whether we can be any good at rugby sevens, isn't it? Or, is it about your good looks?' Dave stretches the words 'or' and 'your' into a few more syllables than necessary. 'Well, in my experience, good looks never won any matches, yeah? Although Jonny Wilkinson might disagree with me, yeah?' Coach Dave laughs at his own joke.

'Who's Jonny Wilkinson?' says Jasper from behind his helmet.

'He's fine, hoo's yersel'?' says Dave, in a terrible Scottish accent. 'He only used to play for England, yeah?'

Jasper raises his eyebrows. Bet you anything you like he'll Google Jonny as soon as he can.

'I see you're into your American football, mate?'

'*Moi*? What do you mean?' says Jasper, looking around.

'What you're wearing, mate! We don't dress like that for rugby, yeah? But thanks for making the effort today.' Dave winks at Jasper. 'Lose the helmet, mate, you don't want to injure your colleagues, yeah?'

Jasper blushes. He takes his helmet off and looks across at Mason. He leans so far to one side he almost falls over.

'So who else of you has never played?' says Dave.

All of us, except Karo, Binny, Ash and Barry, put our hands up, and Coach Dave asks us if we know anything about the game.

'I've watched a lot of rugby, so I kind of understand how it works and have a vague idea of the rules and everything,' I say.

'Well, tbh, had no interest in rugby until the RWC15,' says Mason.

With a loud and dramatic intake of air, Jasper says, 'Me too! Small world, wow.'

'It's probably fair to say that's true for a lot of people, yeah?' says Dave. 'Anyone else want to tell me what brought you here today?'

'Yeah. So me and my mate played a bit of club rugby. I'm okay at it, but yeah, that's me,' says Binny, looking at her nails.

'Fair play, fair play. Anyone else?' says Dave.

'I used to play football in our garden, with my brothers,' says Storm. 'I loved it. But I also used to watch rugby with them – especially the Lions. Ooh.'

Dave nods.

'Well, I've ordered a book of the rules,' says Robyn. Dave gives her a thumbs up.

'And I've been into the Scrum Room and Tight-head Nook *hundreds* of times, obviously,' says Tracy, cackling.

Dave looks at Coach and shrugs.

'That's very funny, Tracy, ja? Sorry, Dave, that's an in-house joke. We have actually in our office meeting rooms with those names.'

'Nice one, Coach, I like that,' says Dave.

'And you've all watched also the training videos I sent, ja?'

155

We all nod at Coach. Storm's nod isn't all that convincing.

'Cool, cool, cool. Good thinking.' Dave gives Coach a thumbs-up. 'Okay, so rugby sevens in a nutshell, yeah?' He picks up a rugby ball and bounces it between his hands. 'It's a game played by two teams of seven fighting over an oval ball.'

'Ooh, fun!' says Jasper, clapping.

'Yeah. Right, so your job as a team is to try and get the ball over the white line at one end of the field, at the same time trying to stop the other team doing the same at the other end. You have to defend your white line to stop them doing that, and they have to do the same with their white line too. Understood?'

'Can I be the defender?' asks Charlie from volunteer services.

I had no idea Charlie was Irish; this is the first time I've ever heard him speak in my whole life.

'You *all* need to defend, mate, unless you're on the attack, yeah?' says Dave. 'Every time your team touches the ball down over the white line, you get points, and then you get a chance to try and kick the ball through those two posts up there – what we call the uprights – for extra points. That's called converting the try.'

'To what?' says Jasper. 'Sorry, Dave, I'm still learning all the lingo and stuff.'

'Yeah, I clocked that one, mate! When you dot the ball down over the white line, it's called a try, yeah, and it's worth five points. Then you *convert* the try, which means someone in your team kicks for posts, in other words tries to kick the ball through those uprights over there. If they do, you get an extra two points, giving you a total of seven. Yeah?'

'Yay!' Jasper claps. 'And if they don't?'

'Then you don't get the two points, duh!' says Tracy.

Jasper puts his hands up in surrender.

'Right, so what's important is that you all bring your own strengths to the team. It could be speed and a bit of dexterity, to move the ball down the field and over the line, or it could be skill with the boot to get the ball over the posts, or to gain some ground. And we need weight and strength to get over the line or push your opponents away from it.'

'Right, now I know my role,' says Storm, picking up her phone.

Jasper looks terrified. He jumps up and down, and tries to hide from Pat's camera.

'I think I overestimated what I could do,' says Jasper, looking at Dave.

'Don't worry, young man. If all else fails, a positive attitude never hurt no one. Yeah?' says Dave. 'Believe me, we need them attitudes and all, yeah?'

He reassures us he's taught plenty of players from scratch – most of them under the age of ten, to be fair – but he promises to get us match-ready. Not being funny or anything, but that sounds like a massive ambition. He must know what he's doing, right? Fingers crossed. (This is how I say fingers crossed: *holding thumbs.*)

'That puts nicely everything into a nutshell, ja,' says Coach. 'Thanks, Dave.'

'That's all right, Pauli.'

'I think we start now calling you Coach Dave, ja?'

'Whatever blows your highlights back, guys. That's what they call me at school. Okay, right, let's get you lot moving!' says Coach Dave, clapping. 'And from the off, yeah, I don't want to see you on your phones at practice, yeah? You won't be taking calls on the field and all!'

Storm puts her phone away and waves an apology to Coach Dave. He gives her a thumbs-up and steps back. He bumps into Richard, who's moved closer to him again, looking straight into Pat's camera.

Coach Dave gives us some warm-up stretches, and then gets us to do some sprints across the field and back. Karo surprises everyone with her speed and everything, as do Barry, Mason, Tracy and Ash. Storm, Robyn and I come in last. This is how speedy I am:

1. Nought miles an hour.

I'm so slow I almost move backwards, so sometimes I pretend I'm just running on the spot, if I'm honest. But if what Coach Dave said is true, I won't be in the team for my speed, or my boot; I'll just be making up the numbers, I think. Otherwise I don't have much else I can offer. That's pretty much my role in life, in a nutshell, now that I think about it and everything.

We don't have enough players for two full teams today, so Coach Dave gets us into two teams – one of six and one of five – and gives one team high-vis bibs to put on.

'Right, you might be surprised that you're going to start playing now. Bibs team, you'll play left to right and you'll kick off. Other team, right to left, yeah? I want to see what you lot are made of, yeah? I want to see your instincts for the game.' Coach Dave bends his knees a little when he says the word "instincts", while some of us put our bibs on. He waves us off on to the field. 'Oy, don't skip, yeah? I said run!' he shouts at Jasper.

'Soz, Coach Dave! So-oz,' says Jasper, jumping up and down and waving at Coach Dave.

'Something to remember: when you kick off at the start or re-start, you have to kick the ball for at least ten metres, yeah?'

Our team's going to kick off, so Ash walks to the halfway line, bouncing the ball on his boots as he walks. Coach Dave blows the whistle and Ash kicks the ball along the ground towards the far corner. It bounces skwonk. Ash shrugs and starts jogging towards the ball.

We all follow but Karo speeds after it, scoops it up and tucks it under her arm. She heads straight towards the try line. Barry, with his team behind him, runs at her and hesitates a bit before leaping at her ankles. He stretches wide, tapping the edge of her boots enough to make her stumble and drop the ball. His team mates scatter and jump away from the ball, as it bounces into touch.

'Oy, don't just run after the ball wherever it goes! Think a bit!' says Coach Dave, tapping the side of his head. I have no idea what he means, but at least I'm too slow to get anywhere near the ball anyway.

'Now when the ball goes into touch like this – over the sideline, yeah – there's usually what we call a line-out. But let's save the mechanics of how that works for another day, yeah? I'll show you what to do and then explain it next time, all right?'

Coach Dave tells Mason to throw the ball in from the sideline, demonstrating an over-arm throw. Mason throws it, Storm catches it and hesitates before throwing it underhand and out wide to Ash. He snatches it at speed and heads straight towards the try-line, watching either side of him as he sprints. No one reaches him, and he takes another quick look around before taking a wide loop to the right. He stands behind the posts for a second before launching into a dramatic, painful dive to the ground, slamming the ball down under the posts. We all run to him, screaming his name and high-fiving him.

'Just like on the telly, yeah?' shouts Ash, celebrating by dancing the floss – hardly rock'n'roll, but his eight-year-old daughter will love it.

Ash looks to Coach Dave, who tells him to give the ball to Storm.

'And oy, you! Don't do that! Don't *ever* do that!' Coach Dave throws his arms in the air, as Jasper jumps up from a celebratory roly-poly on the field.

'Sorry, I'm so excited because we're going to get converted,' says Jasper, blushing.

Coach Dave rolls his eyes.

'Oy, oy, oy. Okay, right, different type of ball skills for you to try,

159

yeah?' Coach shouts at Storm. 'Reckon you can kick for posts? Up that way, straight through the middle, yeah?'

'I'll give it a go. I'm quite good with a football, so let's see.' Storm shrugs and takes the ball from Coach Dave. She swings her foot back for the kick and drops the ball as she swings it back. The ball lands on the lower part of her shin and she kicks it straight up in the air, missing her head by a whisker.

Coach Dave draws a low horizontal line with his right arm and blows the whistle. Pat runs on to the field as we all turn around and run in different directions.

'Back to your own halves, yeah, for what we call the re-start!' shouts Coach Dave. 'Good effort, you in the pink, yeah? Try to get your foot properly *under* the ball next time, yeah? You'll get there and all.'

Storm blushes. It's so weird, you know. Fair play to Coach Dave, to be honest, for looking at someone who looks like a bright pink marshmallow and going, 'Yeah, they look like they'll be good at kicking for posts'.

That reminds me; here are three more words I like:

1. Oxymoron.
2. Juxtaposition.
3. Whip-smart.

The game continues for ten more minutes, gathering momentum in the midst of increasing chaos on the field. We're like Monty Python's Olympics for Twits, where no one really knows what they're doing and we're all wildly running after the ball wherever it goes. It's quite funny, really, and bloody exhausting, if you ask me.

When Coach Dave blows the half-time whistle, Coach runs on to the field with water bottles. There are only seven bottles, so everyone has to share. Mason takes out some handy wipes from his pocket and hands them around. You don't want to pick up germs from anyone else, especially not when you've only just started training and everything.

The second half starts slowly and five minutes in, I stop a try-in-the-making because the person with the ball, who's wearing a high-vis bib and everything, runs into me. I'm trying to conserve my energy, but clearly not concentrating enough on what's going on. Probably better if I stop the other team's try rather than our team's, though, hey?

Karo scores three tries – Coach Dave calls them "soft tries" – before the end of the match, and Tracy has a go at converting one but hooks it to the left, under the uprights. Barry takes the ball for the other two, converts one and shanks the other. Ash scores another try, mainly because Jasper screams and runs away as Ash runs towards him.

Storm has another bash at kicking; this time she heeds Coach Dave's advice. The ball goes nowhere near the uprights, but at least it goes forward. Barry's team wins the match, and we all shake hands at the end of the game.

Coach Dave huddles us together, and Pat films us as we try to catch our breath. Richard makes his way into the huddle.

'Do you reckon we'll become a team, guys? A proper team?' shouts Coach Dave.

'Yeah, a proper team an' all!' shouts Richard, looking straight at Pat as he jumps in the air.

'That was total chaos, yeah, to be fair. But you've given me something to work with,' says Coach Dave. 'I can see what you're all made of. We've got time to get you playing a half-decent game. I'm not a miracle worker, and we're not expecting you to become the Lions. But we can give you a bit of shape and direction, yeah?

'Next time we'll talk more about the rules, about scrums and knock-ons and line-outs and rucks and mauls. Maybe you'll want to watch some matches on the old YouTube, and maybe you'll want to look up some of the words you've heard today. Let me tell you, matches are won and lost here,' Coach Dave says, tapping the side of his forehead.

'It's all in the old watch and chain, yeah? It's a game of strategy, as much as it is skill. But we'll learn together, we'll build strength and endurance together, and, if we believe it, we can achieve it together. It's always down to who wants it more, every time, yeah? And how much do we want it?' says Coach Dave.

'SO MUCH!' Jasper and I are the only ones who shout, and clap. Pat's filming us and everyone else is watching. Oh, boy.

'That's the spirit, yeah? More of that, please. Right, Coach Pauli?' Coach Dave claps.

'Team, I know you'll do me and The HAMP proud, ja? We're going to make actually history, ja? I can feel it in my bone structure. We can do this for The HAMP!' says Coach.

We're back in *Invictus*. We look nothing like the Springboks, but I'm sure we're starting to feel like them. Like winners. Or maybe-winners. I feel waves of exhilaration and joy rise up through my whole being.

'Let's do this thing, ja! Coach Dave will mould you into the shape of a team, and you'll play really rugby. There'll be no stopping The HAMP. I'm so excited, team. I can't even think of the words,' says Coach.

Pat is now running around the huddle to capture the mounting wave of excitement. She taps my leg to let her into the middle of the huddle, and she lies on her back to film us. I'm not sure why she wants to film up our noses, but she knows what she's doing. She asks Richard to get up off his knees and step away from the middle of the circle.

I can't stop myself, I jump up and punch the air with both hands, shouting, 'Yes! Let's do this for The HAMP!' I look for someone to high-five and reach over to Jasper on the other side of the huddle. I just miss jumping on Pat.

I was hoping my excitement would spread like a kind of Mexican wave through the huddle, but no one else moves; no one else high-fives anyone else. Karo looks around to see if she should join in just to make me feel better, I think, but she doesn't.

Something else you've probably noticed about me is that I get easily caught up in the moment, especially when it comes to sport and everything. And to be honest, I kind of forget I'm not watching *Invictus* or anything. I forget this is real life and we aren't the Springboks – these guys are just my colleagues – and we aren't winning the World Cup.

We're just a random bunch of people standing in a huddle on a freezing cold field under the dark clouds of a winter's morning in Bermondsey. I'm making an idiot of myself and Pat's caught it all on film. Oh well, you just have to get over yourself when you're part of something like this, I guess. Best you forget the camera's there at all, and leave your dignity in your backpack. You sure won't be needing it much on the field, I can tell you that for free.

'Right, team. It's a good first day out on the pitch, yeah? You're a great starting squad,' says Coach Dave. 'I need you to work together, to watch each other's every move. Anticipate *every* action – you need to scratch your team-mate's back before they even know they have an itch, yeah? Not literally, Jasper, yeah? Let's not do that, Jasper, yeah? But fair play to you guys, this was a good start and I'm sure you'll all learn how to play the game soon enough, yeah? I'd like to see you twice a week for practice, and we'll have practice matches with some of our teams here too. Sound good, yeah?'

'*BLAT* squad goals. Yeah, sounds good, Coach Dave,' says Mason, with a thumbs-up.

'Fantastic. See you next … what did we decide, Pauli, Tuesday? Yeah? Same place, same team, yeah?'

'Yes, Tuesdays and Thursdays after work, ja. Great work, team,' says Coach, clapping. 'This is a fantastic start, ja. Get in, The HAMP!'

'Crikey Moses, got to run!' says Richard, looking at his watch. He waves and runs backwards, still looking at Pat's camera.

Chapter 19

It's Monday morning. We have two big things coming up in the next six months or so at The HAMP: our annual report, and *BLAT*.

I've been in touch with Alex, that Zimbabwean consultant, and she's thrilled we want to feature her story in the annual report. I've sent her some questions to think about before Ash and I meet with her next week.

'Hey Mase, how're you and Pat getting along with the filming?' says Storm.

'Fine,' says Mason.

'Are you and Pat getting on okay, Mase?' I ask.

'Yep, fine,' says Mason.

'Don't you find her a bit irrit–' says Gennypha.

'*Massively.*'

I know what he means.

Gennypha is still waiting to hear from Cali's agent, Vanessa, to let us know if she'll join the *BLAT* squad.

'Shit, Gennz, I keep forgetting to ask you about Quinn. Have you reached out to his people? And have you done any more digging into his background, yet?' says Storm, taking a massive bite out of her cheese and ham breakfast toastie.

Storm still wants us to feature Quinn in the annual report, somehow, as she thinks it'll help him relaunch his career and everything.

165

Sometimes Storm thinks our annual report is way more than it is.

'I've done a little more, Stormz,' says Gennypha. 'Basically, I can't find anything about him that looks dodgy, apart from the issue with him and his wife, obvs.'

'Okay, cool. Well, there's a piece around ... well, you have to ask him about coming in to meet with Coach, yeah? So it makes sense for you to ask about the annual report at the same time, yeah?' says Storm, with her mouth full.

'Yeah? I can do that today. Basically, I haven't had an answer from Cali's agent yet either, so maybe I can call team Quinn while I'm waiting to hear from her. I'm giving Vanessa another day or two before I follow up. What do you think?'

'I hear where you're going with this, Gennz, but we're up against it, you know. We don't have a lot of wriggle room, yeah? So I'm going to need you to go ahead and reach out again to Vanessa...' Storm holds her toastie in her mouth and scrolls through her phone calendar with her little finger. She takes the toastie out of her mouth. '...by tomorrow at the latest, yeah?'

'I was hoping to take tomoz as TOIL, remember? I emailed you about that. But basically, I guess, if it's okay with you, Stormz, I can push my time off in lieu back to Friday. Then I'll be able to follow up with Vanessa tomorrow, and I'll call Quinn's people today. I'll stick those both in my calendar now,' says Gennypha, typing. 'Done! I'll keep you posted, Stormz, okay?'

'Brilliant.' Storm licks her fingers and studies her toastie for the next bite. 'Okay, so action points moving forward: you're going to reach out to Quinn's people today, and you're going to go ahead and touch base with Vanessa tomo-'

'Unless she replies to me today of course, yeah?' Gennypha chuckles.

'Sure, Gennz, sure. Absolutely. So, to recap: you're going to reach out to Quinn's agent to find out if he's down for coming in to meet with Coach, and for being featured in our annual report. And then you'll go ahead and follow up with Vanessa tomorrow, and you'll report back to me ASAP, with their answers, whether yes or no. Does that cover everything, Gennz?' Storm eyes the last bite of her toastie.

'Yes, Stormz, all covered. I've made a note of my action points.'

'Great, thanks. Won't you do me a favour and send your notes through to me too?'

'Seriously? I don't want to say that's *overkill* or anything, but …'

'Gennz, you know how fastidious I am about my paper trails. Send me your notes within the hour, please.'

Storm has zero intention of doing any of these things:

1. Opening Gennypha's email.
2. Reading her notes.
3. Keeping a paper trail, ever.

'Great chat, Gennz.'

'Yep.' Gennypha looks exhausted from one conversation focusing so much time, attention and effort on this many topics:

1. Two.

The finance director's office door opens and Barry steps out, laughing. It seems he wears a HAMP T-shirt to work every day, unless he has a finance committee meeting. He pops his head back into the office to say something to Robyn, and you can hear her laughing too.

Things are different now that Chester's left and Robyn's taken over as finance director. There's a lightness in the air over there, and Barry and Robyn seem to get on well too.

Barry walks over to our pod, full of confidence, like he's the guest of honour we've all been waiting for.

'Morning, team comms! Hope you're all *Welsh*,' he says, looking around for the laugh. He taps his signet ring on the desk. Storm giggles; the rest of us smile. He looks at Storm. 'Not gonna lie to you, but this is one pretty pod of humanity, like.'

'Yeah, Barry, is that right?' says Storm, with a coy flick of her ponytail.

'Not gonna lie, Storm. All right?'

'Yeah, well, I'm not *Welsh* but all good here.' Storm does a mini storm-clap.

'Not everyone's perfect, right enough.' Barry opens his mouth wide and forces out a shout-laugh. He's a bottomless pit of well-rehearsed throwaway lines.

'Tops here, cheers,' says Mason, giving Barry a thumbs-up.

'See you all later at training, yeah? It's been quite tough, like, don't you think?'

'Yep,' I say. 'I thought I was fit and everything, but I'm going to have to do lots more at gym, I think. Otherwise I won't be able to keep up, to be honest.'

Barry's too busy scanning the office behind me to bother listening to me. He turns to Storm.

'I'm not being funny or anything, but the other night I could hardly walk home, me. Coach Dave trains us even harder than my club coach back home used to, he does. But as I always say, it's short-term pain for long-term gain, right enough.'

'I thought I was the only one struggling,' says Storm. 'Glad we're all feeling the same. To be honest, I'm chuffed to be getting fit, moving forward.'

'And sometimes backwards, to be fair.' Barry chortles and surveys the office again. 'Right, comms pod, I'm away back to my desk to do a number or two. Keep doing your words and pictures, yeah? See you lot at practice.'

'Cheers, Bazza,' says Storm, with a shy look I've never seen on her before.

Whaaaat? Is there something going on between those two? Who'd have put *them* together? It makes sense, if you think about it and everything; words and numbers do kind of go together. But Barry and Storm, the *actual* people? That thought completely blows my mind, to be honest.

It's Tuesday, and Storm walks into the office on time and with purpose.

'Gennz, lovey, have you heard back from Vanessa yet? And have you called Quinn's guys?' she says, throwing her bag down on to her desk. Five Tupperwares of different sizes roll out.

'Morning, Stormz,' says Gennypha, unpacking her bag. She sounds annoyed.

'Gennz, hi. Good morning! Sorry, that was very rude of me. How are you, lovey?' says Storm, righting all her Tupperwares and looking for the one with porridge in it.

'Lolz. Good thanks, Stormz. Nope, still no word from Vanessa – I checked my emails on my way in this morning to see if she'd replied last night, but still nothing. I'll give her a call in a bit. And I reached out to Quinn's people yesterday, and basically they said they'd get back to me today.'

'Cool, thanks. Do you think you could call Vanessa, and maybe chase Quinn's guys before lunchtime, Gennz? Will that be okay?' Storm can be syrupy-sweet when she needs something from you, like answers before her catch-up with Coach or something.

Gennypha gives her a thumbs-up and rolls her eyes as she slumps down in her chair.

'And Morag, lovey, have you had a chance to draft something about *BLAT* for the newsletter?' Storm's ticking off her whole to-do list.

'Yep, it's in your inbox, Storm. Remember? You wanted it last Friday, so I sent it to you at the end of Thursday.'

'Oh right, Morag, of course you did. Won't you do me a favour and send it to me again, my lovely? And this time just put in the subject line: *"BLAT* draft article to review today", yeah? Maybe in caps.'

'Like I did on Thursday? Sure, I'll do that again for you, Storm.'

What's funny, no what's really flipping *annoying* about this, is that no matter what subject line you put on your emails, Storm will *never* read them. You can mark them as *urgent*, give them desperate and demanding subject lines like *READ THIS NOW* – even add a blaring siren that goes off when you open the email – and this is how much difference any of those things makes:

1. Zero.

And this is the likelihood Storm will open or read your email, any time, ever:

1. Zero.

I email and print the article and put it on Storm's desk – belts and braces and everything – but it's going to gather dust along with all the other drafts that have been there since the dawn of time. Not exactly the dawn of time, but at least since she started at The HAMP.

'Super, thanks, lovey,' says Storm, when I put the article on her desk. 'Can't wait to read it. Your last article was quite a good effort, I think.'

FFS.

Gennypha walks back to her desk, puts her phone down and walks over to Storm's desk.

'So I called Vanessa and basically, she says Cali's *intrigued* by the invitation to play rugby sevens with us. They want to have a chemistry meeting with us at The HAMP, so they can, as she says, meet our team and check out the vibe between the two tribes. That sounds cheesy but positive, right, Stormz? And I felt pretty bad about chasing Quinn's people, but they said they were still considering our requests and they'll get back to me, yeah?'

'I'm guessing you've told all of them about me and that *I* lead the team, yeah?' says Storm.

'Basically, I told Vanessa I'd organise things from our side as soon as she gives me some dates. And Quinn's people are going to come back to me once they know more. Maybe tomoz. Is that okay, Stormz?'

'Sounds good, thanks. But I'm going to need you to go ahead and leave me to deal with Vanessa, going forward, and with Quinn's people if we'll be working with them, yeah? I really appreciate all the groundwork you've done, Gennz.' Storm looks all the way down her nose at Gennypha.

'Cali is low-hanging fruit, to be honest. Like pushing on an open door, really. But still, I'm really proud of how you're growing as I'm coaching you into this role. The best compliment you can give your mentor is to do great work, and that's exactly what you're doing for me, Gennz. It's *really* brilliant, *really* brilliant. Thank you.'

Gennypha stares, open-mouthed, at Storm.

'You know, what you do makes my life so much easier, but at this stage I think we need to escalate these relationships a little further up the food-chain, yeah?' Storm points her spoon in the air to show just how much further up. 'Oh, and set that chemistry meeting for Friday. That works best for me, okay?'

'But not for me, Stormz, remember? – I'm taking time off.'

'Oh right, Gennz, of course. But if Friday works for Vanessa and Cali and them, let's do it. It is what it is, yeah? We can't let *your* TOIL stand in the way of a chemistry meeting, can we? I'll just go ahead and meet with them if they want to do Friday, yeah?'

Gennypha's whole demeanour changes. I feel sorry for her, really, because this happens *all* the time. When Storm gives her things to do – a lot, if not all of her work, to be honest – it's always sugar-coated with the promise that she can lead on them. But once Gennypha's done all the groundwork, Storm rushes in and takes over the best parts of the work, and all the glory. Storm's definition of teamwork is: get your team to do all the hard work and then take over when everything looks good and shiny.

Storm's approach is so unlike Coach's; I don't think Coach can have any idea Storm works like this because if she did, I'm sure she wouldn't stand for it. Coach is fair and just, she acknowledges everyone's contribution to any success, and she's always generous with praise. Always. Bet you anything you like Storm won't even tell Coach Gennypha did this. It happens every single time.

If I were Gennypha, I'd be feeling really frustrated and everything. Doing the same thing over and over and expecting a different result *is* the definition of insanity, of course, and it really can do your head in. It's like emailing her the same thing over and over, with different subject lines, and expecting she'll actually *read* the fucking email.

Gennypha walks back to her desk, throws her phone into her handbag and walks out of the office, trailing her handbag behind her. Storm builds a little tower out of all her Tupperwares and carries them through to the kitchen, oblivious to Gennypha's frustration.

To be honest, I don't know if Storm has a thick skin, or if she just chooses to play ignorant. Or if she really *really* needs to put her Tupperwares in the fridge.

Chapter 20

We're at the rugby club again for training. Gennypha told our team the chemistry meeting with Cali and Vanessa had gone really well, and Cali and Coach had hit it off straightaway. Whether it was Gennypha, Storm, Coach, or all of them who charmed Cali and Vanessa, Cali has agreed to play rugby sevens for The HAMP.

And Cali's coming to the training session this evening. We're all super excited about it. An actual celebrity in our team, and she's going to train with us.

Gennypha walks towards us with Cali. Pat runs ahead of them and jogs backwards, filming them as they join the rest of us. Storm pushes me to the side and steps forward.

'Oh super, Gennz, thanks so much for bringing Cali to the training. You should have said, Calz, I could have met you and travelled here with you.' Storm gives Cali three air kisses. 'Lovely to see you again, Calz. How're you doing?'

'Well, Gennz is a proper legend, she is. When we went for lunch, Gennz said she'd bring me to the club to meet the team. Ace, that was,' says Cali, mock-punching Gennypha on the arm. 'Yeah, I'm all right, Storm, ta. No point complaining, right? I'm looking forward to getting back in the game. Just saying to Gennz, I hope my gym sessions are enough to get me through the training, yeah? It's been a while since I've played, to be honest.'

'Oh, absolutely! I know what you mean, Calz. Do you mind if I call you Calz, by the way?' says Storm.

'Cali's good, yeah? Don't want to sound like a pizza, now, do I?' says Cali, laughing.

'Of course. Sure, no worries. Cali it is,' says Storm, shifting her nose back into joint.

'Cali! Good to see you, ja!' says Coach, jogging towards us. 'Glad you could make it this evening, We're all so happy you're doing this for The HAMP. The producers are happy too, because you'll help absolutely to bring nicely up the viewer numbers, ja?'

'Ah, I don't know about that, Coach, but I'm glad to be here too. Something different but right up my alley, really. And as I told you the other day, your helpline was my lifeline; I don't know how or if I would have survived without it,' says Cali. 'The people you have at the coalface, they're amazing, they are. So I'm doing it for them and, of course, all of you guys. It's my way of giving back, you know.'

'That's amazing, Cali,' says Coach. 'Stories like yours remind us why we do every day what we do every day. Cali, this is Morag, she writes our newsletter, ja?'

'Hi, Cali,' I say, only just managing to stop myself from waving.

'Hey Morag,' Cali smiles.

'Hi. So I was just thinking your story would be amazing for our newsletter, hey,' I say. 'If you're happy to share your story, can we have a chat some time? We can arrange it through Gennz, if that's okay?'

'Yeah, sure thing,' says Cali, winking at me. 'Sounds great.'

'Oh you know, Coach, you and I are so alike,' says Storm, her imagination taking a wild leap as she steps in front of me. 'Like I always say to my team, the best thing about working as hard as we do, is sharing awesome stories like Cali's. That's what we talked about the other day when we were chatting at the front door, didn't we Calz? Sorry, Cali?'

'Probably! Wouldn't surprise me if we did,' says Cali.

'So Cali, with your height and speed, you'll be a super useful member of our team, ja?' says Coach, looking all the way up and down Cali's height.

'You see, Coach! I was going to say exactly the same thing. Perfect for our team,' says Storm.

To be honest, it's quite exhausting watching Storm's efforts to elbow her way into a conversation. Cali is being gracious and everything, but it looks like she'd rather just chat to Coach without all the needless comments and grovelling affirmations from Storm. Gennypha looks bemused.

'Yeah, I played centre, back in the day. Right in the thick of it, yeah? How about you, Pauli?' says Cali, looking all the way up and down Coach's height.

'Oh, I used to play fly half or full back in my day. I had some speed, believe it or not, and was quite good with the boot, ja?'

'I'm pretty sure you were.' Cali smiles, and Coach smiles back. I could swear Coach is blushing too, but I might be wrong. I've never seen her blush before.

Coach Dave calls us into a huddle and sends us off on our sprints across the field. Gennypha says something to Cali, then waves and jogs away, with a bit more of a spring in her step than I've seen for some time. Huge clouds seem to be gathering over Storm's head.

Practice goes well, and Coach Dave and Coach are pleased we're all starting to understand how to play the game. Adding Cali into the mix makes a huge difference to the flow of the game, and she's really quick. She's also patient and helpful, giving those of us who've never played before hints and tips.

'You don't want to throw the ball like that, and *never* forward,' she says to me.

'And, as Coach Dave always tells you, you don't want to do roly-polys or cartwheels on the field either,' she says to Jasper. 'I know it's tempting, but it's just not rugby, yeah?'

Jasper mock-salutes her, and mutters, 'Just. Not. Cricket.'

'Robyn, is it? Yeah? You don't need to guard the uprights. Keep your eye on the ball and make sure you're always available and accessible to your team mates, yeah? Otherwise, you'll find the ball landing on your head, with the other team in hot pursuit. Ask me; I used to get into trouble for daydreaming on the field when I first started playing at school!'

Robyn blushes, and gives Cali a thumbs-up.

Karo shines out wide, and has a relentlessness on the field like you never see in the office. She's focused, she's hungry and she's fast. It's funny, you know. You think you know someone in the work environment and then you see them playing sport and it's like they're a different person on the field. It's like they come alive and everything.

Coach Dave huddles us.

'Right, guys, you're all looking good out there. I don't want you to get complacent or anything, but now we're a few weeks in, it's starting to look like you know how to play rugby, yeah? I liked how you spread the ball out wide tonight. Karo is hungry for the ball out on the wing, so feed it to her whenever you can, yeah?' He nods towards Karo.

'And next month, we've got a practice match, yeah? I've asked one of our Sunday league teams to come along, so please don't disappoint me – I've promised them you won't be rubbish!' Coach Dave laughs.

'Pretty high bar,' says Mason, indicating knee height.

'It is high, and all,' says Coach Dave. 'Right, you ugly lot, four laps to cool you down, then off you jog and I'll see you next week, yeah?'

We jog away from Coach Dave and, after Barry finishes his first cool-down lap, he turns around and runs into a dip in the field. He falls to the ground, screaming and grabbing his ankle.

Coach and Coach Dave run to him and we all gather around him. He writhes and moans, curled up on his back, holding his ankle with both hands.

'I've heard something go, Coach,' yells Barry. 'I think I've ruptured something, it's bloody killing me, Coach.'

Coach calls 111.

'Hello, yes, we have a medical emergency ... Bermondsey Rugby Club, ja? One of our players has twisted badly his foot and his uncle is swelling. Like he has actually a pair of rolled-up foot socks around his uncle. Okay, ja, thank you very much. Yes, we will do absolutely that. Thank you. Yes, thank you. Goodbye.'

'Right, someone get the first aid box. We need an ice pick. The paragliders are on their way,' says Coach.

At home, I tell Jamie what happened at practice this evening. He feels gutted for Barry; he had a similar experience at school. When Jamie was thirteen, he'd become his school's star wing. He'd earned his place in the school's first team, after spending his earlier rugby years messing around and pranking his team mates. That all changed when he was in Standard Four (year six), and he played in the D team. Their coach was the father of one of his team mates, and Jamie credits Mr Hanckley with teaching him not only the basics of rugby, but how to behave on and off the field, and some key lessons for life. He still talks about Mr Hanckley today.

He used to say things like:

-'Pull your trousers up, Jamie!'

-'Shake hands with your opponents, gentlemen. Win or lose, behave like gentlemen. It's as important as the game itself.'

-'Practise, prepare, anticipate. You can't rely on a shot in the dark during a match.' And the boys would run around, pretending to shoot each other in the dark. Pyiuw, pyiuw, pyiuw! They got his point though, and all began to take their game a bit more seriously. But the most important lesson Mr Hanckley taught them was about teamwork.

'We don't need heroes,' he'd say. 'We're a team. We train, we win, and we lose as a team, and every one of you matters. There's no "I" in team.'

The boys would cover their eyes and run around the field.

'Practise, prepare, antici*pate*, gentlemen. Antici*pate!*'

Again, the boys would mimic Mr Hanckley and shout "antici*pate!*" into each other's faces. Jamie still pronounces the word like that, and it makes me laugh. Every time.

Jamie said he had fun that season, but he also appreciated and respected Mr Hanckley. He never spoke down to the boys and he always treated them like, well, gentlemen. Jamie tried harder, ran faster, antici*pated* moves and felt like he began to make a difference in the team's performance and everything.

Their final derby was coming up and it was an important grudge match to win. Jamie knew that other coaches would be there amongst the big crowd that day, watching his team. If he played well, who knows – he could even have moved up to the school's first team the next year. Jamie set his heart on doing just that.

But it wasn't to be. When he arrived at the field on that Saturday, Jamie set off a bit too fast on a warm-up run and felt something snap in the back of his thigh. He'd torn his hamstring, and was out of the final match; Jamie forever felt robbed of that opportunity.

Mr Hanckley gave Jamie the 'most improved player' award at their team's year-end BBQ (this is what I call a BBQ: a *braai*), and despite the injury, he did make it into the school's first team the following year. Jamie grew to love rugby, and he excelled at it throughout his school career. He'd often spot Mr Hanckley on the side of the field, cheering him on and everything.

It turns out Barry has torn a ligament in his ankle. The paramedics rushed him to A&E last night, and the doctors say he'll be out of action for six to eight weeks. They've given him a moon boot to wear and some heavy painkillers to take, so he's off work for the next few days.

Coach calls a quick team huddle in the Tight-Head Nook.

'Thanks, team, I know you're all busy, but I wanted to have a quick chat about Barry. As you'll have heard, he's now out of activity already for up to eight weeks. We have more time than that until the festival, but he'll miss too many practices. He's said he'll step down, so he won't play any more in the team.'

There's a sharp intake of breath around the room.

'I'm now a bit worried, ja, because we need another experienced player. No one else came forward when Warren emailed, ja?'

'Hey ho,' says Tracy.

'I'm not meaning actually to be rude, I hope, but we've lost one of our star players, ja. One of the four experienced players we're allowed, actually. Any ideas who can replace him?' Coach says, looking hopefully around the room.

'What about someone from Coach Dave's club team?' says Storm.

'We're allowed only players from our charity, Storm, ja. Plus one celebrity, and we have already Cali. I could play, myself, but I'm not fit enough. Do we know of anyone else who can play for The HAMP? Any of our colleagues?'

None of us has any ideas for Coach.

'Okay, well, let's all give it some thoughts, ja? If anyone has any ha-ha moments, just ping me, ja?' says Coach.

This feels like a bit of a crisis. It sounds a bit dramatic and everything, but Barry had already started to take a real leadership role in the team and on the field. Although he's annoying and everything, he worked hard to make sure we all knew what was going on, and we played together as a unit.

We haven't just lost a strong player, we've lost a potential captain. Well, I don't know if Coach and Coach Dave would have made him captain, but he seemed like the obvious choice. And he acted like a captain and everything, if you ask me.

We all go back to our desks and Karo walks over to our pod, dragging a long piece of toilet paper under her shoe. Warren's drinking tea and watching her out of the corner of his eye. He curls his lip around his mug and takes a sip, preoccupied.

'Guys, this is quite serious, isn't it? Barry's the one who usually feeds the ball out wide to me most of the time, and I'm worried that we're going to lose momentum without him. Or without someone like him there. I was quite excited about our chances, but without Bazza, I'm not so sure any more.' Karo looks down at her coffee-stained top and picks a bit of oatmeal porridge off her sleeve. 'No offence to you guys.'

Warren puts his mug down pushes his chair back. He slouch-shuffles over to our pod, his hands in his pockets.

'Something rotten in the state of Denmark, yeah?' he says.

'What? Yeah, probably,' says Karo, picking another piece of oatmeal off her top.

'What's the probs?' Warren's pretending not to have eavesdropped.

'Barry's injured and is out of our rugby sevens team, and we don't have a strong, fast replacement for him. Coach is quite worried,' says Storm.

'That's bad luck, guys.' Warren bites his lip, concentrating hard on what to say next.

'Yeah, so Coach has asked us to have a think. It has to be someone in the charity. You don't know of anyone, hey Warren?' I say.

'Oh, right. No, not really. Not sure.' Warren's still chewing his lip. He shoves his hands back into his pockets, swivels on his heels and starts to walk back to his desk. After about five steps, he turns and takes slow, measured steps back to our pod.

'Guys, I know this is a bit of a flyer and may not be even vaguely an option, but … nah, never mind,' he says, turning around again.

'Finish what you were saying, Warren. We need all ideas, even stupid ones,' says Karo, with zero finesse.

'Okay. So, well, *I* played rugby at school, if you can believe it. But I'm actually in training for the Great North Run again this year, and I didn't put myself forward for *BLAT* because I didn't want to get injured before the Run. Not in a bad way, you know, but you know what I mean? I'm fundraising for my mum's charity, so I can't let them down. But my training's going well and my fitness is up, so maybe now there's less chance I'll get injured. What do you think?'

'Fitness is one thing, Warren, but we need strength, speed, and good hands too,' says Karo, checking her hair for split ends or porridge.

'Well, what do you think of them apples?' says Warren, yanking his hands out of his pockets and offering them to Karo for inspection. 'I played centre at school. At primary school, my coach always said I had safe hands. He also used to call me "Moses" because he said when I ran straight, the waters parted ahead of me. Not in a bad way, or anything. Not trying to big myself up, or anything.'

'You? Wowzer, that's surprising. Impressive,' says Karo, letting go of her hair and raising her eyebrows in an impressed kind of way. 'Better go speak to Coach – she needs good news, and maybe you can be the bearer of it for her today. Show her those hands, Moses!'

'Ha! Okay, I prefer to call myself the good news guy!' Warren slouch-shuffles to Coach's office, walking a little faster and carrying his head a little bit higher.

At lunchtime, Ash and I leave the office to go and meet Alex in a coffee shop near St Paul's. I'm going to interview her for the annual report story, and Ash is going to take some photos.

It's not raining today, so we can take the beautiful walk from our central London office, past the Tate Modern and along the River

Thames. There are a few buskers singing and playing next to the river, a guy sitting at a small wooden desk offering to write you an "instant poem" on his ancient typewriter, a few static statues, and a crowd of children screeching. They've gathered around a guy who's creating massive bubbles by dipping what look like string-less tennis rackets into a bucket of water and washing-up liquid and waving them in the air. The huge bubbles move slowly and shimmer against the backdrop of the river, silver in the gentle winter sunlight.

We cross the bouncy Millennium Bridge, packed with lunchtime runners and walkers jostling with tourists taking selfies. It's hard to know which way to turn with so many views to choose from and everything: St Paul's, the City, Waterloo Bridge, and the London Eye in the distance, Shakespeare's Globe, and the Tate Modern. I still feel like a tourist in this city, and I never want to take these views for granted. Even Ash stops and takes a few creative shots of the boats making waves in the river.

Alex is waiting for us when we get to the coffee shop. After grabbing a coffee, we go and sit at a quiet table in the corner where Alex and I chat through the questions I'd sent her. Ash takes some candid shots of Alex as she's talking, and he's loving the sunlight streaming through the window next to our table.

'It's a mood,' he says.

Alex's story is very much as she'd shared it at our think-tank meeting. But she also tells me about where she grew up, where she went to school and how she went into management consulting with the hope that she'll be able to go back to Zimbabwe one day. She wants to use her skills to help rebuild the economy and everything.

'I want to give back. Zim gave me such a beautiful, healthy and, frankly, privileged upbringing, so I want to do what I can to help. Plus, I really miss home and my friends and family, hey.'

Alex is one of five children, all of whom studied and now work overseas. The Zimbabwean diaspora. They all go back to see her parents and grandparents as often as they can. They all went to public schools in Harare (this is what I call public schools: *private schools*), and I went to a government school. Although it wouldn't have been at the same time, because she's a bit younger than I am and everything, our school used to swim and play netball against their school. We always lost, but we loved the half-time snacks we used to get there.

It's not long before Alex and I have discovered people we both know, and we're reminiscing about our childhoods in Zimbabwe. When you're from Zim and you're talking to a Zimbabwean you've just met, it doesn't take long before you find people you know in common. This is how many degrees of separation there are between Zimbabweans:

1. One. Okay, sometimes two.

When you've just met someone from Zim, this is how a typical conversation might go:
'What school did you go to?'
'XYZ School.'
'Oh, right. Did you know so-and-so?'
'Yes.'
Or, if the answer is 'No,' it'll be followed by:
'Okay, do you know so-and-so?'
'Yes.'
It takes about this long to get to someone you both know:

1. One minute. Okay, maybe two.

And once you've established that connection, the conversation opens into infinite territory and you can lose all track of time, as poor Ash discovers.

183

'Hey, guys, sorry to break up this Zim-chat, but can we do the outside pics quickly?' says Ash. 'Before it gets dark.'

Alex and I have been talking for almost an hour. What a blast, hey.

Chapter 21

Kevin is standing at the printer, doing squats. Every time he has to wait for a big print run, he uses the time to do one of the following:

1. Squats.
2. Lift his eyebrows into forehead stretches.
3. Pace up and down, and talk to himself.

If it's a really big print run, he'll do all of those things, in that order.

I stand at the printer to wait my turn to use it. Kevin doesn't notice me at first, and I don't want to disturb him – he's counting squats. When he gets to a hundred, he spots me.

'Ah. Morag. Yes. They say the printer is the new water cooler. Where the cool kids hang out. Good,' he says, making eye contact with my shoes.

'Oh, that sounds about right, Kevin!'

'Yes. Black and white copies for Colour-blind Kevin,' he says.

'Why Colour-blind Kevin?'

'Mason will tell you.'

'Oh, okay. Are you nearly done?'

'Another hundred to go.'

'Squats, or copies?'

'Ah. Squats. I think I have about two hundred more copies to print.

Sorry,' he says, starting his next hundred squats.

'No worries. I'll just come back when you're finished, then?' I say, but Kevin's already up to seven squats.

Back at my desk, Mason looks up at me.

'Colour-blind Kevin – want the back story?'

'You heard that?' I laugh.

'Miss nothing, me! So when I started at The HAMP, Kevin told me the charity was chuffed to have me because of my digital skills (duh!) but also because "the charity has too many whites", yeah? Couldn't believe he put it like that, but you know what, I told him it was better than pretending not to see my skin colour.'

'Wow, that's a gracious response, hey Mase?' I say. 'Very big of you.'

'Guess so. Had it *so* often, you have to choose the gracious, yeah? Anyway, Kevin felt terrible. But he also said if anyone couldn't see my skin colour they'd be lying, which just made me laugh even more. So that's how I gave him the nickname, "Colour-blind Kevin".'

'That's a cool story, Mase,' I say. 'I can't believe I'd never heard that before. But I like it, and the name.'

'Think Kev's a bit embarrassed by the story, to be fair. But he likes the name. Preferred it to "Captain Stating-the-bleeding-obvious".'

Here are three things to know about Kevin:

1. He has calendar reminders for when to put his sandwich in the fridge, when to take it out, when to have lunch, when to do a tea round, when to do squats at the printer, and so on.
2. He loves going out for drinks after work and, once he's had about two half-pints, he gets loose and chatty, and he even makes eye contact. That's usually when the next point comes into play.
3. He has a huge crush on Tracy, and tries to go home with her after every Christmas party. It's hard to picture them together, to be honest, but then you never know.

It's unusual for someone with such a blunt personality as Kevin's to work in HR, if you think about it and everything. Not in a bad way, or anything. From interactions like the one I've just had with him at the printer, you'd think he might be awkward when he's dealing with people, but he behaves quite differently when he's in full HR mode.

He's really good at his job and is super approachable. If you have any issues that you want to discuss with him, he'll always fit you in around his scheduled sandwich-or-whatever times, and he'll take your concerns seriously.

One of the things I appreciate the most about Kevin is that, despite the colour-blind story, he doesn't judge, and nothing shocks or surprises him. He's always honest, that's for sure. But he's also kind and respectful, and you can trust him to treat everything you tell him as confidential. And he's a good listener. Unless he's doing squats at the printer, I guess.

An email from Kevin pops into my inbox:

Subject: Status of printer

Squats and black and white copies: completed.

Printer status: free (apart from the 7p/page cost, lol).

Many thanks, Kevin Wells

Gennypha looks across at Kevin. She jumps up and goes to say something into his ear. He looks up at her and cups his hands around his mouth to say something into her ear. He looks at his screen, picks up his notebook and pen, stands up and motions for the two of them to walk into the Tight-head Nook. He closes the door behind them.

One of a few things could be happening in the Tight-head Nook. Gennypha could be:

1. Resigning.
2. Raising a grievance.

3. Checking how much annual leave she has left for the year.
4. Having a catch-up.

Madison looks at me – she looks so different without her screensaver – and whispers, 'What do you reckon they're talking about? Is she leaving? Complaining? My money's on the latter, because she's been having a hard time with Storm. Last time someone had such a hard time with Storm they lodged a bullying grievance with HR but then left because Storm was so passive aggressive. So what do you think?'

Madison's screensaver glides back up and she turns away to look towards the Tight-head Nook.

'Not sure, really,' I say to the back of Madison's head.

Everyone gets curious whenever anyone goes behind closed doors with Kevin. Gennypha and Kevin come out of the room after about ten minutes.

'Thanks, Kevin, I'll keep you posted, yeah?' says Gennypha.

'Good. Thanks, Gennypha. I'll wait to hear from you, then. Yes? Hmm? Good.'

Kevin draws his feet together as a kind of full-stop to their conversation. He turns on his heels and marches back to his desk to check his calendar, before sprinting into the kitchen to take his sandwich out of the fridge.

Gennypha comes back to her desk, looking pleased with herself. She smiles and winks at me, and flops into her chair.

Ping! An email pops into my inbox from Gennypha:

<no subject>

Want a quick chat? G x

I look up at her and nod, and she jerks her head towards the front door.

'Just going for a quick smoke break,' says Gennypha, grabbing her cigarettes and walking to the front door.

I stand up and pretend to yawn and stretch.

'Just going to the loo.' That's a bit stupid, because I would never normally announce that to everyone. What an idiot.

When I walk past Richard in the front lobby, he's on the phone, and puts his hand up to stop me. I wait, expecting him to give me a message from Gennypha. When he gets off the phone, he saunters round to the front of the counter and stands next to me.

'All right, Morag?' he says.

'Yeah, good thanks, Richard. How about you?'

'Not bad, yeah. A *bit* down in the dumps,' he says, nodding his head to emphasise the word "bit" and not looking one bit down in the dumps. Sometimes Richard tells me so much about his wife and daughter, even I need to get to the office to get a break from them. What have they done now?

'Guess who's only gone and died?' he says.

'Sorry?'

'You'll never guess who's gone and died, Morag. Will ya?' he says, jerking his tie straight.

I shrug and wait for a clue of what he's about to tell me or how the hell I'm supposed to respond. His words and the smirk on his face don't go together, but that's standard for Richard, I guess.

'Only Joyce off the telly. The one off that music show, yeah? When was it on, again?' he says, looking up at the ceiling. 'The 80s. Yeah, back in the day when I was a lad. Had a proper crush on her an' all. Not exactly *Top of the Pops*, but that kind of show, yeah? She was well fit, and had them big, round ...'

'Earrings?' Jeepers, that was going to end badly.

'That's 'im!' he says, and laughs like a drain. 'Phwoar!'

'Sorry, Richard, for your loss. I'm sure you're distressed.'

'That's all right, Morag. I didn't know her, and all. But you just never know when your time's up, do ya?'

'No, Richard, you don't, hey. Actually, I really need to ...'

'We'll all pop our clogs one day, won't we? You just never know, though, do ya?'

'No. That's true, Richard. Life's too short.' I stop myself from adding: *for conversations like this.*'I need to find Gennypha, though. Did you see where she went?'

He puts his hands up in the air in surrender, nods and points to the right of the front door. I offer him my sympathies once again, thank him, and walk out on to the street to look for Gennypha. She's around the corner, finishing her cigarette.

'Thought you weren't coming, lolz.'

'Richard...' I start.

'Enough said, lolz. So basically, Morag, I've just spoken to Kevin, and I'm thinking about taking another job I've been offered. Cali wants me to work with her, as her kind of PA. I'm really tempted but not too sure yet. Basically, Kevin thinks I must work out what's best for *me*. He said The HAMP won't want to lose me, but I need to look out for myself. Obvs.'

'Wow, Gennz, that's huge. Congrats! That's quite flattering too, hey? What do you think you'll do?'

'Not sure yet, Morag. And yeah, I guess it is flattering, to be honest. Basically, I really love what I do here but Storm is doing my head in. News alert!' She waves her hands around her head.

'And it feels like I'll never progress as long as I'm working with her. I can't see a career path for myself here, and basically Storm doesn't give me anything to handle on my own. I mean *really* on my own. She tempts me with stuff, but I just end up doing all the basic stuff and she just swoops in and grabs all the glory. I fall for it. Every. Single. Time. Shit! I don't know if I can do this any more, but to be honest, I'm also getting some good experience. So basically, I'm super confused.'

'I can imagine.' I have no idea what I would do in her situation.

'This last thing with Cali and Quinn felt like the last straw for me. Basically, I did everything, made *all* the asks, and Storm tried to take over. To grab it all from right under my nose. I decided I wasn't going to let that happen, so I took the initiative with Cali and basically made contact with her without Storm knowing. You should have seen Storm's face when I arrived with Cali at that first rugby practice. Basically, she could have killed me with that glare of hers.'

'I saw.'

'So, basically, I don't know what to do next. What would you do?'

I was hoping she wasn't going to ask me that, because it's such a difficult question to answer when you're not in that situation or anything. Also, when you've never had the luxury of actually making a choice about a job and everything, it's quite hard to think what you'd do.

'I'm not sure, Gennz. I've never been in a situation of being head-hunted or anything, so I don't have any experience to draw on. If you want to stay on and get more experience here, have you thought about maybe lodging a grievance or something, rather than leaving? Do you have a feeling one way or the other, in your gut? Sometimes your instinct can be a good indicator, hey?'

'True. So basically, I do want to stay but I'm not sure if that's just because it's a safer option. Or because of *BLAT*! I'm also really excited at the thought of working with Cali, though. I mean *the* Cali Shannon. Come on! But here's my struggle: on the one hand, basically I love working here and I *so* respect Coach – I mean, I've learnt such a lot from her about leadership and how to get the best out of your team, and stuff.' Gennypha looks up at the sky.

'But on the other hand, the thought of working with Storm for another minute longer ... aaaaarrrrgggggh, it's so bloody confusing, yeah? Kevin also mentioned the grievance thing as an option, but I'm not sure. I'm thinking about it, but basically Storm could just catch the hump with me for doing that and make life even more difficult, you know?'

'I know. It's a tough situation, hey Gennz? Where do you feel you'd learn more – here, or with Cali? And, if you think about it, what's the worst that could happen if you took a leap into the unknown and everything and went to work with Cali?'

Gennypha nods and shrugs her shoulders, as she lights another cigarette and takes a long, deep drag.

'I don't know, really,' she says, blowing smoke out of the side of her mouth. 'I have rent to pay every month, so basically the worst that can happen is that if it doesn't work out, I'll end up without a job. And potentially homeless. That's pretty bad, I guess. But then I do have some savings ... Ah no! Why does this have to be so bloody difficult?'

'Maybe it doesn't. Maybe the answer is staring you in the face, don't you think?'

'I guess. And I guess, basically, I do hit it off really well with Cali. I know she has a bit of a temper but I can deal with a temper – my dad was basically like that, and we just shouted a lot and dealt with stuff really loudly. Lolz.

'What I can't deal with is Storm's bullying, and her fake *sugar-sweetness* while she bullies me. Basically I don't want to leave because of her. I'd rather leave on my own terms.' She stares into the distance.

'Anyway, thanks, Morag, it really helps to talk to you about this. *Please* keep this under your hat, yeah? Soz for asking, but basically I'm not ready to talk about it with anyone else yet.'

'No worries, of course. Always safe with me,' I say. 'Better get back to my desk. This is a long loo break!'

'What on earth have you been eating, Morag? Lolz! But thanks, Morag, see you in a bit.'

Gennypha stays outside to finish her cigarette. Just as well, otherwise we'd walk back into the office together and everyone would know we'd been outside talking. As if they didn't already know that, hey?

I don't know what it is about me but, you know, people often confide in me and tell me stuff they don't want anyone else to know and everything. It happens a lot. I never break other people's confidence, ever, but it can sometimes be a bit of a burden when you're asked to carry someone's secret, if I'm honest.

When I walk back through the front lobby, Richard seems to have got over his recent bereavement. He's cutting his fingernails with a pair of large, industrial-sized scissors. Niko, the other receptionist, offers him a small pair of nail scissors.

'Nah, you're all right, Niko, cheers.'

Richard looks up at me, nods and smiles, and carries on with his desk-based manicure.

I get back to my desk and, to avoid all the questioning looks from everyone, I offer to do a tea round for the pod. As I take everyone's mugs and orders, Madison grabs my arm without looking up from her screen.

'My eyelashes fell into my mug earlier, Morag. Soz. Just throw them away, yeah?'

That is so gross.

'Are you sure? I can always give them a shampoo and blow-dry, if you like?' I can't resist the sarcasm to the back of Madison's head.

Warren's also in the kitchen doing a tea round and, while he's waiting for the kettle to boil, he's juggling three teaspoons. He looks up when I open the door and all the spoons crash to the floor.

I turn to close the kitchen door behind me, and almost close it on Bernard, our office cleaner. He strides past me without a word, and replaces a notice on the wall above the sink. He then moves one of the tables right up against the wall in the corner, and leaves the kitchen. He's always struck me as a bit of an oddball, if I'm honest.

The notice he's put up says:

Polite notice. This is a shared kitchen, please wash up your own cups and bowls and put them away.

It's the same as the previous one, but without the handwritten *Mum xx* at the bottom of it.

'So, Morag, all right?' says Warren, as he stands up from picking up the teaspoons off the floor.

'Yes, I'm well, thanks. And you?'

'Great, thanks. Ooh, hello, what's that then?' Warren squints at the new notice.

'I was just looking at it too, Warren, and I find it quite strange that these notices are called *polite notices*, don't you? Why not call them *bossy*, or *telling-off* notices? I've often wondered about that, hey.'

'Interesting,' Warren stretches out that word when he's not sure how to respond to what you've just said. 'So I don't mean to change the subject or anything, but I spoke to Coach the other day, and she said I can join the rugby squad. I'm coming to this week's practice – pretty excited, I have to say,' he says, pouring hot water into the mugs.

He looks up at me.

'I hear Karo is quite the star on the wing, yeah?'

'Oh, definitely, for sure. She's amazing,' I say. 'She surprised everyone when she said she played at all, but she's brilliant, hey. So fast and quick-thinking. She's kind of our secret weapon, I think. Coach is really impressed with her and everything. And so is everyone else. She's great.'

'Amazing,' says Warren, stirring the teas. 'You can never really know people, can you? I mean, Karo? Karo, a talented rugby player? Who'd have thought? Not in a bad way, but she's so surprising. *So* surprising.'

He starts to juggle the teaspoons again, looking through the kitchen window at Karo. There's a real longing in his eyes.

Poor guy; unrequited love must be so tough. And so can juggling teaspoons when you're not really concentrating; he drops all of them again and one lands in a mug and splashes tea all over his white shirt.

'I'm better with a rugby ball, I promise,' says Warren, laughing.

'I'm sure you are! At least you didn't start a fire today, hey.'

I walk back to my desk, carrying two mugs in each hand. Gennypha's still outside, so she'll just have to miss out on this tea round. Jasper's at our pod, talking to Mason. I interrupt them to offer Jasper a drink, but he says he's okay. They're talking about the rugby and it's quite funny because Jasper is, well, a bit *coy* around Mason.

'Oh hey, Mason! I *love* your shirt, is it new?' Jasper leans to his right, clasping his hands to his chest.

'This old thing? Lol. Yep. New.'

'It's amazing. So smart.'

Jasper hovers and you can see he's trying to think of something else to say.

'My mum went to school with David Bowie,' Jasper says, apropos of absolutely nothing. His statement sounds like a question.

'Yeah? She knew him?'

'No, he'd already left when she got there.'

'Oh, right.'

'Okay, byeee!' Jasper waves at Mason and skips back to his desk.

'Cheers,' says Mason, smiling.

Jasper turns back and blushes. He puts both hands to his face.

'Hey Mason, talking of shirts, do you wear slim or classic-fit shirts, yeah?' says Ash, craning his neck to look over his PC at Mason.

'Erm, depends,' says Mason. 'Why?'

'I'll tell you for why: my belly is making my slim-fit shirts feel tight, yeah. Don't know, must be something about having kids and not going to the gym as much any more, yeah? So I've had to go and buy myself classic-fit shirts, yeah. *Classic fits!* Are you joking me, yeah?

That's why this rugby thing is brilliant, because I'm way too young for a belly like this, yeah,' he says, patting an almost non-existent belly.

Here are three things to know about Ash:

1. He's really stylish and takes a lot of care in how he dresses. He often talks about clothes, and told us he used to do some modelling "back in the day". He met his wife on a shoot too.
2. He keeps his hair short and gelled at a backward angle. I've often wondered how he gets it to look like that. I imagine he gels his hair before he goes to bed and then sleeps with his face in the pillow. Not likely to be even vaguely true or anything, especially given point 1.
3. He *loves* Google. You can mention anything like a play or a gig or a holiday destination or a word and, while you're talking, Ash will be Googling it. And you can ask him absolutely anything, and he'll Google it for you.

'So, Mase, yeah, I'm thinking about doing some running at lunchtimes to get myself proper fit for the rugby, yeah. Want to join me, mate? I thought twice, maybe three times a week? We can run down to the South Bank and find a half-hour route around there, yeah?' Ash says.

'You and me? Running, I mean? Yeah, guess that could work … starting when – tomorrow?' says Mason.

'Yeah, could do, yeah. What you reckon, mate? Sound like a good idea?'

Mason gives Ash a thumbs-up, just as Jasper appears at his desk again, breathless.

'Ah, guys, can I run with you too, please? I've been running on my own, but it would be *much* more fun with you two. Pleeeeeeease?' he says, with praying hands.

'Sure, cool with me,' says Ash. 'Mase?'

'Long as you don't wear your American football kit.'

'Oh, don't!' says Jasper, fanning his face. 'I'll never live that down, will I?'

'Nope! And unless there are any more social media disasters, tomorrow's good. Putting it in the calendar as we speak,' says Mason.

'Cool. Nice one. Yeah, start tomorrow,' says Ash.

'Yay,' says Jasper, clapping and beaming.

Mason smiles and nods, and Jasper stands next to him. The two of them watch Ash get up from his desk and walk to the kitchen in his classic-fit shirt.

Chapter 22

It's Monday. Again.

'You'll *never* believe what I did this weekend, guys!' says Wendy, my direct marketing colleague, dumping her bag and backpack on her desk and switching on her PC.

'We probably won't, Wendy-Wends,' says Madison, on a brief sojourn from her screensaver. 'Put us out of our misery, my love?'

Wendy's just had a big birthday. An "oh" birthday", as she calls it. Or sometimes an "oh-oh" birthday, when she's trying to be cute. (I think the "oh" might have a "six" in front of it, but I'm not a hundred percent sure.)

For the past few weeks, Wendy hasn't stopped talking about her birthday. She asks us to guess what we think her husband Lance will plan for her birthday, whether we think it'll be a surprise or not, to guess what we think it will be or won't be, and what we think he'll give her. She tells us what she *definitely* doesn't want him to give her, so I just hope he knows that too.

It's been pretty exhausting guessing so many things, to be honest, and I can't imagine how it must be for Lance, poor guy. He always seems to be under pressure to surprise her and everything, and it sounds like Wendy demands a Wendy-approved surprise. Seems that started way, way back.

When I joined The HAMP, one of the first things Wendy told me was how Lance proposed to her. She's very proud of the story, and tells it to everyone when she first meets them. It's a kind of Wendy-induction for new starters. This is how it goes.

When they were both in their twenties, Lance "surprised" Wendy by arriving at her office one Friday, dressed in a white three-piece suit with a black open-neck shirt and wearing a gold medallion. His ginger hair was slicked back.

'One of my favourite movies of all time is *Saturday Night Fever*. Have you ever seen it? You *must*. It's the best movie ever, and you'll love it. Tony – that's what John Travolta's character is called: Tony – is so *dreamy* in it. You'll go mad for him. Everyone does,' according to Wendy's script. 'Lance knew that was my favourite movie, so you know what he did?'

'Rented it from the video shop?' I said.

'No, silly! He actually bought himself the whole Tony Manero outfit. If it wasn't for his hair colour, he'd be a dead ringer for John Travolta. *Everybody* says so.'

(As you know, Wendy and the truth often go their separate ways.)

'So this one Friday morning at work, someone in the office suddenly put on the cassette of *Night Fever* and I screamed when I saw Lance shimmying over to my desk. Then, in time with all of Tony's signature dance moves, he asked me to marry him. In front of *everyone* in the office. They'd all turned around when I screamed.'

(How else would they know to turn around and watch her?)

She then showed me the video on her phone, which she'd filmed from her TV. I watched the bumpy, grainy footage of Wendy putting her hand to her mouth, looking around the office and then straight into the camera her colleague was holding.

(Either Lance or Wendy – my money's on Wendy – had conspired with Wendy's colleague to make sure it was all captured on film;

life wouldn't have been worth living if Wendy didn't have footage she could share with everyone.) I watched Wendy say "yes" into the camera, and turn back to Lance.

'The office erupted. Lance gave me the biggest bear hug, grabbed my hands and danced me out of the office. *Everyone* was in tears.'

In the video, you can't see anyone in tears but you can actually feel the awkwardness and everything right across the office. And the silence as people look around at each other. They join Wendy when she starts to clap.

It's quite sweet, though, to be honest. Especially the way it all happened. Lance looked sheepish, like he wanted to get everything over and done with as quickly as possible. He also got quite breathless when he asked Wendy to marry him. It was her "dream proposal", she says. Fair play to her for getting Lance to do it, I have to say.

A few things struck me when I watched that footage:

1. Lance's awkwardness was tangible.
2. What he lacked in natural rhythm, fitness and co-ordination, Lance more than made up for in courage. Sometimes he got the Travolta moves right but when he got out of step and had both arms in the air at the same time, he looked like he was about to dive sideways into a swimming pool. But what a sweet act of love. Embarrassing and awkward and everything, but still, really really sweet.
3. I don't want to be horrible or anything, but if you're a little heavier than you should be and you're wearing a white suit that's a bit small for you and everything, you might end up sharing a little more than you intended.

'So, guys, who's going to guess what we did for my birthday?' says Wendy.

'I give up, Wendy,' says Barry, who's just appeared at Storm's desk. 'You'll have to put us out of our misery!'

'You didn't even try, Barry. But okay, if you insist. Well, guys, it was the *most amazing* thing. Ever. Lance told me we were going out on Saturday evening, but he wouldn't tell me where we were going. He told me to wear something nice. I said to him, "As if I would wear something horrible", so he said, "I know you always look lovely, but just in case". So I put on my new Monsoon trousers, my new floral blouse from New Look.'

(This is how Wendy pronounces floral: *flawrill*.)

'And I wore my new Manila Blatnik shoes.'

'Don't you mean Manolo Blahnik?' says Gennypha.

'Mine are so similar, you'd never tell the difference,' says Wendy. 'I got them off eBay at about a quarter of the price.'

You can get exhausted from so much detail, I tell you.

'Lance couldn't believe his eyes when he saw me. Anyway, we get on the tube and get off at Baker Street station, and start walking to a church building. I'm thinking, "This is weird, why would we be going to a church building for a birthday surprise", but that's where he takes me. And guys,' she says, looking around to make sure *all* the guys are listening, 'it was a *Bonnie Tyler* gig, in that church building. Can you believe it? There were *so* many famous people there, I couldn't believe it. It must have been some kind of exclusive gig, and *how* Lance got tickets to it, I can't even imagine. Bonnie Tyler, guys!'

'Whaaat? Oh God, should have told my parents about that gig, right enough,' says Barry. 'They bloody *love* her.'

'Really?' Wendy can't decide how to react to that. 'So Lance just wouldn't tell me how he managed to get tickets. And I can't even think about how many arms and legs those tickets must have cost him. Bless him. Lance is like that when it comes to birthdays, though, he's *so* generous. Money seems to be no object.

'Anyway, the evening was *amaaaaaazing!* If I tell you how amazing it was, you won't believe me! You should see how amazing Bonnie looks, Barry. You won't believe how young she looks. I didn't know she was as old as she is – she certainly doesn't look like she's in her sixties. You would never say she was that much older than me.'

You'd think Wendy might start jogging back towards the truth, but it's still not happening.

'Didn't take you for a gig-goer, Wendy,' says Mason. 'Which other artists do you like?'

'Oh, Mason, Lance and I are *always* going to gigs. We like anyone really ... our taste is quite *eclectic*. We like Bonnie Tyler, and well, loads of other artists, really. It's hard to remember all their names. We have *all* the music CDs at home – Bonnie's, Cheryl Cole's, *all* the NOW albums, anything they play on Magic Radio, really. We're *really really* into our music.' Wendy's struggling to find literally *any* other name to add to her list.

'Cool,' says Mason.

(Something else to say about Mason is that he's never rude, even when he knows someone's talking rubbish. He'll always listen and he usually just says "cool" or something like that.)

'So, you guys won't believe who else we saw there at the gig. Take a guess?' says Wendy.

The guessing that Wendy always asks us to do is kind of impossible, really, because you never know where to start. Like when Wendy says, 'Guess what we're doing this weekend?' and you know it could be anything from going away for a romantic weekend in a Travelodge to having a colonoscopy. Sometimes when you do guess, she'll say yes because she thinks that's a better thing than the thing she was about to tell you anyway.

It's quite ironic and everything that the "honesty" value is the one bouncing around on our computer backgrounds this month, but we all know this about Wendy and the truth: they've never been that close.

'Bonnie Tyler,' says Mason.

'Duh, Mason!' Wendy slaps her thighs and screeches. 'Silly billy! I mean, who *else*? Guess!'

'Katy Perry,' says Mason.

'No, I don't *think* she was there. Well, I didn't see her, anyway,' says Wendy, her eyes darting around, wondering if she'd know Katy Perry if she fell over her.

'Guys, you're all useless. The morning show presenter from Magic Radio was there. He's so handsome, and quite a lot shorter in real life than you think he'd be. I can't remember his name. And that old lady from *Gogglebox* was there too, I think, and so was the whole cast of the Southend production of *Dreamgirls.* And the *entire* England rugby sevens team. I nearly fainted. *Everyone* was there.'

Wendy's now about to burst, her untruths knowing no bounds.

'You can't believe how star-studded it was, and there were little old Lance and me, right smack bang in the middle of everyone, chatting to everyone and having the best time ever. They were all so friendly. Say what you like about famous people, I've always found them to be quite friendly when you're in a small venue,' Wendy says, rolling her closed eyes in that show-offy sort of way.

'Guys, it was awesome, the *best* birthday surprise ever!' says Wendy, looking around to see just how awesome we all think this birthday surprise was.

'I can't even *begin* to think how much Lance spent on those tickets. Money's no object for my Lance, and he really went all out for this big "oh" birthday. He made it an "oh boy" birthday celebration. He spoils me *so* much.'

We all believe about one percent of Wendy's story, and it's hard to know how to respond. But this is what we all say at once: 'Cool.'

Mondays are busy days for meetings. Our team has a weekly "catch-up" meeting that Storm leads, and today she's in the office on time, so our meeting won't start late. We get to the Scrum Room just before ten.

'So hi guys, hope you're all doing okay and had good weekends, yeah?' says Storm, putting a tower of Tupperwares on to the table in front of her.

She takes them down and puts them in a row, biggest to smallest. She opens a medium one with yoghurt in it and pours it over the biggest one with fruit salad in it, shakes some muesli from a smaller one over it and then spoons honey out of the smallest one and pours it over the lot. We all get kind of lost in the activity of Storm's breakfast, and forget to respond to Storm's question about the weekend.

'Guys? Your weekends?' says Storm, looking up briefly from her breakfast-building.

'Storm, mine was amaaaaaaazing,' says Wendy. 'For those of you who didn't hear, it was my *big* birthday over the weekend – I know, no one believes how old I am. *No one.* Lance took me to the most awesome, exclusive, intimate event near Baker Street – I got to meet *so* many famous people. The *whole* Chelsea team was there too.' Her eyes and her mouth widen with each new fib.

'*And* the England rugby sevens team?' says Mason.

'Sorry, did I say Chelsea? I meant to say the England rugby sevens team,' says Wendy, trying to remember what else she'd made up. It's hard work trying to remember all the details when you invent them.

'Okay, sounds super, Wendy. And happy birthday, my love. Hope you enjoyed your day. Guys, anyone else have anything exciting to tell us?' says Storm, her mouth full.

'Watched some more rugby vids. Super cool,' says Mason.

'Me too! I had to keep asking Jamie what was going on, but it kind of made sense, I think,' I say. 'We also went to see the movie, *Bohemian*

Rhapsody. It was awesome. The movie's had mixed reviews, but we *loved* it.'

'Freddie Mercury! That's who else was at the gig,' says Wendy, clapping and looking around the room.

No one has the energy to put her right.

'Oh, and we also met up with friends from Cape Town who are here on holiday. We went exploring –'

'You guys are *forever* exploring, Morag,' says Gennypha. 'You've probably seen more of London than all of us. But basically you guys do it on purpose, right?'

'I guess, Gennz. Makes sense. So we met up with our friends in Little Venice. Have any of you been there?'

'Yes, I've been there – it's awesome,' says Madison. 'I love going on the water-bus from there to Camden too, it's so cool.'

'Ah, we couldn't get tickets. But we loved walking around there and catching up with our friends too. My favourite kind of day.'

'Isn't every day your favourite kind of day, Morag?' says Mason.

'Ja, I suppose so. I think Jamie gets tired of hearing me saying that. Sometimes he looks at me like I think he really wishes I'd just shut up. You probably all think the same, hey?'

'I know what you mean,' says Madison.

'Not me, Morag.' Sometimes Mason knows just when to say the right thing.

'Right, can we do some work now? Glad you had super weekends because it's going to be another busy week. I'm going to need you all to go ahead and put your shoulders to the wheel, yeah, because we've all got lots to think about and do for the annual report and for the *BLAT* programme, yeah? Even for people at my level up here, believe it or not,' says Storm, indicating sky-high level.

'We all need to roll up our sleeves and do things we normally don't do.' (This is how Storm pronounces you guys: *we*.)

Mason chokes on his coffee, and puts his hand up to apologise.

'So, shall we do a bit of a round robin?' Storm makes a circular motion with her finger as she spoons her breakfast out of the biggest Tupperware.

One by one we list what we're working on and, while we talk, we wait for Storm's response. She's not really listening because she's focusing on scraping out every last bit of her breakfast. She looks up when we've all finished speaking.

'Right, super, guys. Thanks. That all sounds super, I'm really pleased. Okay, so this is where we are with Cali Shannon – or Calz, as I like to call her – and Quinn, and their teams.'

Gennypha and Mason look at each other, "whatever" all over their faces.

'Soz, Storm, so as I said, I haven't had a chance to feed back to you about Quinn. Basically, it's a no from him. He's happy to draw a line under this whole shebang but reading *between* the lines (see what I did there, lolz), I think he just doesn't want to have anything to do with us. Maybe Coach can reach out to him a bit further down the road, yeah?'

'Oh, right. Thanks, Gennz. I love a surprise in my own meeting, yeah?'

'Soz, basically that's what I said in the round robin, Storm.'

'Right. So Morag, we're still on track with Alex for the annual report feature, yeah?'

I give Storm a thumbs-up. 'Yes, as I said in the round robin, I've sent you the draft to review. Hers is a lovely story, so moving.'

'Of course you did, lovey! Won't you print it out for me too?'

'Sure, no worries.'

'So, where we are with Calz and her team is this: they're super keen to work with us. Calz has said, as you all know, that this isn't so much about exposure for *her*, but more about giving back to an organisation that helped her sister through a really dark patch in her life ...'

'No, Storm, it was Cali who went through the dark patch. When she basically lost her shit that evening in Soho. Remember?'

'Of course, Gennz, you're quite right, but to be honest, the details don't really matter, the point is...'

'Soz, Storm. Of *course* the details matter! Her story is what I need to sell in to the red tops and magazines and the breakfast show and everything, ahead of *BLAT*. We *have* to go to them with *her* story, exactly as she told us –'

'Excuse me, Gennz, *I'm* selling in the story to the media, yeah? We talked about this the other day. I'm taking this on, moving forward, and I'm going to need you to go ahead and leave this with me, yeah?'

'So you *didn't* hear what any of us said in the round robin, did you Storm?' says Gennypha. 'You didn't hear me say that I'd had some bites from broadcast media, and that the breakfast show is keen to get Cali on to the sofa to share her story. It's mental health awareness month soon and they thought it would be a good fit to have her sharing her story to tie in with all the other work they're doing to raise awareness. You didn't hear a single word, did you?

'But sure, I'll pass all of this over to you, Storm,' Gennypha's voice is shaking. 'As you wish, Storm. And you can go ahead and stuff it up like you do to every other thing you work on, Storm. Basically, this is rubbish. And you're bang out of order.'

She pushes her chair back, grabs her stuff and storms out of the door. As she reaches the door, she pauses briefly and turns to look at Storm.

'And, just so you know, she fucking *hates* being called Calz! It's Cali – she told you the other night at practice! We *all* heard her say it. This is such shit!' She leaves the room and slams the door behind her.

We all turn to Storm. She pulls herself upright in her seat, leans over to chuck her plastic spoon into the bin, rebuilds her Tupperware tower from biggest to smallest. She brushes some crumbs off her skirt and picks up her pen.

'Okay, super, guys. So action points moving forward,' she says, giving us all action points that bear no relation to any conversation we've had at this meeting. She's reading a to-do list from her notebook, and ticks our (her) action points off one by one.

'And if any of you have any questions, going forward, we can take them offline, and you can just go ahead and ping me an email. I know there's a lot on at the moment, as you can see from Gennypha's behaviour today. I understand, but moving forward, I'm going to need you to go ahead and focus on what you're working on. We were going to develop a new WOW process, ways of working, but we'll have to circle back to it when the dust has settled after this unprecedented uptick of activity over the next few months, yeah?'

'Cool,' says Mason.

We're all trying to figure out which world Storm lives in. And for how much longer Gennypha is going to be part of it. Storm surely can't be that unaware of her own behaviour, can she?

It's no surprise when I get back to my desk that Gennypha isn't at hers. Kevin isn't at his desk either, and the door to the Tight-head Nook is closed. If anything would sway Gennypha's decision to leave, I guess this would be it. I've never seen her lose her temper like that – things must have just built up and up.

When Storm knows where Gennypha's going to work, basically, she's just going to lose her shit, hey. I kind of do and don't want to be there when that happens.

Chapter 23

This morning, Gennypha and I get to the office at the same time. 'Basically, I can *never* find my door pass,' Gennypha says, scratching around in the bottom of her handbag.

'No worries, Gennz.' I pull my door pass out from the front pocket of my backpack. 'I always keep mine here, otherwise I'd never find mine either!'

We walk in together, and throw our bags down on our desks. Wendy and Mason are already at their desks, and Gennypha offers us all a drink. She motions for me to join her in the kitchen.

'So, basically, I've done it,' says Gennypha.

'Resigned?' I say.

'No, I've lodged a grievance. I still don't know whether or not to take the job with Cali, but basically, I need to deal with this issue first, you know? I couldn't leave under this cloud. More like that shit, Macleod.' There's an insecurity in her eyes I've not seen before.

'Wow, Gennz, that must have been a tough decision to make, hey?'

'Yeah, it was, but basically Kevin was ever so sweet and helpful, and gave me excellent advice. He's a good egg, that one. Someone you can count on in a crisis, yeah? Lolz.'

'Everyone says that about Kevin, actually. So what happens now?'

Gennypha looks around to see if anyone's coming into the kitchen.

'Well, basically, Kevin told me to put my grievance to him in writing, which I've done. I sent it to him and copied Coach in – Kevin said he couldn't advise me to do that, but it wouldn't harm to do that. So basically, he was saying I should do that, but he couldn't tell me I should, if that makes sense, yeah?'

I nod.

'So he and Coach acknowledged my email yesterday, and Kevin told me he'd let me know what the next steps were. Basically, I think, they need to get a grievance review panel together, or something, and then they'll meet with me and her separately, and then they'll either uphold or deny the grievance. I'm *so* glad we don't both have to meet with them at the same time. She can be such a bully and talk such bullshit, I'm not sure how that would go for me. But basically, I've put my side of the story to them so there's always that, yeah?'

'Wow, that's huge, Gennz. It sounds like quite a scary process and everything.'

To be honest, I'm also worried about the fall-out from Storm during all of this not only for Gennypha, but for the rest of us too. Storm isn't the best at hiding her feelings, as we all know. But I don't want to take the focus away from Gennypha or anything.

'That's a really brave thing to do, you know. I'm sure it's the right thing, Gennz. You have to get it resolved one way or the other, and this process will make you feel empowered and everything, hey?'

'Thanks, Morag. It's always good to chat to you, you're so helpful.'

'No worries, Gennz.'

I get back to my desk and give Wendy her rooibos tea (this is how she pronounces rooibos: *roobois*.) She asks me how my evening was. It's rare for her to ask me that; it's usually a springboard for her to tell me about her evening. Like when people ask you when your birthday is and you tell them, and then you ask when their birthday is and they say "today".

'Ah, not too great, hey Wendy,' I say. 'We had a bit of a disaster with our boiler. It blew up last night. Well, not completely, but enough to put us out of heating and hot water for a while. So annoying.'

Wendy's mouth gets bigger and bigger; I think that's where she absorbs all her gossip. She holds it all in there until she decides who she can impress with it first.

'You know, *we* would never have a boiler like that in our flat,' she says. 'We prefer to spend a bit more money on the more *reliable* brands.'

With a sharp intake of breath, she puts her hand on my arm. 'Oh, you poor thing, I *forgot*. You probably can't afford the best appliances, can you? When you own property in that part of London, it's not worth investing too much because you know what the people are like who live there. They just destroy everything, don't they? You poor thing, it must be so scary living there.'

She makes a kind of harmonica-smile, where you show how sorry you feel for someone by showing all your teeth. It absolutely sucks.

I've never been great at thinking on my feet. I'll think about this and later today or tonight I'll come up with a retort I wish I'd thought of at this very minute. For now, I choose not to say anything otherwise I might be rude, and that will make me feel even worse.

'So how was your evening, Wendy?'

'Funny you should ask, Morag. Especially after the *disaster* with your flat. I can't stop worrying about you.' She puts her hand on my arm again, worrying about me not even one flipping bit.

'Anyway, now that our kids have left home, we have a bit more *cash* available to replace all of our appliances. Thank your lucky stars you don't have kids, Morag, because honestly, they are much more hassle and expense than they're worth.'

Wendy's children don't seem to have made the choices she'd hoped they would. She and Lance had much higher aspirations for them both. Her son, Thaddeus, is a plumber.

'I always thought he was going to follow in his dad's footsteps and become an estate agent, you know. Or become a brain surgeon like … like … well, you know, you get good wages for that work, you know? That's a really good job, isn't it? There's a real social stigma around being a plumber, you know.' (Wendy says "social stigma" in a kind of nasally mime-whisper.)

The first time Wendy said that, Ash chirped, 'Said no one, ever.'

Anyway, Thaddeus also doesn't have a partner, although he spends a lot of time with his flatmate, who's a "chap". (Wendy says "chap" the same way she says "social stigma".)

And Rivonia, her daughter, lives in a shared home *south* of the river. Wendy can't really bring herself to mention the area her daughter lives in, but she doesn't mind that Rivonia works in telesales, as there are "endless opportunities for her career to skyrocket".

Not being funny or anything, but sometimes I think Wendy's ideas are just messed up.

'So when we buy appliances, Morag, we *only* buy high-end brands, but you'll be surprised even *those* don't last forever,' she says, winking at me. 'That surprises you, doesn't it? So anyway, Lance bought us a new dishwasher and we used it for the first time last night. It's *amaaazing*. It works *so* well. On the reviews page, it sounded like *all* the celebrities use this brand, so no wonder it works so well.'

'Cool. Which brand of dishwasher is that, Wendy?' You know, even if I dug through all the crap on Madison's desk, I still don't think I'd find a shit to give about Wendy's answer.

'Oh, my dear Morag, it was *really* expensive. You probably won't even have heard of it. It's the same one they use in all the top-end guest houses.'

Wendy has put her hand on my arm again and I want to scream or punch her in the face, or both.

This is what I say to Wendy:

1. Cool.

Also, when Wendy talks so negatively about her children, and points out that I don't have any, I flipping well can't stand it. And this is why:

1. It's horrible to talk about your children like that, no matter how disappointed you are in their choices. (To be honest, I've sometimes wondered if they've made choices to annoy their parents in return for the names they've given them.)
2. She has *no* idea why Jamie and I don't have children. She doesn't know about the nights we've cried over dashed hopes and failed attempts at IVF. I can't even bring myself to say any more about it or even tell you about it; my heart hurts too much. Wendy isn't the first person – and won't be the last – to hit that nerve. On the surface, I try and brush it off, but inside it hurts like hell. It really does.
3. My parents always hated the word "kids"; they thought it was "common". But they did always want to be grandparents, and they never were.

When Storm walks in today, she has no food in her hand but she has a *huge* cloud over her head. That cloud is an early warning system for all of us. She's like a punctured hosepipe; instead of spraying her anger in one direction, anyone even vaguely anywhere near her gets soaked when that cloud bursts.

'Morning, Stormz,' says Madison, removing her screensaver for seven seconds.

'Madz, I'm going to need you to go ahead and cancel our catch-up this morning. I would never normally do this, as you know, but something else has cropped up,' says Storm, over-enunciating the word "cropped", and eating not even one thing.

We all know she *often* cancels meetings, but anyway.

'Okay, sure, Stormz,' says Madison, bashing her keyboard harder than normal.

'And guys, I'm going to need you all to go ahead and get on top of all of your work today. I'm tired of chasing you all for everything all the time, yeah? I expect more of you,' she says, taking a sandwich out of her handbag.

'Morag – where's that email draft I asked you about yesterday?'

'It's in your inbox, Storm,' I say. 'I told you I'd emailed it to you again yesterday, remember? I put "SUPER URGENT FOR STORM TO CHECK" in caps in the subject line.'

'Guys, guys, guys. Just because you email me, doesn't mean I read your emails. Is it really that difficult to understand? You can't just email me and expect me to read it. How many times must I tell you that?' says the head of comms.

This is how many unread emails Storm had in her inbox the last time I looked at her screen:

1. 1,765.

'Guys, at my level you can't just read every email that comes into your inbox. I'm *way* too busy, and I'd spend my life doing nothing but reading and replying to emails. I *need* you guys to get that into your heads. We need to work as a team and, as your head of, I really expect more from you. I need you to leave it all out on the field, go the full nine yards, dig deep to grind out the win. Every day.'

We're all incredulous, gob-smacked.

'Morag, not sure how many times I need to tell you this. I'm going to need you to go ahead and print out your email draft and put it on my desk. Right. Here!' Storm slaps the side of her desk, upsetting two mountains of papers and a cosmic cloud of dust.

'Storm, I've emailed it to you four times and you have three copies of it on your desk somewhere on that pile there,' I say, pointing to the higher of the two mountains of paper.

'I don't need stories, Morag. I need ...'

'Storm, leave Morag alone!' yells Gennypha. I nearly jump out of my skin and the whole pod goes silent. 'Just fucking stop it. Stop bullying everyone! Basically, you'll never get the best from your team by being like this ... *no one* likes a bully, Storm. Just *drop* it. Jesus!'

What just happened?

'Quite finished?' says Storm, looking at Gennypha.

'For now,' says Gennypha, shaking and close to tears.

Storm raises her eyebrows, bites the inside of her cheeks and looks around the room. Everyone across the office has been looking at our pod, and all the heads bob below their computer screens when Storm looks around. She stands up slowly, picks up her bag and walks out of the office. We all watch her closely, not sure what to think. This has never happened before. Storm has never left an unopened sandwich on her desk.

'Now what, guys?' says Gennypha, when she comes back from lunch.

'I guess we wait and see, Gennz,' says Madison, looking at the door and then her phone. 'She hasn't text me at all. I thought she might have come back by now, but maybe she's just gone home.'

'I'm going to ask Kevin,' says Gennypha, getting up from her desk.

'Good plan,' says Mason, ripping open a packet of crisps.

'I guess ...' says Gennypha.

I get up from my desk to get away from Mason's crisps, and Gennypha walks over to Kevin and whispers something in his ear. He looks at her, his screen and then his phone, gets up from his desk and walks to the kitchen to fetch his sandwich from the fridge. I follow him into the kitchen and close the door when he leaves, watching through the window as the two of them walk into the Tight-head Nook. Am I the only one in our team who knows what's really going on here?

I pour myself a glass of water, sit down at a table and page through last night's *Evening Standard*. I check to make sure Mason's finished his crisps before I go back to my desk. When I get there, Gennypha walks back to her desk.

'So what did he say, Gennz?' says Madison.

'Well, basically he hasn't heard from Storm at all. He said *everyone* saw her, basically, *storm* out of the office earlier. He said he had to go and speak to Coach about something else, so he said he'd ask her if she'd heard anything. And then he'll get back to me, er, I mean, us.'

'Job's a good'un,' says Madison, giving Gennypha a thumbs-up.

'I wonder what's going on with Storm?' I say to Madison's screensaver.

Chapter 24

Storm doesn't come back to the office for the rest of the week. Coach tells us Storm has been booked off sick. Gennypha tells me Storm has missed her grievance hearing twice because of that and, if she doesn't come to the hearing Kevin has scheduled for Monday, Coach will have to do something. She doesn't know what that could be, but Kevin says he wouldn't miss Monday's hearing for anything, if he were Storm.

It's Friday, and Storm has also missed our rugby training sessions and the practice match this week, and Barry isn't happy either.

'Morning, team comms, how are we this Friday morn,' he says, leaning on a crutch and tapping his signet ring on the desk. 'Bit tired, mind, after ironing fourteen shirts and five pairs of trousers last night. Felt proper knackered, I did.'

'Wow, Barry. Huge news. Let me tweet that – you said how many shirts?' says Mason, laughing.

'Very funny, Mr O. But seriously, like, I'm not being funny or anything, guys, but if our Storm doesn't come to practice next week, we're going to have to drop her and all,' he says. 'Look you, Storm's reliable with the boot right enough, but if she's unreliable as a team member, we're in trouble, right?'

'It's tricky to know, Barry.' I'm unsure how to respond. Storm is our head of comms and everything, so I decide not to say anything further.

'We may have to drop-kick her, right enough.' Barry laughs out loud at his own joke. He doesn't realise how much some people in our team would agree.

The grievance hearing takes place off-site on Monday morning, and Gennypha beckons me outside when she gets back to her desk, to tell me what happened. Kevin had called Gennypha into a meeting with him and Coach, and told her Storm had made it to that hearing. They said she's thought about and reflected on what had happened, and acknowledged that her behaviour had been unacceptable. She also said she hadn't given Gennypha a chance to lead on projects, or to grow in her role.

Kevin and Coach upheld Gennypha's grievance and, during the next month, Storm has to:

1. Meet with Gennypha to apologise unconditionally. (Gennypha also has to apologise to Storm for her outbursts.)
2. Put a plan of action together for Gennypha, outlining how she's going to give her more responsibility and her own projects to handle.
3. Go to one of our volunteer-led anger management classes.

'Morag, this is pretty amazing and basically I feel validated. I told Kevin and Coach I was nervous Storm might hold all of this against me, and they said I have to tell them if I feel that's happening. If she does anything that makes me feel uncomfortable, they want to know – how amazing is that?'

'That's pretty amazing, Gennz,' I say. 'You must feel so chuffed and everything. So good that Coach and Kevin are supporting you like this, hey?'

'Deffo. Basically, they told me our HAMP policies protect me, and so do our values. Storm's behaviour doesn't chime with our values here at The HAMP. Nor has my recent behaviour, to be fair, which is why I have to apologise to Storm too. Lolz, but fair play, yeah? I had no idea how the grievance procedure would work, but it feels like The HAMP values me and my well-being. Storm has booked a meeting with me next week, so we'll see if she's prepared to do the right thing. If she does, I'll try to too.'

Gennypha gives me a double thumbs-up.

Rugby practice this evening is quite tricky. When Pat is filming our warm-up, she asks me where Storm is. I motion to her to stop filming and tell her Storm might be a bit late for practice tonight and, if she does come, Pat shouldn't focus on her. I don't know how much anyone else knows, or how Storm is going to act, so I don't say anything further to Pat.

'Oh, right,' says Pat. 'I haven't seen her at the office for a few days, and I was wondering what was going on with her. I'll get the low-down from Coach and let you know.' She taps the side of her nose. This is what I say to her:

1. No worries.

This is what I wish I had the courage to say to her:

1. Stay out of it, Pat, this is none of your bees-wax.

Tracy jumps sideways towards me. 'Oy, Morag my love, all right?' she says.

'Yep, great thanks, Tracy. How about you? How's the world of fundraising?'

'Not bad, my love. Kind of like, I don't know, like, not bad at all. So what's this I hear about Storm and all?' she says in a stage whisper. A funny thing about Tracy is that when she talks to you she looks just beyond and slightly below the side of your shoulder.

'Not sure, Tracy. What is it you've heard?' I'm not great at lying, but I am pretty good at playing dumb.

'Well, when I went down for a fag at lunchtime, my mate Richard said he thought she'd gone and left and all. It's kind of like a bit strange, obviously. I don't know ...'

'Oh wow, that's interesting,' I say. 'No, she hasn't left. She's been unwell for a few days.'

'Ah, that's a pity, yeah? I'd be kind of like glad to see the back of that little fucker. She gets right under your skin that one, obviously, and it's kind of like, I don't know, she doesn't ever seem to do any actual work. I've had quite a few argy-bargies with her, I have.'

'Mason calls them RG-BGs,' I say, trying to change the subject.

'What?'

'Never mind, sorry. Yes, I guess Storm isn't easy to work with,' I say. As much as I struggle with Storm, I still don't want to say the wrong thing.

'Come on, my love, wouldn't you be kind of like, I don't know, glad to see the back of her?' says Tracy.

I smile and shrug.

'Oh, and me and Richard think there's something going on between Mason and Jasper. I've seen them on their lunchtime runs with Ash, and they seem a bit googly-eyed with each other, if you know what I mean?'

Here are three things to know about Tracy:

1. She's been at The HAMP for about ten years, and is a world champion gatherer of gossip. If there were an award for gossip, Tracy would win it, no contest. If you ever want to know

anything about anything or anyone, ever, Tracy is your person. She uses her smoke breaks to gather gossip too, I've discovered.

2. She's super confident – the kind of person who walks through a doorway or around a corner like she has the right of way.

3. She's not unaware of Kevin's attentions, and it's hard to tell if she finds him annoying or not. She told me once, 'Old Kevin's told me when he's come in this morning, he's only gone and kind of like, I don't know, put on the wrong fucking shoes! What does that even mean? I mean, don't. Don't, even. Yeah?'

'Right, you lot, give us six laps round the field, yeah?' Coach Dave shouts.

Tracy and I run off together and I stop to tie my laces, trying to avoid any further questions from Tracy. When I stand up, Mason is waiting for me and slows down to my pace to jog with me. Pat jogs alongside us to film us for a short while, and when she drops back to catch the others coming around the field for the second time, I chat to Mason about the day's events.

'Amazing outcome for Gennypha,' says Mason. 'Well deserved. Storm can be a proper tosser sometimes.'

'Yep, she sure can be. I hope she doesn't punish us all for this.'

'She'd better not.' Mason sprints ahead. 'Dice you to the end!'

I stand absolutely zero chance of getting anywhere near Mason. As I've said, I was born with no aptitude for speed. At school, we had to run sprints at our inter-house sports days, and it was super challenging for me. I ran my heart out, and my legs felt shorter the faster I tried to run. The effort wasn't rewarded with much forward movement, and although I always came stone last, I usually got the loudest applause. I loved that until I learnt what the word "patronising" meant. I guess everyone does love a trier, hey?

At the end of our practice, Coach Dave calls us all together.

'Right, you lot, that was a good run, that was, yeah? I'm well pleased with how you're all playing, yeah? You're starting to play as a proper team.'

Coach steps into the circle and raises her hands.

'Great work, The HAMP team. I also like what I see. All credit to you guys, ja?' she says. 'You're giving it hundred and ten percent, and leaving it all out under the wire. I'm proud of you, ja? And thank you to you, Cali, for bringing your experiences to the team. I think it's a good motivator to have you in the team, ja? You agree, team?'

We all nod and wave and shout our agreement.

'We have just eight more weeks until the big day when we play in the festival, and if the other teams aren't quaking in their foot socks at the prospect of taking on us, then they're living in another planet, ja? They need to pull instead their foot socks together, ja!' Coach claps hard and walks around the circle. 'Who's the best charity sevens side?'

'WE ARE!'

'Who's going to win the festival?'

'WE ARE!'

'Who's going to lose?'

'WE ARE!' We all shout, and laugh when we realise we fell into Coach's dunce trap.

'The best charity sevens side since chopped liver! That's who we are! We're winners. Winners, ja?' says Coach, slapping each of us on our shoulders.

'Thanks, you ugly bunch. We're done for tonight, yeah, see you Saturday,' says Coach Dave.

'THANKS, COACH!' we shout.

I remind Coach and Coach Dave that I won't be there on Saturday, as I've booked a long weekend away. They say it's fine.

Jamie meets me outside the clubhouse after I've showered and changed.

'That was interesting, Rags. While I was waiting for you, I saw …
well, did you see who was in the restaurant as you walked past?'

'No, I wasn't even looking that way. Who was there?'

'Coach. She was there with someone, having a meal.'

'Cool. I know she lives in the area, so she must have arranged to
meet a friend there. And ding-dong, now for some more boring news
from Jamie.'

'Hey! No, it isn't boring at all, Rags. She was having a meal with
Cali. It looked kind of cosy, Rags – they were talking and laughing
and drinking wine. Cali! And Coach!'

'What? Coach? And Cali? Together?' I stop and look at Jamie.

'Yep! Now it's not so boring, hey?'

'No, not at all. Sorry for saying that, Jamie.'

'It's okay. Don't do it again, though,' Jamie laughs, as we start walking
again.

After a few minutes, I stop and look at him. 'Do you think we
should keep this to ourselves for now? I think Coach might feel super
embarrassed that we spotted her. I think she'll let us all know when
she's ready to. What do you think?'

'Yeah, Rags, you're probably right. But you know her better than
I do. I guess it would just be gossip if we talked about it before she
does, though, hey?'

'Yep, I guess. But then, if they wanted to be discreet, they wouldn't
have had a meal right there under everyone's noses, would they?
Maybe they wanted to be seen … who knows?'

It starts to rain, so we grab each other's hands and walk quickly
towards the tube station. The wind is starting to feel icy too.

We're going to Corfu for a long weekend because we both feel we
need a proper break from the busy-ness of London life. Work has
been quite full-on for us both and Jamie hasn't been sleeping well.

And when I start feeling stressed about work and stop feeling like every day is my favourite kind of day and everything, then I know I need a holiday too.

I now have my indefinite leave to remain, but I still need to get a visa for this holiday. I can't wait to get my British passport next year, so I can travel freely throughout Europe.

I get a bit crazy-excited that our hotel room is right on the ocean and our view is awesome. The water is crystal clear, the temperature is perfect and I want to stay here forever. The weight of work and Storm and all the tension of the past while fall off my shoulders and I dive like a dolphin into the turquoise water.

If paradise were a place on earth, this little corner of Corfu is it.

Chapter 25

Having a few days away was the best idea Jamie and I have had in a long while. It was everything we needed it to be. I arrive at the office on Tuesday morning, feeling perkier and holding my head a little higher than I have recently.

'How was your city break?' says Madison, as I pop my bag on to my desk.

'It was awesome, thanks,' I say to the back of her head.

'Where did you go again?' says Mason. 'Crete, was it?'

'No, Corfu. Have you been?'

'Years ago, with my parents. It was okay, a bit too hot for my liking,' he says.

'Ah, yes, Lance can't stand the heat either,' says Wendy.

'It was hot,' I say. 'But we spent most of our time swimming and in the shade on the beach. The food was amazing too, and we found some beautiful little villages and small, sheltered coves for swimming. It was perfect, my f –'

'Your favourite kind of holiday,' says Mason. 'Mind-reader, me.'

'I'm just super predictable and everything, hey,' I say, embarrassed by the truth.

'Yep,' says Mason. 'But in a good way.'

I'm nervous about interviewing Cali today. It's the first time I'll ever have interviewed a celebrity and, although celebrities are just people

225

too, I can't help but second-guess myself. I'm going to interview Cali for a feature in the charity's magazine, *The News HAMPer*, and Pat's going to film it for our *BLAT* programme too. I'm glad to have Gennypha coming with me; she'll be a great support, and Ash is coming along too to take some behind-the-scenes photographs and others for the magazine.

The four of us meet in the downstairs lobby to travel to Cali's flat together.

'Awesome,' says Ash, looking up at the clear blue sky. 'The light will be good enough to shoot some images outside, maybe.'

'Super. But I can't film outside because of the ambient noise, you see. Always such a privilege to empower you folks with learning. Such a privilege.'

Ash rolls his eyes.

'Anyway, chaps, I'm going to run ahead, if that's okay. I need to buy a ticket and get a receipt, yeah?' says Pat. 'Need to keep a record of incidentals to claim back, yeah?'

'No worries,' I say. 'See you at the turnstiles, Pat.'

'Okey dokey.'

'Cheers, Pat.' Gennypha waves, and turns to me. Ash is now engrossed in his phone and nearly walks into Bernard, our office cleaner, near the front door.

'Mate!' says Ash.

'Sorry, my love,' says Bernard, winking at Ash and stepping back. He pretends to stand to attention with his broom, and bows as Ash walks through the door. Ash doesn't react.

'Weirdo,' says Ash, when we get outside.

'So, basically Morag, Storm came in really early this morning for our meeting. You saw, yeah? I was pretty scared, not sure how she was going to be after all that stuff from last week. Anyway, basically, she apologised to me. Without any ifs or buts or maybes. A totally unconditional apology, like she was told to do. And you know what? It actually felt sincere.'

'Wow, Gennz, that's awesome. A miracle, hey?'

'At first I thought she was just doing it because she'd been told to. Well, basically she was. But I really saw some remorse and regret in her eyes, you know. I think she genuinely felt bad about treating me like shit all this time. But you know what, I also saw something new in her eyes – a kind of softening or something. Do you think she and Bazza are ... you know?'

'Wow, maybe! Love can do that to you, hey?'

'It can basically soften even the hardest hearts, yeah? So anyway, you know what? I apologised to her too, and I decided to forgive her. I think forgiving someone takes almost as much courage and risk as apologising does, don't you think? So that's what I did. Basically.'

'That's very big of you, Gennz. I'm proud of you.' I immediately regret my words. 'Sorry, Gennz, I don't mean to sound patronising. I just think that's a generous and gracious step you've taken.'

'Thanks, Morag. It didn't sound patronising at all to me. Not to say she isn't going to irritate the shit out of me again, but if she's prepared to make an effort and do things differently, then I'll give it a go too. What's there to lose?'

'Well, we could maybe lose our way,' says Ash, looking up from his phone.

We've followed his shortcut to the tube station, which has taken us through a park, around a block and through a really, really narrow alleyway I've never ever seen before. We meet up with Pat at the tube station and go down the escalator together.

We get on to the tube, find four seats together and wait for the doors to close. They don't for a while, and we watch people rushing to get on the tube. I don't know if it's just me, but I find it funny seeing how awkward and sheepish people look when they run on to the tube thinking the doors are about to shut, and they don't.

Another of my favourite things is watching people on the tube. You try to look invisible and there's no eye contact, but there's always so much going on. A young sad-looking woman opposite me hugs an *Addicted to pasta* shopping bag, while the woman next to her is engrossed in putting on her lipstick – staring into a little mirror and when her hand slips she mouths 'Oh, fuck off' to herself.

A young mum with a hairstyle like a helmet is furious with her little daughter. 'You ain't listening, Mia! I told you not to lick that pole – it ain't a straw, Mia. You ain't going to get to do them things you wanted indoors because you ain't listening, Mia. Are you listening to me, Mia?'

Almost everyone who isn't listening to Mia's mom is looking at or listening to a phone or a device.

'Morag! This is us!' says Gennypha. 'You're miles away!'

'Sorry, I was.'

Ash Googles how to get to Cali's flat. We set off from the station, but a block away, he stops and stares at his phone, turning it upside down.

'Google maps! Soz, guys, it's this way.' He turns around and leads us back past the station. 'Told you we might get lost!'

When we get to Cali's flat, she and Vanessa greet us at her door. Cali looks fresh and happy, and invites us in. We pile our jackets on her banister, and put our shoes under the radiator.

'Do you need me to stay with you, Cal, or are you okay to do this without me?' Vanessa says.

'I think I'll be all right, Ness, but feel free to stay if you like. That'll be okay, right, guys?' Cali looks at Gennypha.

'Yes, sure. What do you think, Morag and Pat?' Gennypha says.

'No worries. Whatever works best for you, hey,' I say.

'You can stay if you li-ike, Vanessa,' says Pat. 'But to be honest, I'm not convinced it would be the best use of your time to stick around. Up to you, though. Whatever you want to do, yeah?'

'Oh right. Oh okay, cool, that's great. I think. Actually, much as I'd love to stay, I do have a few other things I need to do today, so let me pop out quickly. I'm sure I'll be back before you're finished, yeah?'

Cali nods, shrugs and gives Vanessa a thumbs-up. 'Sure, Ness. See you in a bit, we will. I won't say anything I shouldn't. Promise.'

'Better not, Ms Shannon,' says Vanessa.

Cali offers us all something to drink and invites us to sit in her front room. Pat says that's the best place to film the interview, and follows Cali into the kitchen. She returns and dishes out some orders.

'That's brilliant. Cali says we can move some furniture around for the filming, and we can open the blinds fully too, to let more natural light into the room. Give me a hand, won't you, chaps? And Morag, when I'm filming, you can sit next to me so Cali can keep eye contact with you while you two are chatting. Sound good, chaps?'

When Cali walks back into the room with our drinks, Pat asks if she can move the big vase of roses on the mantelpiece into shot, for the filming. Cali smiles and offers to move them herself. She takes a card out of the flowers, and studies it closely before shoving it into her pocket.

'Lovely, Cali. Thanks, those add so much colour to the room. And they smell divine, don't they, guys?' says Pat.

'Yeah, don't they just? They're from a new friend, a lovely surprise,' says Cali.

Pat sets us up for the filming, and I ask Cali my first few questions. She tells me about her difficult childhood and how she got involved in sport.

'My mum and dad had very little money, and they had us four children to feed and get to school. Mum was in and out of jobs – she just couldn't stay away from the booze, really. My dad worked for the local newspaper and didn't earn a big wage, so he took on other jobs to make up the money Mum was drinking away. He got so angry with her when she was drunk, especially when he'd given her money to buy groceries, or something.'

'That must have been really difficult for you and your siblings,' I say.

'Yes, awful. I *hated* the fighting. Mum was an aggressive drunk, and she'd be so unreasonable – like someone we didn't even know. Me and my brother and sisters were scared *all* the time.'

'I'm sure it was hard to make sense of what was really going on. You probably wished you could be somewhere else.' I suddenly worry I'm putting words into her mouth and everything. (That's exactly what I'm doing. I'm such an idiot.)

'That's right. I tried to get away from it as much as possible. Sport was my life-saver, you know, and I was lucky I was good at it, I was. Athletics and rugby were my favourites. My sisters played netball and spent as much time as they could practising at school or out on the road.

'My brother was a bit of a loner, he was. He preferred staying at home, escaping into his books, bottling up his fear and anger and frustrations, though. Literally. He'd drink himself into oblivion whenever he could. Just like our mum.'

'Sometimes addictions can pass down from generation to generation, hey. Would you say that's what happened with your brother?' I say, hoping it didn't sound too obvious.

'Yeah. I don't know if he was copying our mum or if it was something in him that he couldn't change. Anyway, he began drinking when he was a teenager, and he's never stopped really. I don't even know where he is now, to be honest. We haven't talked in about ten years, we haven't. It's really sad.' Cali looks up. 'Not sure I want that last part on the film, mind. It's a bit too painful, and personal, to be honest.'

'No worries. We can edit that out.' I look around and Pat gives me a thumbs-up.

'Do you miss him?' I immediately regret asking this. She didn't want to talk about this on film, so why would she want to tell me? Jeepers, I'm such an idiot.

'Yes, I do. But it was too difficult to see him in self-destruct mode. He became a different person, he did. He said awful things to me, and to my dad.' Cali grabs a tissue from her pocket and blows her nose. 'Sorry, I don't often talk about this. I didn't realise how much this still hurt. And I do miss him.'

'No worries,' I say. 'And sorry, you asked me not to go there so I shouldn't have. Would you like a short break?'

She puts her hand up, and holds the tissue against her mouth. 'You're all right, Morag. Sorry, I'll be back in a minute.' She stands up and walks out of the front room.

'Oops, do you think I'm digging too deep, Gennz?' I ask.

'Maybe, Morag. Basically, she didn't want this part on film. So ask her what she'd like to talk about when she comes back, yeah?'

I can't seem to stop myself from asking that extra question, or that extra *stupid* question. It *always* ends up driving me crazy and everything.

Cali comes back into the room, wiping her hands on her trousers.

'Sorry, guys. This is so unprofessional. I haven't talked about this for years. I can usually avoid it, so not sure what's going on today. Anyway, shall we get back to this?'

'Yes, sure. If I'm overstepping the mark with my questions, just let me know and I'll change gear,' I say.

'Thanks, my love. I don't want to get too personal on film, or in the article, mind, but let's see what the first edits look like, yeah? Shall we get back to sport? Ah, before we do that, do I look okay? I touched up my slap a little, but do I need more?'

'No, you're okay, pet,' says Pat.

231

'Okay, great. So, at school I had to deal with a lot of stigma. In those days, there were a few girls in my town who played rugby. My parents thought I should be dancing or doing gymnastics, anything they thought girls should be doing instead of playing rugby. I think they felt embarrassed; thought I behaved like a boy. I guess that made me feel like I wasn't good enough, like I fell short of their expectations or something.

'But I absolutely loved the game. Playing sport made me feel alive. My coach saw my potential and fought for me to keep playing. He was an amazing man – quite a lot like my dad, really. But a dad who wasn't embarrassed I played rugby! He was so much more than a coach – he saw everything I was going through and tried to make things as easy for me as possible. A true mentor, he was. I miss him.'

'Where is he now?' I ask, without thinking.

'He passed away five years ago. A huge loss, he was.'

'I'm so sorry, Cali. I wasn't thinking.' I'm driving myself crazy again.

'Not at all, my love. You weren't to know. Anyway, I sound like a real case when you think about it, yeah?' Cali smiles and looks down at her hands.

'Not at all, Cali,' I say. 'We all have our own stories, and everything that happens to us shapes us into who we are. That's what my mom always said to me, anyway.'

'Sounds like she's a wise woman. You're lucky.'

'Yes. Well, she's no longer around. I miss her a lot,' I say, feeling awful that I'm now trying to one-up Cali Shannon. What an idiot I am.

'You'll edit that out, right?' Pat gives me another thumbs-up.

'So, Cali, you must have an incredible strength of character to have pulled yourself through all those struggles.'

'I guess. I've never really thought about it like that. I just did what I felt I had to do, you know. Sometimes it felt like I had no choice.

232

I pushed myself as far as I could go. I was determined to make the Welsh women's rugby team, and when I did, I wanted to be the best. I had to prove myself every step of the way. It was great for a while, but then I started to feel all the things I'd experienced in my childhood bubbling up to the surface. I'd spent so many years trying to push everything down, pretending everything was okay and not dealing with anything, you know.

'I worried my anger was going to spiral out of control. I'd read something about The HAMP in the paper, and so I'd call your HAMP helpline, sometimes in the middle of the night. The volunteers were so amazing. I got angry with them sometimes too, because they helped me see the truth, and I really didn't want to see it or hear it. There's only so long we can pretend to ourselves, and then – well, who the hell are we kidding, right enough?

'And then it all caught up with me, I guess. It all became too much and exploded in the face of that poor lovely woman in Soho. Poor, lovely soul. I broke her nose, you know.

'All she did was hold up a mirror to my face – not an actual one, mind, but she made me see the ugliest face I'd ever seen and I didn't want to admit it was me.

'Punching her was the worst and the best thing I ever did. She threatened to press charges, and I had to do something about my anger, and my drinking. I apologised, and offered to pay for her medical treatment and counselling, and promised to sort myself out, so she decided not to go ahead with the charges.

'I booked myself into rehab. It was the last thing I wanted to do and was the only thing that helped me turn my life around. That, and your helpline.'

'That's amazing, Cali,' I say. 'You knew exactly what you needed to do, hey? Not many people have that kind of self-awareness, you know. I'm so glad you had that help. And that The HAMP has been so helpful to you,' I say.

'Thank you, that's very kind of you. I've never thought about it like that. And wow, I can't believe I'm telling you all this. I don't think I've shared my whole story with anyone other than Vanessa or my family. All your fault. You ask good questions, Morag, and you listen even better. It's a gift, I'd say.'

'Thank you, Cali, that's such a kind thing to say. A friend once told me I listened so much, that I listened even after he'd stopped talking. I'm not sure if that was a compliment or not,' I say.

'Lol, could go either way, right enough,' says Cali, laughing.

'Cali, you know, your story is amazing. You're so inspiring and everything,' I can't help myself saying. But oh, my word, that's such a stupid, lame thing to say – I'm going to go over and over everything I've said today and think about it all night tonight and cringe. I can feel it right now.

'Ah, thank you, Morag. I've always hoped my story will inspire people experiencing what I did as a young girl growing up in south Wales. I want them to know they are good enough, and that it's okay to be yourself. You don't have to be like everyone else, or do what other people might expect of you. That's one of the reasons I wanted to get involved in your charity and this rugby programme too.

'I love the rugby, and it's great to be playing again and so on, but I really wanted to share my story with people, your supporters, anyone who needs to hear and learn from it. It's something I've wanted to do for a long time; it's like a "coming-out" for me. Not that kind of coming-out – ha-ha, *that* happened a long time ago – but a coming-out of my story. It feels good. It feels quite liberating, it does. I'm grateful, I am. Truly.'

'That's so lovely,' says Gennypha.

'Connecting with your charity also feels like a huge life-changing experience for me in so many other ways, it does. You're all so lovely, you are. It's all been quite beautiful, really.' She looks at her hands again, before looking up and smiling at Gennypha and me. 'Wow, I'm getting proper carried away, aren't I?'

'Not at all, Cali. It's a privilege to hear your story,' I say.

'Thank you. Anything else you want to ask me?'

'Just one more question, if that's okay? I ask this of everyone I interview. Knowing what you know now, what would you say to your young self?'

'Great question. And something I had to reflect on when I was in rehab. I think I'd tell my young self that you're not responsible for all the crap the adults around you create. Enjoy being young, do what makes you happy, spend time with people who make your soul smile. Don't worry about what tomorrow might bring. Live in the moment. Cheesy, right?'

'Not at all, Cali. Huge wisdom right there, I reckon.' I look at my notebook. 'I think that's all my questions, Cali. Anything else you want to add?'

'No. I think I'm done. Thanks, guys,' Cali says.

'Pat?' I ask.

'All good, thanks, pet. Great job, Cali. Do you want to have a little break, yeah? And then would it be okay if I filmed you doing a few things around the house, and in your garden too?'

'Of course.'

'What about the ambient noise, Pat?' says Ash, with a good helping of sarcasm.

'Well remembered, Ash! I'm so glad I taught you that. But not to worry, I'll be filming that without audio, you see. What about you, Ash? Do you have enough shots?' says Gennypha.

'Absolutely. Yeah. I've been snapping away a *lot*, to be honest. The natural light in here is awesome. Think I've got some great images. Thanks, Cali.'

'No worries at all, my love. Do you think you could let me have some of those pics too?'

'Of course, Cali. I'll send you a good selection once I'm back in the office, yeah?' says Ash.

'Brilliant. Okay, well, I think we probably need to get back to the office, hey?' I look at my watch as everyone else looks at their phones. 'Thanks so much, Cali. You've been amazing.'

'Yeah, you have. Thanks, Cali,' says Gennypha.

'Cheers, nice to meet you, Cali,' says Ash.

'Ace. Thanks, guys. It's been brilliant. Say hi to everyone at the office.' Cali walks us to the door.

As she opens the door, the sun shines on her face and highlights her hair. She looks radiant; maybe telling her story has lifted something inside her.

'So it's just you and me, then, Pat. A drink?' says Cali.

'Go on, then. A tea will be super, thanks. Lovely-jubbly. I must say, these are never easy interviews to do. When we filmed Stephen Fry for that BBC documentary ...' says Pat, as Cali closes the door and we walk down the front steps.

On the way back to the station, I look down a side-street.

'Ah, wow, this is where Jamie and I were flat-hunting, hey. Do you remember? That weird landlady who wouldn't take an offer from me, and thought we'd be better off staying where we were?'

'Here, yeah?' says Ash.

'Yes, down that street there. About halfway down on the left.'

'That was so weird, Morag, wasn't it? Old bat probably didn't like your accent. Or she wanted people with better jobs living in her flat, yeah? Awful,' says Gennypha.

'Wow, double burn, Gennz!' says Ash.

'Oh no, so soz, Morag! I didn't mean it like that, I meant ...'

'Collateral discrimination, yeah. Times two!' Ash shows her two fingers.

'No worries, guys.' I know Gennypha won't have meant to take a swipe at me like that. It does make me feel a bit horrible and everything, though.

'So so soz, Morag. I hate it when I run my mouth like that without thinking. Stupid me,' she says. 'Anyway, the press is going to love our collab with Cali, and our supporters are going to *love* Cali's story. Basically, she's the most perfect fit for our charity, yeah? And she's so open. A great interview, Morag. Well done, team comms!'

'Who are walking in exactly the wrong direction again,' says Ash, turning his phone upside down. 'Google maps is useless!'

'Lolz,' says Gennypha. 'Are you blaming your tools, by any chance?'

We get back to the office mid-afternoon, and I start to write up my Cali piece. I don't notice the time and stand up to pack up my things. Storm is still at her desk, actually working.

'Wow, still here, Storm?' I say.

'Yes, lots of emails to catch up on. Actually, Morag, I've been meaning to chat to you today. Have you got a few mins?'

'Yes, sure, Storm,' I lie. I was hoping to get to another gym class straight after work today. I guess I can make up for it another time.

'So, I'm sure you know what's been going on between Gennypha and me, right?'

'Sort of.' I don't want to betray Gennypha's confidence here, but I hope this isn't a trap.

'She hasn't said anything to me, so don't worry. But I know you guys are close, yeah? Anyway, we've had a bit of an issue, which she quite rightly took upon herself to sort out. So I've taken some time to reflect, and look at my own behaviour, and I wanted to apologise to you too, for being a total bitch to you ...'

'Ah, no worries, Storm …' I start.

'It *is* a worry, Morag! Please hear me out; this is important. And you're always so polite, which makes it even worse that I'm such a bitch to you so often.' Storm takes a deep breath and rests her chin on her hands. 'Morag, lovey, I'm sorry. I *really* am. You know, when you have to stop and step back and really look at your behaviour, you realise something has to change or you'll start losing everything and everyone around you. You'll end up being old and lonely. And everyone will really start to hate you. I know that sounds dramatic, but I was shocked, myself, when I stopped to think just how awful I was being to everyone. Every day. I actually feel embarrassed when I think about it, you know.

'I know I'm difficult and everything, but Jesus. I didn't realise just how much. And I'm sorry if that's affected you. Actually, I'm sorry it *has* affected you. I'll try to be more aware of when I'm doing that, and you can tell me too.'

'No worries, Storm, I'm sure you'll do fine,' I say.

'Morag, I'm really not so sure. You really don't have to keep being so nice. Sometimes people walk all over you when you're too nice. Like I've been doing, and before you say anything, I absolutely know I've been doing that.'

'Okay, well, I'll try and be horrible, then. I can be quite mean and everything. Actually, I won't be mean to you. I'll just tell you if I think you're being mean to me, as you say.' Here I go again, being an idiot; I just can't help myself.

'Please do. I really mean that, Morag. It'll help us both. I know you've got your gym bag with you and you only have it with you when you're going to a class after work. Thank you for staying, and I'm sorry if I made you miss your gym class. I know it's not the first time I've done that. Now go! Say hi to Jamie from me, and enjoy your evening. See you tomorrow.'

The following things about this blow me away:

1. Storm is genuinely apologetic and she really seems sincere.
2. Storm seems to want to help me and everything, and for the first time, this doesn't feel like it's all only about Storm.
3. I believe her.

Maybe she really is in love.

Chapter 26

Pat has booked time with each of us in the sevens squad to film our back stories. The producers have told us to film about two minutes per story, so Coach and Pat tell us to share briefly. Our stories will fill in the gaps around the main feature on Cali.

We have to say something about ourselves, how we came to work at the charity, why we work at The HAMP, how we came to be part of the sevens squad and what we hope The HAMP will achieve by being part of the *BLAT* programme.

This is approximately how much we can say about each point:

1. One sentence.

To cut down costs, we're going to do the filming in the Scrum Room. Pat managed to get some budget to buy a sofa and some turquoise cushions from a charity shop to create a "homely" environment. The whiteboards and the big screen on the walls, which we can't move, obviously detract a bit, but we'll do our best.

If we can't find a permanent home for the furniture, it'll go back to the charity shop when we're finished. Chester will be proud that we're maintaining our excellence in recycling.

Day one, Karo, Ash, Warren, Mason, Tracy, Binny and I will do our bits. Day two is Storm, Robyn, Charlie and Jasper. Coach, Barry and

Coach Dave will do theirs on day three. We're allowed to take a bit of time away from our desks because this programme is so important to the charity, so we each sit in on a few of the filming sessions.

Karo goes first. She's wearing a once-white blouse with pulled threads, tea stains on the sleeve and a fraying hem at the neck. Pat asks her if she wants to put a HAMP fleece on. She agrees.

'So, I'm the older of two sisters and I come from Dorset. Well, I was born in Poland but then we moved to UK when I was three. When I was four, I started at the local …'

'Perhaps not so much detail, love,' says Pat. 'Just the headlines, yeah? We only have two minutes, pet, remember?'

'Sorry. Yes, of course. Sorry. Should I start again then? I haven't done this before.'

Pat gives her a thumbs-up.

'So …'

'Perhaps don't start with "so". Is that okay?'

Karo nods.

'I'm the older of two sisters and our family comes from Poland, originally. This is my first job in the charity sector, and it's nice to be working here because it's not boring. You know, you get to work with different people every day, and you help them to get their computer problems sorted. It's quite a challenge, really.' She laces her fingers together and pulls her arms out straight in front of her, looking up at the ceiling.

'So by helping my colleagues do their jobs properly, I feel like I'm helping people we help too … if that makes sense?'

Karo's voice goes really high at the end of each sentence.

'Great, thanks, love,' says Pat. 'Shall we move on to the rugby sevens bit? And remember, try not to start your sentences with "so", yeah?'

'Okay, yes. Sorry,' she says, extending her neck and darting her eyes around the room. 'So, I … sorry. Ummmm … okay. I started playing rugby when I was at school. I absolutely loved it. At first, I was one of only two girls in the team, and I think my parents were proud of me for that. They liked that me and my sister did things that weren't typical for girls, so they encouraged me, which I thought was pretty cool.'

'So, then?' says Pat.

'Okay, so … sorry, sorry! I also played at uni, but it was quite a challenge, really. I managed to ace my degree and …'

'Waaaay too much detail, love!' says Pat, slicing her forefinger across her neck.

'Sorry!' says Karo, putting her hand over her mouth.

'I'll have to edit that a lot.' Pat nods as she over-enunciates the word "lot". 'Okay, so just tell me what your hopes are for The HAMP in the *Britain Loves a Trier* programme, yeah?'

'So … sorry!' Karo squeezes her eyes tight and shakes her head. 'I'm so excited and feel privileged, really, that The HAMP is taking part in *Britain Loves a Trier*. It's a brilliant programme to be part of. We have the drive and we're developing the skills to win, and the prize money will help us support *so* many more people struggling with anger out there,' says Karo, making a huge "o" with her mouth when she says the word "so".

'Great stuff.' Pat puts her camera down. 'Well done. That's it. But don't move just yet, love, I need to take your mic off you, yeah?'

I have to finish some work before doing my bit later. It's hard to concentrate because I'm suddenly quite nervous about going in front of a camera and talking about myself and rugby. I feel a bit of a fraud, really. My friends back home wouldn't believe I was going to play rugby sevens; let alone on TV.

I'm running through what I'm going to say when I hear a commotion near the front door.

'Leave me alone!' The voice sounds vaguely familiar. 'I need to speak to Storm!'

Storm looks up from her chicken tikka wrap.

'Oh shit!' she says. 'Shit shit shit!'

'What – chicken fell out of your wrap again?' says Mason, smirking.

'Storm! You told me you were happy to meet me, and you said my work was amazing. Yeah? Yeah?'

Tom, the guy Storm had been interviewing the day of the Warren fire-drill, runs from the front desk to Storm's desk, a crazed look in his eyes and Jasper on his heels.

'Sorry, Storm, he literally just …'

'It's okay, Jasper, I know. Don't worry. Tom, good to see you too.'

Tom's sweating and panting, and looks kind of grubby.

'You said I stood a chance at getting that freelance gig! But you lied, just like everyone else in my life has lied. Storm, you *lied*!' Tom sniffs loudly, and wipes his nose with his sleeve.

'Tom, do you want to come and sit in the kitchen with me?' Storm licks her fingers and puts her wrap into a medium-sized Tupperware. 'Let's go and have a little chat, yeah?'

'No! You're a bloody liar! I thought I stood a chance here, yeah, like I could make a difference, yeah. I thought this time I'd actually get the contract, but you lied to me, Storm! You bloody lied to me!' Tom's sobbing and shaking and flinging his arms out in front of him as he yells.

'I didn't lie, Tom. I'm sorry you think I did. I'm sure it's just a misunderstanding, yeah?' says Storm, standing up.

Pat pops her head out of the Scrum Room.

'Hey, guys, would you mind keeping it down a …'

Gennypha runs over, waving her arms to gesture for Pat to go back into the room. Gennypha whispers in her ear, and Pat nods and turns her mouth into an "eek" shape as she peeps over Gennypha's shoulder to see if she can see Storm and Tom. Gennypha kind of pushes her back, and she ducks back into the room and closes the door behind her.

'*You're* a misunderstanding, Storm! *You're* a bloody misunderstanding. You *lied*. I thought I'd get that freelance work and I didn't. Just like every other job I've tried to get. Why is it so fucking hard to get any kind of job in London? Why? *Why*, Storm? What's wrong with *me*, Storm? Why not *me*?' Tears and snot merge and bubble around his face and he wipes his whole face with his hoodie.

Storm tells Tom to follow her to the kitchen. She closes the door behind them.

'Yikes, do you think she'll be okay?' I ask our pod.

'Yeah, she's done some counsellor training and she's pretty good at dealing with other people's anger. And she's pretty good in a crisis. Remember Chestergate?' says Gennypha.

'Watching the kitchen from here,' says Mason, still typing. 'Storm might be shit at a lot of other things, but she's ace at this, tbh.'

I walk over to peep through the kitchen window. Tom's shouting and Storm's sitting next to him, listening and nodding. It doesn't look like she's saying anything back to him, which is unusual for Storm, if you think about it and everything. I go back to my desk and try to carry on with my work. It's not just the upcoming video that makes me feel so distracted; I'm quite concerned for Storm too. That surprises me, really.

I go back to the kitchen window and Storm's just handed Tom a pile of tissues. She says something to him as she stands up and walks to the kettle and switches it on. She takes two mugs out of the cupboard, and gestures to Tom to sit back down. She puts teabags into the mugs, then puts her hand up to stop Tom talking. He blows his nose, and Storm picks up her phone.

Storm punches a number into her phone, and stands still as she talks to someone. She ends the call, and says something to Tom across the room. There's a flicker of relief on his face. Storm spots me at the window, and I give her a thumbs-up to check she's okay. She nods and winks back at me, and pours the boiling water into the mugs.

Back at my desk, I try to distract myself with the Cali piece for the magazine. I'm struggling to find the right words today.

'What's another word for *furious*, Mase?'

Mason looks up at me and nods his head to the left. I almost jump out of my chair, as I see Jasper standing behind me.

'Wow, Jasper! I never heard you coming! How long have you been there?'

'Ah, literally just a minute or so,' he says, fiddling with his cuffs.

'That's quite a long time, Jasper! Did you want to ask me something?'

'Ah, yes. Of course. Thanks. There's someone here to see Storm. I told them she was busy, but they said it was urgent. I don't know if I can go in there right now,' he says, pointing to the kitchen, and smoothing the front of his shirt. 'Er, would you mind letting her know? I'm a bit scared, I mean, I don't want to disturb her.'

'No worries, Jasper,' I say, pushing my chair back.

'Thanks, Morag. That guy's quite upset, isn't he?' Jasper follows me to the kitchen.

'Yes, very.' I can hear Mason saying something about Jasper's detective skills.

When I knock on the kitchen window, Storm and Tom both look at me, and I point to the front desk. Storm gives me a thumbs-up, so I go back to my desk and Jasper goes back to his.

Storm and Tom come out of the kitchen and walk to the front desk. Kevin has also been pacing between the kitchen door and his computer screen all the time they've been in there and, as soon as they leave, he sprints into the kitchen to fetch his sandwich from the fridge.

When Storm and Tom get to the front desk, Jasper jumps to his feet and tugs at his cuffs. Storm tells him to sit down. She greets the woman waiting there for her, and walks her away from the front desk, with Tom. Jasper looks around at me, and stands up to give me a double thumbs-up.

Storm speaks to the woman and, after a few minutes, Tom walks out of the door with her. Storm walks back to her desk.

'Enraged. Maddened. Livid, even,' says Mason.

'Huh?' says Storm.

'Morag's question. All right, Storm?' says Mason.

'Yeah, just about. I managed to talk him down a bit, I think. I hate it when that happens. I can normally see it coming, but this time I didn't. I missed all the signs when I interviewed him, but it's super that he'll get the help he needs now. It took a bit of time for me to get him to his come-to-Jesus moment. To get him to reflect on what was actually going on. He also seemed relieved to be getting help. I'm happy about that now, I have to say. Phew!'

'Great work, boss,' says Ash. 'Who's helping him?'

'That was one of the triage volunteers – she said she could fit him in as an emergency session today. I'd worked with them last week when I did that, you know, that *thing* I had to do, so I knew exactly who to speak to. It helps when you have a name, you know. Otherwise it might have taken a bit longer. I'm so proud of The HAMP team, you know.' Storm opens her medium-sized Tupperware and takes a huge bite out of her chicken wrap.

Three things really floored me about this whole episode:

1. I never knew Storm could remain calm like that, in the midst of a drama. Gennypha and Mason are right. I'd seen glimpses of it before, like with Chestergate, but I never knew she had such composure in a personal crisis like this. You know how when the sink's full of bubbles, and they disappear when you

put soap in the water and everything? Well, Storm's calmness and composure completely dissipated Tom's anger. It was quite amazing and impressive to witness, to be honest.

2. This is kind of linked to point 1, but I'd never seen Storm's capacity for compassion. She was kind to Tom today, when he really wasn't being kind to her at all. You really never know people, you know, hey.

3. That was the first time I'd *ever* seen Storm make a cup of tea.

I go for a walk at lunchtime to clear my head before my filming and to get a break from all the drama at the office and everything. I walk through a little park and, on the way to the river, sit on a bench in a little piazza. A small band's setting themselves up to play in the shade of a plain tree.

The guitarist sings some slow, poetic songs, before a violinist and a double bass player join him, and a young woman cycles past, dressed like an old-fashioned washerwoman, with a knotted scarf wrapped around her head, and a fluffy toy penguin as her pillion passenger.

The band plays a livelier song, and when someone shouts to the singer that the song sounds "quite happy", the singer apologises. There's a chalkboard next to the small wooden stage that says: *"No stage diving"*.

With the blue sky and the sunlight streaming through the leaves of the trees, this is one of the most London lunchtimes I've had in a long time. And it's just what I need. When you take the time to look up, London will show you random, bizarre, funny, and unique and everything, like nowhere else in the world.

I finish a few things on my to-do list before I have to go into the Scrum Room for my story filming. I've been dreading it, I have to say, and my palms are sweating and everything. I hate doing this kind of thing.

'Okay, let's mic you up, love, and can you do something with this hair?' says Pat, as I sit down. She pats the top of my head and tucks my hair behind my ears, as she pins the lapel mic to my collar.

'No worries,' I say, putting my hair back where it belongs and pushing my fringe out of my eyes.

'Okay, what did you have for breakfast?' Pat says, as she gets the camera to focus on me.

I'm a bit surprised she needs to know this much detail. 'Well, I normally just have a bowl of fruit salad but today I was quite hungry so I...'

'That's enough, thanks, pet. Just checking the sound levels. You'll have to speak up, yeah?'

Is there no end to how embarrassing I can be?

'You know the drill, right? Something about yourself, how you came to work here, why you work here, how you got into the sevens squad and what you hope The HAMP will achieve by being part of the *BLAT* programme, blah, blah, blah. Okay?'

(This is how Pat pronounces okay: *ay-kay*.)

'Okay, Morag, ready when you are, love. Don't worry if you make a mistake. The beauty is born in the edit, as they say.'

'Yay, so you can cut me out and all the stupid things I say and everything.'

Pat's not listening. She hurries me on.

'Okay, cool. I'm Morag Williams, and I've worked at The HAMP for six years. If you're wondering about my accent, because most people do, I'm from South Africa, well originally from Zimbabwe. But I went to university...'

'Stick to the basics, my love. The basics. We don't need your life story.'

'No worries, Pat, I'll start again,' I say, feeling stupid all over again. 'My name's Morag Williams, and I've worked at The HAMP for six years after moving here from South Africa. I'm the storytelling manager and I really love my job. I'm a writer, and I get to write stories about all the amazing people in our community, who are dealing with their anger management problems. We all get angry, and that's okay. It's okay not to be okay.' Oh, for goodness sake, this isn't the Oprah flipping Winfrey Show. What's wrong with me?

'Sorry, Pat.'

'Just get on with it, love. Quickly.'

'Okay. I'm so happy to be part of the sevens squad…'

'The seavens squad? Can you say it again so people can understand, please. Okay?'

'I'm so happy to be part of the sevens squad.' (Although I want to say, 'Only if you'll say okay like a normal person, Pat. See how that feels?')

Pat makes me say my bits over and over until I say them without hesitating, evangelising or sounding like a complete idiot. Or all of the above. She also struggles with my accent like you've seen, so stops me every now and then to ask me what I've just said.

I'm super relieved when it's over and everything, but the worst is still to come – we'll have to watch it all when the programme airs. I'm holding thumbs they'll just edit me out altogether.

Chapter 27

I wait until Madison leaves the office today so I can finish writing an article for the magazine before rugby training. I've been struggling to get it done because Madison has been making loads of calls looking for corporate sponsors for some of our events. She talks *really* loudly on the phone, and it's super distracting if you're trying to:

1. Proofread.
2. Write.
3. Speak to someone at your desk.
4. Speak to someone on the phone.
5. Think.
6. Do literally anything else.

Warren and Mason are throwing a rugby ball to each other at the other end of the office while they wait for Ash and me to finish work. We're going to walk with them to the station for training.

'Careful, guys. Health and safety, remember?' Storm says to Warren and Mason as she walks past them. 'See you at the station, yeah?'

'Yes, boss,' says Mason, saluting Storm.

'Come on, guys, hurry up! Let's go,' says Warren, watching Storm walk out of the door. He turns around quickly and throws the ball across the office to Ash.

'Think quick, Ash!' he shouts.

The ball flies through the air and bounces on Madison's keyboard and over her desk right into Ash's hands. With Madison's keyboard surrounded by piles of stuff, it falls to the floor when the ball hits it, and it takes every single thing down with it. I knew her desk was chaotic; I didn't realise it had its own, entire, connected ecosystem.

'Oh no! Can you guys help me clear this lot up?' I stand up and look at Ash, as Warren and Mason run over.

'Nah. Leave it, Morag,' says Ash. 'Honestly. I'm pretty sure Madison won't even notice.'

'Fair enough! Let's see.' I feel a bit mean and everything, but I'm curious to see if that's true. Plus, I don't have time to sort this lot out.

'Guys, I'm just logging off. See you at the front door now now,' I add.

Bernard is waiting at the front door when I join the others there.

'Working the late shift, Bern?' says Warren.

'Yes, chaps. Today's your training day, yeah?' says Bernard.

'Yeah, that's it. Off you go, Bernard, the office isn't going to clean itself, yeah,' says Ash.

'Right you are. Have fun, boys. You people always look great in those shorts,' says Bernard, waving and watching us walk away. (By "us", I don't mean me.)

'Total fucking creep,' says Mason, as we turn into the next block. 'Always watching us.'

'Really? I haven't noticed him watching me,' says Warren.

'Nah, he's got taste,' says Mason, laughing. 'He's only human.'

'Too right! Gives me the heebie-jeebies, though, for real,' says Ash. 'And how about the "you people"? Really?'

'I know, right?' says Mason.

'Anyway, enough of that weirdo,' says Ash. 'Not loving our chances for the festival, to be honest.'

'Ah, Ash, that's not the spirit,' says Warren. 'Not in a bad way, but everyone loves an underdog, right?'

'Everyone loves a trier,' I say, immediately regretting being so cheesy. Again. I'm such a loser.

'Yeah, Morag,' Ash exhales.

'Anyway, we're going in with zero chance of winning. All the odds are against us, but with the crowd on our side – and they probably will be – who knows what magic we can produce? Nothing to lose, yeah?' says Warren.

'Fair play to you, mate. That's what we need: optimism, yeah?' says Ash. 'What you reckon, Mason?'

'Tbh, chances are limited af. Always been a glass half-empty kind of guy irl.'

'You think?' says Ash, punching Mason's arm.

'That obvs?'

We all say 'yep', as we get to the tube station. Storm's waiting for us near the turnstiles, and she looks up from her phone as we get to her.

'Hey, you guys took *ages*! But go ahead and travel without me, guys. Bazza's on his way and we'll join you there.'

So I was right. Something has been brewing between those two. Maybe that explains a softening in Storm's attitude, too.

'Whaaaat? Bazza and Storm?' says Ash, at the bottom of the escalator. 'How long's *that* been going on for?'

'Been brewing for a while, hasn't it, guys?' says Mason, smiling. 'Not sure it's a thing yet, though. WYT, guys?'

We guys all shrug.

'I've thought something was going on for a while,' says Warren, the world champion of eavesdropping. 'But not in a bad way.'

At the club, Coach Dave is talking to Coach and Cali, and the three of them are laughing. Coach looks at Cali, and she puts her hand on

Coach's shoulder. Coach Dave waves to us when he sees us. Cali pulls her hand away and the two of them turn around.

'Oh hey, guys! You snuck quietly up, ja?' says Coach.

'Ninjas! Trained in sneaking up, we are,' says Ash. 'Did we interrupt you, Coach?'

'No, you didn't. We were just shooting quickly the wind,' says Coach. We all laugh.

'Right, you lot, jumpers off and give me five laps, yeah?' says Coach Dave, clapping. 'Where are the others?'

'I think they're still on their way,' I say. 'We were the last ones to leave the office, so maybe they called in to get some food en route. Not sure.'

'Oy, Ash, before you run off, mate, any news on the shirts for the festival?' says Coach Dave.

'Yeah, Coach, the company called this afternoon. They're sorted and all, and they were supposed to deliver them tomorrow but there's been another delay. Nightmare, mate, but they've promised to get them to us by Monday. I'll ask Coach to call you when they're in the office, yeah?'

'Cheers, mate, nice one.' Coach Dave slaps Ash on the back as he runs off.

Ash has been struggling with getting the shirt design signed off by Channel 53. His contact is a press officer, who has to go through his line manager, who has to go through her line manager, until it goes up to the Commissioning Team (CT) press manager who makes the decision and then cascades it back down the food chain. There's been a lot of back-and-forth about the size of our logo on the T-shirt compared with the size of Channel 53's logo; about whether our logo has to be to the left or the right of their logo, and whether medium turquoise works for Channel 53.

'It's not really *us*,' says the CT press manager, through the various channels down to the press officer, but without offering suggestions of what would be *more* 'them'.

Ash has been frustrated at having to *design-by-committee.* He says they peck his designs to death. And, as he keeps saying, 'It's just a friggin' shirt. No one's going to die or anything if their logo is 2mm narrower than it normally would be on the website. And anyway – who *cares?* Really, who cares?'

I'm glad they liked my line, though: "The HAMP and Channel 53: together, tackling anger management issues." It's the first time I've ever used a pun that my colleagues can get behind.

I throw my hoodie on to my backpack, and spot Storm and Barry walking across the far side of the field. Barry is still on crutches, and pretends to trip Storm with one of them. She laughs, throwing her head back and flicking her hair.

'Bazza, you're crazy,' she says, as they reach our side of the field.

'Oy, you two,' says Coach Dave. 'Storm, it's five around the field, yeah?'

Storm blushes as she looks at Barry.

'Off ya go, babe,' he says, pointing to the field with his crutch.

Practice is tough this evening. Coach Dave reminds us how close we are to the festival and how much work we still have to do. Warren's getting used to running with Karo, and is more confident in distributing the ball out wide. And Karo seems to be warming to Warren's way of playing.

'Great hands this evening,' she says to Warren after practice.

'Thanks, mate. Cheers, nice one.' Warren looks at his hands before shoving them back into his pockets. He looks up at the sky and everywhere else except Karo.

'We're working pretty well together, don't you think?' Karo says.

'Yeah?' says Warren. 'You want to come home with me?'

'Excuse me?'

'Sorry, mate. I meant, shall we walk to the tube together?'

'Yes, sure,' says Karo, twirling her hair.

'Cool. Shall we go, then? Cheers, guys, see you tomorrow, yeah?' says Warren, before anyone can even think about joining them.

I'm the first one in our pod to get to the office today. I go into the kitchen to make some coffee, and get back to my desk as Madison arrives.

'Hi, Madison,' I say.

'Hi, all right?' she says, not waiting for an answer as she yanks her keyboard back up on to her desk. She shrugs her coat off and sits down on it, jumping a little when she realises her stapler was on her chair.

'Oh wow, I wondered where that was!' she says, putting it back on her desk. She starts her computer, and literally doesn't notice the avalanche of stuff around her chair and under her desk. It's become her own private landfill.

'Hey, Morag, how was the rest of your evening?'

Karo's behind me, looking chirpy and bright.

'Hey Karo, it was cool, thanks. We just stayed in and caught up with a few episodes of *Breaking Bad*,' I say.

'That's nice. My sister loves that series. She's *always* talking about it.'

'Great. How was your evening?'

'Oh, my evening? It was good, thanks. Warren and I just went for a cheeky drink after rugby; quite chilled, really.'

I don't think I've ever heard Karo say "chilled", or "cheeky drink" ever before. I don't think I've heard her talk about anything other than rugby, or her cats, even when you ask her about her weekends, or her evenings and everything. And I can't quite put my finger on it, but something else about her seems quite different today.

'Nice!'

'I wanted to ask you something, Morag, if that's okay? It's kind of personal.'

'Sure, of course. Not sure how much I'll be able to help, though – it's been yonks since I've been on dates. Jamie and I have been together forever!'

'What? Who said anything about dating?' Karo swings round to look at Warren. He waves at her and she smiles and waves back at him.

'Sorry, Karo. I misunderstood your question. So sorry, say what you were going to say.'

'No worries. Everyone just needs to calm down,' she says, pushing her hands downwards.

'Right, sure. How can I help?' I wish I hadn't said that; I hate it when people ask me that. Not sure why, I just hate it. Maybe because it can sound a bit:

1. Rude.

'Well, I know you always say you're super fussy about your hair, yeah? I wanted to ask if you could recommend a hairdresser for me – I really need to do something about this,' she says, grabbing bunches of her hair. 'I have *so many* split ends, and my hair is just growing wild. I haven't had a good haircut for years, and I might even do something with this colour too. What do you think?'

'Wow, that would be amazing,' I say, a bit too quickly. 'Well, not that I thought your hair looked bad, or anything. It's always lovely to have your hair done, isn't it? It's one of my favourite things. My hairdresser might be a bit far away for you, though? I can ask her for a recommendation near you, if you like?'

'That would be great. Thanks, Morag.'

'No worries. I'll let you know as soon as I hear from her.'

'Brilliant,' says Karo, turning to walk away. She hesitates and turns back to me.

'Hey Morag? Sorry for snapping at you just now.'

'No worries,' I say. 'I know what it's like when someone says something that hits a nerve.'

She blushes, and walks over to Warren's desk. I realise this is what's different about her today:

1. She's wearing clean clothes.
2. There's not one bit of oatmeal in sight.

'Sorry, what hit a nerve?' says Madison, surfacing above her screen-saver briefly.

'Long story, Madz. It's very sweet and everything – you'll see soon enough.'

Madison lost interest after the word "story". She still hasn't noticed there's a box file on her chair behind her back.

Chapter 28

The festival is just around the corner, and you can feel the rumblings of nervous excitement and everything around the office.

'So Pat's video clips are pretty crap, tbh,' says Mason. 'Mine is, anyway. Look like such an amateur.'

'Well, we are amateurs, aren't we?' I say. 'That's the point, hey? But we *are* going to get slaughtered at the festival, aren't we?'

'Yes. Probably. But basically that's pretty pessimistic, Morag. That's unlike you,' says Gennypha.

'I surprised myself, too,' I say. 'I go between thinking we'll be brilliant or we'll totally embarrass ourselves, to be honest.'

'Speak for yourself, but I think we're in with a chance.' Warren's eavesdropped his way into the conversation again. 'I think our chances are pretty good. There's no stopping that Karo once she's got the ball in hand.'

'Well, Warren, I *am* speaking for myself. Not sure what I was thinking when I signed up to play actual rugby sevens in an actual tournament. I'm starting to feel a bit sick about it all, really,' I say.

Thinking about it and everything, I do feel a bit sick. Not sure if it's nerves, or last night's curry making me feel that way.

'We're all in the same boat, lovey,' says Storm. 'And I personally think we'll do amazing as a team. Going into this as the underdog and looking amateur is the narrative we're wanting to create, moving

258

forward, no? The media bloody *loves* stories like ours. So will the Channel 53 audience, I'm sure of it.'

'That's supposed to make us feel better?' says Mason.

'You'll all be heroes,' says Gennypha, giving Mason a thumbs-up as Coach appears behind her.

'In my book, you're already anyway heroes,' says Coach. 'But no more of this negative speak, ja? We need absolutely to talk to ourselves into the winning corner. That's what winners do already, ja? We need to believe it so we can see actually the trophy on our shelf. Envisualise it; just over there,' she says, pointing to the reception bookcase. Jasper turns around and waves.

'I like how you think, Coach,' says Storm, beaming and storm-clapping. 'Yay for Coach! Yay for positive thinkers like us!'

'Absolutely, yes. Okay, team, I came to tell you that all of our *BLAT* shirts have just arrived in the office. I've been hovering over cloud seven with them – I'm so happy! Ash has done an incredulous job, ja, and the printers have got exactly to a T-shirt our medium turquoise. For both the match-day shirts and the T-shirts. Good, ja, Storm?'

'Brilliant, Coach! That'll look perfect on the telly and at the stadium, yeah?' says Storm. 'When Ash gets in, I'll ask him to put all the shirts in the Scrum Room so, team, go and collect yours as soon as you can, and –'

'Not the match-day shirts, ja? Coach Dave is going to give actually those out in Cardiff. The charity T-shirts are there, so you can all go and get some for your journey to Cardiff and for any friends and family who'll be at the festival.'

'Yes, of course, Coach. That's what I meant. So guys, why don't you go ahead and fetch your charity T-shirts for your friends and family. Remember, we're wanting the punters on the telly and in the stadium to notice us, yeah? So let's turn the Cardiff Arms Park medium turquoise – we want The HAMP's medium turquoise *everywhere*!

It'll be *wild.*' Storm's jazz hands morph into a manic storm-clap.

I've always found our charity colour quite funny, and the fact that people get so excited about it. For Ash, Storm and Coach, the medium turquoise is much more than a colour; it's a point of pride. It would be so much easier to say we wanted to turn the stadium red or orange or blue, or any other one-word colour. I don't know if it's just me, but "medium turquoise" always sounds too weirdly *specific*.

It's our final practice before the festival. In a nod to Coach for her enthusiasm and malapropisms, we sometimes talk about our *Cloud Sevens* festival. Coach rather loves it.

Pat is running up and down the side of the field, filming our practice, and Coach Dave pushes us harder than ever. Richard has come to cheer us on, but focuses more on trying to get into Pat's shots than on cheering. He runs to the other side of the field from her, and jogs up and down the field and everything to get in line with her camera. Pat runs over to him, unaware his moves have been deliberate.

'Sorry, pet, but would you mind staying behind me while I film? I seem to be getting you in shot while you're probably trying to stay out of it, aren't you?' says Pat.

'No problem, young lady,' he says, saluting Pat and looking a little disappointed.

I'm really struggling to keep up in today's training, for some reason – I feel a bit slow and tired, but I keep going anyway. In our practice match, Karo and Warren are on fire, crashing through the opposition, despite Cali's and Ash's best defensive attempts.

We form a circle around Coach Dave for our final huddle. Richard circles us to get into view of the camera.

'I have to say, you lot, you're looking pretty decent ahead of the festival, yeah? Cali, you and Ash are working together brilliant, just like Karo and Warren. You go together like pie and mash, you do,' says

Coach Dave, intertwining his fingers.

He looks over at Jasper, who's found a small bucket of sand and has built a small mound out of it.

'Oy, Jasper!' says Coach Dave, as Jasper jumps on the mound to flatten it. 'Over here!'

Jasper jogs over to us, laughing behind his hand. 'Sorry, Coach Dave! I see sand and I have to build something! Do you think someone brought that back from the beach somewhere?'

'Nah, mate. Some people prefer to use sand rather than a tee when they kick for posts, yeah?'

'Oh, wow,' says Jasper, making his mouth into the smallest, then biggest, then smallest "o" ever. 'I never knew that.' He puts his hands on his hips.

'Yeah, I guessed that, mate. So back to business, guys, there's no room to get complacent, or rest on our laurels or anything – we've got big matches ahead, and we have to have razor-sharp focus, yeah? We need to leave it all out on the field, and remember that winning is down to who wants it more. How much do we want to win, HAMPers?' Coach Dave circles the team, clapping, and slapping us on our backs.

'SO much,' I shout, as everyone else shouts 'BIG!'

'That's what I like to hear! How much?'

'BIG!' I shout, as everyone else shouts 'SO MUCH!'

Richard is jumping up and down behind the huddle shouting 'Team HAMP, Team CHAMP!' never taking his eyes off Pat.

'That's a pretty good war cry, and all! Team HAMP, Team CHAMP! I like that – nice one, squire,' says Coach Dave to Richard. 'Team mascot, yeah?'

Richard jumps up and down and gives Coach Dave a thumbs-up, still not taking his eyes off the camera.

'Sweet, yeah, I'd love to do that!' says Richard.

'Right, before I send you lot home, Coach has something to tell you.

Coach?' says Coach Dave, bowing and ushering Coach into the centre of the circle.

'Thanks, Coach Dave. We have actually a joint announcement to make, ja? First of all, we are pleased to let you know that *all* of you will be playing at the festival. We'll announce the starting seven just before the festival, but we'll try and give actually everyone the opportunity to play at some point on Saturday, ja?

'And as you know, we had a team vote about this last week, and Coach Dave and I have made now our casting vote: we're happy to announce finally that Karo will be your captain for the festival. I know you'll all agree but Karo has stepped absolutely up to the plate on the field out there. She makes good decisions on the hoover, leads by example, and is a good all-round egg, ja?'

'If eggs were round, and all,' laughs Coach Dave.

'Yes, but that's the saying, ja?' says Coach, putting her hand to her forehead.

'Yeah, Coach, a good egg. Spot on,' says Mason.

'Karo, would you like now a moment to say a few words to your team?'

Karo steps forward, and pushes her hair away from her face. She suits the shorter, layered look, and the highlights make her eyes look bluer than ever.

We all applaud Karo: I'm not just speaking for myself or anything, but she's a popular choice as captain.

'Wow, that's a lovely surprise,' says Karo. 'I feel a bit emotional actually. I've always wanted to be a team captain, but I've never been picked. Thank you for this honour, Coach and Coach Dave. Team, I feel not only honoured, but privileged and chuffed as anything that you've selected me as your captain. So I'll do my best to do you proud, Coach and Coach Dave, and all of you, every time we run out on to the field in Cardiff.'

'Fantastic. Nice one,' says Coach Dave. 'We'll leave you to speak to your team, yeah, and then we'll see you at the pub later. Not too many bevvies tonight, guys, and try and get some rest before Cardiff, yeah?'

Karo nods, and puts her hands to her heart.

'Thanks, Coach and Coach Dave, cheers.' Karo takes a deep breath. 'Wow, you guys. Thank you for voting for me. I think this is honestly the best day in my life. I don't really know what to say to you. In the words of someone special to me, *Don't aim to be the best in the team, aim to be the best for the team.* I've seen that's what we all do. I haven't seen any ego out on the field from any of you guys, and if we keep it that way, there'll be no stopping us in Cardiff.

'That's about it, I think. You all bring something important and unique to the team, and you bring it when it counts. We'll be up against teams in the same boat as us, yeah? Still learning. But I want you to know I'll be proud to lead us on to that field. Unbelievably proud. And now, to the pub!'

'To the pub! In the words of someone we once knew, let's crack onwards, yeah' says Ash, laughing.

We all clap and jump and high-five each other before running to the benches to get our stuff.

It's not like me, but I just wish I could duck out of going to the pub tonight, but I can't really. I also don't want to miss out on all of us being together and everything. I go along but can't face even one glass of wine, so I just have a lime and soda. I chat to Coach and Cali for a while, and then leave. I'm *so* tired, and can't wait to fall into bed. I don't know what's wrong with me; training wasn't that tough this evening. I really really hope I'm not getting sick; this would be the worst time for that to happen, ever.

I get to the office later than normal today. I struggled to wake up this morning, and I feel sluggish and everything; it feels hard to get moving.

When I get to our pod, everyone's talking about what happened at the pub last night.

'*So* into each other, not even hiding it,' says Mason.

'Morning, guys. Who're you talking about?' I say.

'Oh, hey, Morag. Coach and Cali – did you see, or had you left already? You ducked out super early,' says Mason.

'Yes, I did, hey. I was so so tired, don't know why. But yes, I chatted to them a bit last night. I've wondered about them for a while, to be honest. Actually, Jamie saw them having a meal and everything together at the club a few weeks ago, so I guess I've been aware of something brewing since then,' I say.

'And everything?' says Mason.

'Sorry, I meant just the meal,' I say, feeling a bit silly for the way I speak.

'So why didn't you say anything?' says Gennypha.

'I don't know, really. Not really my business and ev–, sorry, not really my business.' I kind of hate and love gossip. But mostly I feel a bit irritable today. Maybe it's just because I didn't have enough sleep.

'Well, guys, I've got quite close to Cali over the last while, and basically she confided in me that she had feelings for Coach,' says Gennypha. 'I promised I wouldn't say anything to anyone, but now you've all seen it for yourselves!'

'Yeah?' says Mason. 'Quite close to Cali?'

'Basically, for work, you know? Being the charity's point of contact, I get to chat with her – or Ness – often. Almost daily now, if I'm honest.'

'Look at you, hobnobbing with them famous people an' all.' Tracy's just appeared at our pod. 'Sorry, guys, I don't mean to interrupt your conversation, but Morag my love, I need a favour. Would you have time to proofread my CoTY proposal for that food delivery company? I need to send it by close of play tomorrow obviously. Sorry for the last-minute ask, yeah, but my team sat on it for ages, only gave me their input on Monday. What do you reckon, my love?'

Tracy puts her hands together, as if in prayer, looking just beneath and beyond my shoulder.

'Yes, sure, send it through to me,' I say. 'No worries.'

'Best little fucker in town, you are,' says Tracy, holding her hands to her heart.

That's flattery in Tracy-language, if you think about it and everything. But I'm still irritated. To be honest, I hate having so little time to work on stuff. Even though I should just refuse to do it, I can't really run the risk that she either won't send off the application, or she'll send it off and it'll be crap, with words like 'your' instead of 'you're' or 'should of' instead of 'should have'.

Here are my top three copy errors I've had to correct:

1. T-shit.
2. If you've subscribed but still don't get our emails, please check your junk.
3. The HAMP is here for people who struggle with anger and their families.

Chapter 29

It's the day before the *BLAT* festival, and Jamie and I have just arrived at the hotel in Cardiff. It's one of those budget hotels, right in the centre of the city, and only a short walk from Cardiff Arms Park.

We decided to drive rather than catch the train; I've been so tired I didn't think I'd manage the journey by train. It's difficult just to switch off or have a nap when you're travelling with a whole bunch of people. We sit down in the reception area near the vending machine.

'Oh hey!' shouts Mason as he walks through the revolving doors, followed by the rest of the team. 'Journey okay, you two?'

'Yeah, breezy,' says Jamie. 'Very little traffic.'

'Yeah? I thought the roads would be rammed with all them fans coming to watch The HAMP team play. They'll all be coming tomorrow, they will,' says Barry, winking at Storm.

'Oh yes! Thank goodness we travelled today and avoided the rush.' Storm laughs and throws her head back.

'Anyone know where Coach is?' says Ash.

'Guys, Coach and Cali will be here a little later. They said to meet us in the restaurant at dinner time, yeah?' says Karo. 'Why don't we get settled into our rooms and meet back here at six, yeah?'

I stand up and follow Jamie and our wheelie case to the lift. We get to the fourth floor, walk down the corridor and open the door into what looks like a cupboard. Our charity's on a budget and everything, but bunk beds? There's standing room only between the beds and what must be the smallest, narrowest bathroom in the whole wide world. You could brush your teeth in the bathroom basin without having to get off your bed. We put the suitcase on the top bunk and agree we'll have to put it in the shower tonight when we go to bed.

We've got about two hours till we're meeting for dinner. We'd planned to go out and explore Cardiff a bit beforehand, but I have to have a nap. Jamie goes out on his own, and I fall into a deep sleep within minutes of lying down. What's happening to me? I can't seem to shake off this fatigue.

'Hey, Rags, wake up! We've got to meet everyone in twenty minutes!'

Jamie's shaking me gently.

I open my eyes and try to rub the sand out of them.

'I thought you were going for a walk?'

'I did. It was awesome! We're *so* close to the stadium, and there's such a buzz in the city. I also bought us a few things for our flat and a cool Cardiff shot glass for our collection. I'll show you later. You okay, Rags?'

'Ja, I'm fine. Just so so tired, Jamie. How long have I been sleeping?'

'About an hour and a half, I reckon. You were snoring before I even walked out the door!'

'Jeepers, I don't know why I'm so tired, Jamie. So weird,' I say, stretching my arms above my head and yawning. 'Let me have a quick shower, and I'll try to wake myself up.'

'Okay, sure,' Jamie says, standing our wheelie case up to make room for himself on the top bunk. 'I'll climb on the top bunk so you can get into the bathroom.'

This must be the smallest hotel room ever. Literally.

The shower refreshes me, and Jamie and I climb out of the cupboard for supper. As we close the door, I realise I've left my phone in the

267

room, so Jamie goes back in to fetch it for me. I wait for him outside the door, and a door opens a bit further down the corridor. Storm and Barry walk out of it, laughing and looking like they've just had a shower too. Barry says something into Storm's ear and kisses her neck. Storm turns her head, and stiffens and whispers something to Barry when she sees me.

'Oh, hey, lovey. Hotel neighbours, yeah?' says Storm.

'Oh, hi! Wow. Yes,' I say, trying to look like I've only just seen them. 'I don't think any of us can be very far away from each other in this hotel, if the size of the rooms is anything to go by!'

'Right? Our, I mean, my room is *tiny*! Barry just popped by to help me sort out the AC – it's set on frigid, I think!'

'Barry the handyman to the rescue,' he says, winking.

'Oh, right. That's cool,' I say.

'Hear that? She said "cool", babe! Clever, right enough,' says Barry, giving me a thumbs-up.

I'm so glad when Jamie comes out of our room and we can end the awkwardness and everything. The four of us go down to the restaurant together, and we're the last to arrive. Coach is sitting on one side of Cali, with Gennypha on the other. Gennypha refuses to budge when Storm asks her to, so Storm sighs and rushes for the empty seat opposite Cali. Barry follows her and before he sits down, looks around the room to check first where the cool people are.

'Great, everyone's now here,' says Coach. 'Order your food as soon as you can, and then I have a few words to say to you all, ja?'

'Coach, mind if I say something first about the food orders?' says Barry. Coach nods.

'Right, team, our budget allows for us all to have one main course and an extra – so *either* a starter *or* a dessert. *Not* both, yeah? And it goes without saying, there's no alcohol tonight for any of the team members. For those of us along for the ride, alcohol is for your own account. So if you order a bevvy, right enough, just ask the waiter to bill you separately for that. Everyone got that, yeah?'

We all nod and give him a thumbs-up.

'And look you, for those of you who are drinking alcohol, we're counting on you to drink responsibly. Your support tomorrow at the festival is vital, and we can't afford to have you hung-over. Yeah? We need you at the top of your game too, right? We don't mind what you do in your *own* time, but this weekend you're here for The HAMP. For *BLAT*. Yeah? We want to see a lively block of supporters in that stand, not a hung-over one, yeah?'

Coach lightens the mood.

'Thank you, Barry. You're a very good head prefect for the weekend, ja?' she laughs. 'But that's enough of the rules for now; we don't want anyone to catch absolutely the hump before the festival tomorrow, ja?'

Cali laughs and Coach winks at her.

'Cheers, Coach,' Barry interjects. 'Sorry, just one more thing, if that's okay? You guys, don't forget to keep your receipts from your lunch meal tomorrow. You can claim up to £7 per person from petty cash for lunch. We've upped it from the usual £5. Coach has properly pushed out the boat for the weekend, but that doesn't mean you can go overboard. See what I did there?' Barry winks and mime-shoots Coach.

Here are three things to know about Barry:

1. He keeps receipts for *everything,* which is great and goes with the territory if you're a finance manager and everything. But not so great when he's keeping receipts of favours he's done, or whose drinks round it is, and so on. Or how many hours he's spent tidying his kitchen, or how many shirts he's ironed, and stuff like that. He has a good head for figures, but it can get really

annoying. It's the *small* things that count, if you know what I mean.

2. He likes people and is quite charming when you first meet him. But when he talks to you the next time, he's already looking around the room for the coolest person in the room, and that's never you. (Well, never me.) That's another thing that's kind of annoying about him, really.

3. He's a bit of a knob, if I'm completely honest.

Coach invites Karo to speak.

'Yeah, team, the time has come. So we're finally here, and the festival – our very own Cloud Sevens, *BLAT*, even, is tomorrow. *Tomorrow.* Not later this year, not next month, not next week. It's here. *Actual* tomorrow. I hope you're feeling as excited as I am? I can't wait to lead you out on to the pitch, and to show everyone in that stadium just what The HAMP is made of.

'Our blood runs medium turquoise, and our hearts beat for everyone in this country who struggles with managing their anger. Let's keep that in our minds for every second the clock ticks down, in every match, yeah? We're doing it for them, to keep The HAMP going for *them.*'

'With no thanks to our former director of finance,' says Warren.

'Hashtag loser,' says Mason.

'Let's not go there, guys. We are where we are; it is what it is. Let's move forward, let's keep our eyes on the prize. A wise person once told me,' Karo says, looking at Warren, 'that when you're having a bad day at work, the best thing to do is think about one person whose life The HAMP has helped change. Find a story that chimes with you, and play the game tomorrow for *that* person. *That* family. *That's* why we're here; *that's* why no matter what happens tomorrow, we win, for *them.* Yeah?'

Karo's moved herself almost to tears. And all of us too, if I'm honest. 'Thank you, Morag, for helping me with this speech. The charity messaging was super helpful and inspiring – I hope I got it right?'

I give her a double thumbs-up.

'Cheers! Okay, so Cali, would you like to say a few words?'

'Thanks, Karo, wow. That was really inspiring. And well done too, Morag! So yeah, all right, okay. Don't know about you guys, but I'm starving, so I'll keep this short and sweet. I'm beyond honoured to be joining you in this whole programme. I know I've said that before, but I really mean it. Thinking of how The HAMP helped me in my darkest hours, I'll be wearing the medium turquoise with pride tomorrow. If you think of no one else tomorrow, think of me and how you've given *me* back my life, yeah?

'I'm excited I can use this festival to boast about the work you guys do every day, and I'll use every interview to do that. Gennz, you'll be pleased to know I've been practising the lines and messaging you gave me, and I'll stick to the script, yeah? Thank you for inviting me to be part of this team. You're all ace, and tomorrow we're going to smash it. Win or lose, you'll – we'll – do The HAMP proud. Thanks, Coach, Coach Dave, Karo, all of you.'

Coach leads us in applauding Cali, who blushes and says to Karo, 'Can we eat now?'

'Yes, sure, in half a minute! Just a final word from me, if that's okay everyone? So, I can't describe how proud I am to be wearing the captain's armband tomorrow,' says Karo. 'Thank you, Coach and Coach Dave for giving me the opportunity. It's honestly the biggest honour in my life. I don't think I've ever been happier. I'll be on cloud nine at our Cloud Sevens festival.'

Karo smiles, puts her hand on her heart and steals a glance at Warren, who hasn't taken his eyes off her.

'Right. *Now* we can eat. *Bon appetit* everyone; enjoy your meal, get a good night's sleep and we'll regroup at sparrows' for breakfast. Yeah? Cheers. That's me.'

We all clap and cheer Karo, and I feel quite emotional after her and Cali's words and everything. It's quite amazing to see Karo step up like this. All this time she's kept her sporting talent, her big heart and her leadership well hidden. Under scruffy wraps, if I'm honest. And now she's motivating us; she and Warren are drawing ever closer, she's upped her clothing game and now she's even changed her hairstyle too.

Amazing what love, sport, the right messaging, and a captain's armband can do for you.

Chapter 30

'Rags! Rags! Wake up, my love,' says Jamie.

I open my eyes and Jamie's leaning over me.

'We need to go. I've been trying to wake you up for ages. You okay?'

I'm working hard to keep my eyes open, and struggling.

'What's the time? Why the panic?' I push myself up on to my elbows.

'It's 6.15, Rags. We have to meet for breakfast at 6.30. I've got your kit ready for you, if you want to jump in the shower quickly to wake yourself up. Are you okay? It's usually you waking me up ...'

'Sheesh! I really don't know what's wrong with me, Jamie. I'm *so* tired – no idea why. I've got *no* energy. I'll get up now now.' I fall back on to my pillow.

Jamie catches me and grabs my hands to pull me up out of bed. I drag myself into the shower and try to wake myself up. I've never ever felt so tired.

We go down to the dining room and we're behind a group of tourists, who ask the restaurant manager if they serve "a fry-up" in the restaurant. The restaurant manager assures them they do, and then shows us to our table as most people are getting ready to leave. Binny is finishing off her full English.

'Hey, Binny,' I say. 'That looks good! I thought you were vegetarian?'

'Yeah, except when I eat meat. Mainly veggie, though, yeah?' she says, her mouth full of bacon.

I really don't have an appetite, but I know I'll feel worse if I don't eat, so I have a small bowl of porridge. I'll need the energy for today but I have no idea how I'm going to make it through.

We meet in the hotel foyer at seven, to walk to the stadium. We're playing in the first match so we'll need to warm up and get ourselves big-match-ready. Richard joins us in the foyer; he tells us he got up at three this morning to drive to Cardiff. He's gone all out in the medium turquoise: not only is he wearing a HAMP T-shirt and cap, but his shorts, socks and trainers are all the same colour too. He looks like a medium turquoise jelly bean.

'Mr Blue Sky, Mr Bluuuue Sky!' Barry croons to Richard.

'Yeah, that's me. I take this job serious, yeah? Can't be a bleedin' mascot and not wear the right colours, now can I? The missus found all this clobber for me online and it didn't cost me a lot of *this stuff*,' Richard says, rubbing his thumb and forefingers together. He looks super proud of his outfit. 'You got all this, my love?' he says to Pat, pointing to his whole body.

'Yes, Richard, all good, thanks. You do love the camera, don't you, pet?' says Pat.

'I think you'll find that old camera loves me, don't it?' Richard smiles.

'Dickied up, right enough?' says Barry, laughing to himself. 'See what I did there, guys? *Dick*-ied up, yeah? I'm too much!'

'That you are, Bazza! That you are,' says Storm.

'So, team, looks like we've all got a bit of PMT, yeah? Pre. Match. Tension. Yeah?' says Barry, still laughing at his own jokes.

Richard laughs like a drain and Storm rolls her eyes and punches Barry in the arm. Karo waves for us to follow her out of the door. Pat runs ahead and films us walking out of the hotel. She puts her hand in the air to stop Richard running to the front of the pack.

'Richard, would you mind waiting, my love, so we can get just the team walking out again? Okay, guys?'

A disappointed Richard hovers at the back of the team as we go back in and out of the hotel again. Oh, my goodness, we're going to see so much photo-bombing and everything from Richard in the final footage. It'll be hilarious, and I can't wait to see it.

'Okay, guys, I'll film around you as we're walking to the stadium. Just take no notice of me, as usual, my loves,' Pat says, looking at Richard, who might just get whiplash from trying to get his face into shot.

As we approach Cardiff Arms Park, Karo calls Coach, Coach Dave and our mascot, Richard, to lead us into the stadium. Coach and Coach Dave choose to stay at the back, but Richard steps out front. All those not in the sevens squad wave us goodbye, wish us well and leave us to take the final stretch as a team.

There's an amazing carnival atmosphere at the stadium. Local volunteers are doing bucket collections for The HAMP at the main entrances. We've been allowed these throughout the whole day and, as we're the only charity taking part today, we're hopeful they'll bring in big funds. They'll show clips of Cali's film on the big screen throughout the day, along with text-to-donate asks on the screen and over the tannoy too. Gennypha's given the stadium announcer a full briefing and a short script to read throughout the day.

When we're through the turnstiles, there are murmurs of "Cali" as people in the crowd nudge each other when they see her. Lots of people applaud us and cheer us on as we walk past.

'Yeah, HAMP for the win! Don't let us down!'

'Yeah, HAMP, don't catch the hump!'

If we had a pound ...

We get to the dressing rooms and find our allocated locker spaces. I feel like crying when I see all of our match-day shirts and shorts hanging in our own lockers. Each of our shirts has our name and number on the back, the *BLAT* branding with our HAMP logo on the front and sleeves, and the festival and other branding on the shorts. This is so exciting – I feel sick to my stomach. Actually, I feel really *really* sick to my stomach, all of a sudden. I run to the bathroom and throw up some of the excitement I'm feeling. Wow, that's never happened to me before, but I feel a bit better. Maybe that's what's been wrong; I just needed to throw up. Nerves, maybe?

We get into our practice kit and follow Karo out on to the field to warm up. It's weirdly exciting to jog through the tunnel, and I kind of imagine what the roar of the crowd will be like later when we emerge into the sunlight of a beautiful summer's day, for our first match. But no one in the stadium is paying any attention to us right now. The stadium is still mostly empty and everything, so we get to warm up without feeling like we're being watched. Richard stands wide-mouthed on the side of the field, turning his neck round and round like an owl.

'Crikey! I never done such a thing before, yeah? We're like proper celebs off the telly!' he says, catching up with Pat as she runs along the goal line, filming us doing our sprints. Pat does her best to shake him off, and keep the camera on us.

After warming up, we run back to the dressing room to freshen up, get into our match-day kit and drink from the sponsored water bottles. When Karo calls us into a huddle, Coach Dave speaks first.

'Well, team, the day is here, yeah? We've put in the hard yards over the past few months, haven't we? I'm proud of you all. I don't recognise one single person from the bunch of amateurs I took on all them months back. You've transformed and all. You've all given your all, you've all left it out on the field every single time I've called on you to do so. Even you, Jasper!'

Jasper laughs and blushes, and flashes a look at Mason.

'They say if you can dream it, you can achieve it. Let's keep the dream alive today, yeah? Go and do your magic. I know you can. I believe in you, and I know you'll do me, Coach, and *every*one who depends on The HAMP, *proper* proud.'

I could swear Coach Dave has tears in his eyes.

'Over to you, Captain. I'll leave you to it,' he says, bowing and stepping out of the way. He blows his nose loudly and stuffs his hankie back into his pocket.

'Thanks, Coach Dave, for those epic words,' says Karo, putting her hand on her heart.'Right, guys, this is *our* day. We deserve to be here. We've worked bloody hard, we've earned the right to take our place proudly in this stadium today. I believe we can do what Coach Dave says, but more than that, I believe that we can win *BLAT*. We're already winners. Every single one of us. Yeah?'

A few of us say, 'Yeah'.

'Pathetic, guys! You can do better than that! Yeah?'

'YEAH! YEAH! YEAH!'

Warren gets us jumping up and down, beating our chests and yelling into each other's faces.

Karo raises her hands to speak again.

'Remember, it's not the size of the dog in the fight, it's the size of the fight in the dog. We may be small, we may be unknown, but we've got *fire* in our bellies. Yeah? We're a good team. No, we're a *great* team. A smooth *machine*.'

'YEAH!' we all shout.

'Remember, there's no *i* in team, and there's no such word as *defeat*. Whatever we do today, we do together. And no matter what we do, we've already won. This is *our* day.'

'YEAH!'

'We've got what it takes, that secret ingredient, to make today count. You know what that ingredient is? It's *heart*. Whether our opponents are bigger than us or not, no one has bigger hearts than ours. We have a truckload of *this*,' Karo says, punching her chest with her fist.

'YEAH!'

'And why do we have so much heart? What is it that gives us the *edge*, what gives us the magical *mojo* that will make all the difference today? Anyone?'

We stare at her in silence.

'Like I said last night, we're doing this for Every. Single. Person. Who's made use of our services at The HAMP. Every. Single. Person. Who's struggled with anger. Who's taken steps to change their lives for the better, by seeking the support of Our. Bloody. Fine. Charity. *That's* why we have fire in our bellies. *That's* what fires our engines.'

'YEAH!'

'They're the reason we do what we do. For our supporters, our service users. Let's keep *them* in our minds and our hearts today as we run out and do what we do best.' Karo's voice gets louder and louder. 'Go out and give it your all, guys. I bloody love you all, and I bloody believe in us all. Hands in for The HAMP!'

'Hands in for The HAMP!' we all shout.

Nobody says anything about the clichés flowing from Karo's lips. We don't care; we're The HAMP, we're *all* winners and everything, and we all bloody love everyone today.

Pat asks us to do the hands in again, so she can film it. She squeezes into the middle of the circle and lies on the floor, pointing her camera up to film our hands. We all shout, 'Hands in for The HAMP!' and jump backwards, hands flying into the air.

We're bloody going to win *BLAT*. I bloody know it. I'm so amped I'm going to burst. But yikes, I feel sick.

Coach Dave says a few things in Karo's ear before she walks to the front of our squad to lead us on to the field for our first match. She nods and beats her chest again, while Coach Dave winks and points at her. The whole squad follows her and we jog through the tunnel and out into the sunlight. The stadium erupts! We're rock stars – this is crazy! We run on to the field and look all around us, taking everything in.

There are cameras everywhere, and the stadium is almost full. Richard is running towards the corner camera when Karo calls him back.

'Richard! Here, mate!'

She pivots on her feet and points to the spot where Richard needs to lead the singing for The HAMP.

'GUYS! GUYS!' she yells, pointing towards the eastern stand. We turn to look, and we gasp. Everyone, and I mean *everyone*, from our charity has come to the stadium today to support us. Colleagues, friends and family. Coach waves to us from the bench in front of the eastern stand, gives us a double thumbs-up and waves to the block of medium turquoise behind her. She made this happen, we all know it; what a legend. What a bloody legend.

Fuelled by emotion and adrenaline and everything, we run and hug each other and again yell in each other's faces. The day is becoming more and more epic by the minute.

We follow Karo as she runs towards our bench. The HAMP block erupts into *Song Sung Blue*, joined by the tuneless yet enthusiastic Richard. It's really quite endearing and everything, to see someone who has no sense of tune or rhythm fronting a charity in song and dance. I hope Pat's getting *this* on film.

I take my spot on the bench with Storm, Binny and Charlie, to watch the first match. Coach Dave, Coach and Barry join us, although Coach Dave can't sit still. Karo leads Cali, Warren, Ash, Mason, Jasper and Tracy on to the field, to face our first opponents: a corporate side. The stadium music stops and the announcer welcomes the teams on to the field, introducing each of the players by name.

Led by Richard, the medium turquoise block goes wild at the mention of each name in our team. When it comes to Cali, the whole stadium erupts. She's a local hero; it's going to be a pretty emotional day and everything.

Richard's dancing starts with the sprinkler but he really comes into his own with the funky chicken. He bites his bottom lip, jerks his neck forwards and backwards, grabs his right ankle with his right hand, and flies around in random circles and everything. The HAMP supporters yell his name and the louder they get, the faster he goes. He's got moves. Not great ones, but enthusiastic ones, that's for sure. I hope he's warmed up properly.

There's also a lot of support from all around the stadium for us. If your team's not playing, it's your duty to support the underdogs. It's quite a British trait, I think, and I do love it.

Our first match goes by in a blur. We put up a great fight but are totally outclassed by the other side, who play with ruthless efficiency. We lack discipline (probably just nerves) and they punish us hard. It's a kind of uneven playing field, really, but I guess we always knew that, coming into *BLAT*. That's the point of the programme. Channel 53 wanted the playing field to be level, but let's be honest: if you have the resources, you'll always have an advantage and everything, won't you?

We score two tries in the second half, but we're no match for the opposition's six converted tries. Coach Dave didn't trouble the bench much during the match, so only Charlie gets to run on for this one.

Karo leads the team off the field in a small conga line, each player holding the shoulder of the player ahead. It's quite sweet, really. Karo gathers us around her and tells us to put this game out of our minds.

'We were never going to win against those guys,' she says. 'They're massive and they obviously had an edge over us. We did ourselves proud, though, yeah, and let's chalk that one up to experience. We can't let it spoil our focus for the next game. One game at a time, right? Hands in for The HAMP!'

We throw our hands in for The HAMP, shout and jump up and go back to our bench. Pat's running between and around us and everything, filming us and still trying to shake Richard off. He jumps out of her way and hangs back, craning his neck to make sure he stays in shot.

There are a few other matches to go before we play again, and we need to move up to our stand to watch them. We also want to see how the other teams perform.

'Karo, would it be okay if I went to get myself something to eat?' says Storm. 'I'm *famished*. I haven't had anything since breakfast.'

'Let's stay together, Storm, yeah? We need to see what these other teams are like. But if you're hungry, there are plenty of these,' says Karo, throwing Storm an energy bar.

'Oh, right,' says Storm, with a disappointment she's not even trying to disguise. The chasm between hope and reality can sometimes be, well, enormous.

'Don't mind if I do,' says Mason, grabbing a whole bunch of energy bars and throwing them to each of us as we start to go up to the stand.

I still have zero appetite. I'm feeling a bit sick again, and I don't want to risk throwing up when I run on to play later. That would be way too embarrassing and everything, not to mention gross for everyone else on the field. 'I'll have a bottle of sparkling water, if that's okay?'

'Sure, I'll grab you one,' says Storm, digging in the cold box. 'Here you go. Ah, no, aren't there any Diet Cokes? I hate water.'

'Can you also pass me a *naartjie*, please?' I ask Storm.

'A what?' she says, screwing up her nose.

'Sorry, I never remember what they're called over here. Is it a clementine?'

'Ah, got you! It's a satsuma. What do you call them, again?'

'*Naartjie.*'

'Narchie. Narchie,' says Storm, over and over. 'So exotic. I *love* learning a foreign language.'

I leave the stand a few times during the next matches to go to the bathroom, and Storm wants to come with me on one of my trips. She and Barry have a few words before she leaves her seat, and he pulls out a notebook and writes something in it. We leave the stand but Storm ducks off to buy herself a hot dog, which she wolfs down before we get back to the team. I try not to watch her eat; it's something that makes you feel queasy even when you're not already feeling queasy and everything.

When we get back to our seats, Karo and Coach Dave stand up.

'Great, you're back,' Coach Dave says, pointing at each of us. 'Okay guys, time to start warming up for our next match. I want you all to get moving; but this time I want Storm, Morag, Binny, Warren, Cali, Ash and Karo running on. I'm saving our top team for the later matches, yeah?'

'No offence taken,' says Storm, laughing.

Wow, it's starting to get real and everything. We follow Karo and Coach Dave down to our bench to leave our warm tops there before jogging over to warm up behind the uprights. It feels like my legs are made of lead; I hope I'll feel better once I'm properly warmed up and out on that field. This will be my first match, ever, in front of a huge crowd like this – in front of any crowd, to be honest. I wonder if it's just a massive case of nerves. Would I have had nerves for the past two weeks? I really have no idea.

We run back to our bench as the ref blows the final whistle for the match on the field. People pour out of the stands to go to the bathroom or get food. It feels like both a relief and a disappointment that we'll be playing in front of an almost empty stadium.

Karo leads us out on to the field, and the medium turquoise block on the eastern stand goes wild. Wendy, Lance, Kevin, Madison, Simon, Binny, and all of our team's family and friends are up on their feet and look so proud of us and everything. It's exciting to see even my most annoying colleagues so enthusiastic for us. Gennypha is sitting behind them, with Vanessa on one side, Jamie, Alex, Tom and Ronda on the other. I feel like a rock star. The announcer introduces each of us by name. I can hear Jamie's scream above everything when my name is announced.

We eye our opposition, an NHS team. They don't look too daunting, but we'd be wrong to underestimate them or anything. The ref blows the whistle and the game begins with Ash kicking into our opponents' half. Cali chases, but her opposite number gets the ball and runs with it. He runs straight into Warren, and loses the ball forward as he falls to the ground. Our scrum. As I join the scrum, I start to feel a bit dizzy but I shake my head and lean in.

Warren recovers the ball from the back of the scrum and distributes it out wide to Karo. I stand up again and although I feel a bit woozy, I jog towards the action anyway. Karo runs with the ball, draws her man and kicks the ball ahead – it bounces skwonk and into touch.

Their throw-in, which Ash steals and offloads to Karo. She's running into traffic so looks around and passes the ball to me; I catch it and panic and chuck it wildly to my left. Ash scoops it up, cracks on the pace and sprints to the try-line, side-stepping an attempted tackle. He dots the ball down next to the posts and the crowd goes wild. He converts it and he and the rest of the team run over to high-five me as we run back to our half.

Whaaaat? Did that just happen? Did I actually play a role in that try? I'm giddy with excitement. And then I realise it's not just excitement; I feel like I'm going to faint. I can't catch Coach Dave's eye as he's watching the restart.

I catch Richard's eye, point to Coach Dave and roll my hands over each other. Richard has no idea I'm asking to be substituted, but must think it's a new dance move. He imitates what I'm doing and adds in some exaggerated disco moves. I can't catch anyone else's eye, so I run towards Coach Dave and I'm so relieved when he notices me. He points to Jasper and points to the field; Jasper jumps up on to his feet and on to the field.

As he reaches me, Jasper stops, gives me a high-five and apologises. I have no idea what for, but I tell him it's okay anyway. He cartwheels as he catches up with play on the far side of the field just as Warren scores an audacious try and the medium turquoise block – and disco Dick – go wild.

When I get to the side of the field, I flop on to the grass and lie on my back. Anything to stop myself from passing out. Coach comes over to ask me if I'm okay, and gives me a bottle of sparkling water. I drink a few sips and manage to get myself up enough to sit on the grass.

'I don't know what's wrong with me, Coach. I'm feeling so strange. I've never felt this way before; so sorry I'm letting you down.'

I feel a bit teary, I have to say. I feel like I'm about to start crying. It's so frustrating feeling this way and everything. I hate feeling unwell, but I also hate letting my team down. Not that I'm a hugely important part of the team or anything, but you know what I mean.

Coach puts her hand on my shoulder.

'It's okay, ja. You haven't absolutely let us down. You gave it your all and you played an instrument in that last try. Without you, we wouldn't have scored, ja? Nothing can take that away from you. And if you can't play again, it is what it is. Sometimes our bodies are talking to us and we have actually to listen, ja? You're still team medium turquoise; still Team HAMP all the way. Just stay quietly here. Can I get you anything?'

'No thank you, Coach. I'll be okay.'

'That's all that matters, ja?'

Best. Boss. Ever. I feel so encouraged and motivated by Coach, I start to cry. I want to run on to the field again but I can't. What I *can* do is support from the sidelines and do my best not to throw up over the rest of the team and everything. That's become my new challenge for today. Oh, boy. But why today of all days? I grab a handful of tissues.

When I stop crying, I have a few sips of water and manage to get myself up on to my feet and walk over to the bench. As I sit down everyone jumps up and screams, 'Go Cali! Go Cali!'

With the ball tucked under her arm, Cali sidesteps the defence, crosses the try-line and jogs towards the uprights, taunting her opposite number. She speeds up to dot the ball down between the posts. Team HAMP, all of our supporters and most of the rest of the stadium roars. Richard screams and flings his arms in the air, before running at Coach Dave to shake his hand. He runs at Coach too but she bats him away without even looking at him. He runs back to his spot to do a manic running man, getting in Pat's way again. She runs around him to film the team and to get some footage of the supporters going crazy.

Jamie's walking towards me, and the look of concern on his face is heart-breaking.

'Are you okay, Rags? What's happening? I was so worried when I saw you come off the field.'

'Thanks,' I say, burying my head into his shoulder. The tears start to flow again. 'I don't know what's going on with me, Jamie. I feel so so sick.'

'Oh I'm so sorry, Rags, I can imagine. Shame, man. It's the pits. You must feel really disappointed,' he says. 'But your health is much more important than this match. You know that, hey?'

I nod from the safety of his shoulder.

'I think you should go to the doctor next week to see what's going on, hey? This isn't okay, is it?'

I nod again, and wipe my tears away with his sleeve.

What on earth is going on with me? Not only am I feeling dreadful, but I also can't seem to stop crying. I know I can be quite dramatic and everything, but this is what I really hope isn't happening to me:

1. I'm dying.

Now that I think about it, this is something I'm really good at:

1. Catastrophising.

Jamie sits with me for the rest of the match. We're running all over our opposition in this one. Karo and Warren are having a cracker of a game, playing well and anticipating each other's moves like they've been playing together for years.

We win the match 33-5. I'm so disappointed not to have been on the field, enjoying a win with my team-mates and everything. Not that I would have added anything; I just would have been in the team that won a match. That must feel brilliant, and I try to own that feeling for myself too, but it's hard.

The team runs off the field, triumphant in their conga line. Storm high-fives everyone in the squad – even those of us on the bench – and flicks her hair back like a winner. Barry pats her on the back a few too many times, and does the same to the rest of the squad.

Karo comes over to me to ask if I'm okay. Pat follows her to film the interaction, and Richard runs over to us too. He stops behind Karo and starts doing the sprinkler. He's the most skilled video-bomber, ever.

I tell Karo I'm okay, and apologise again for letting the side down. 'No, Morag, you didn't let us down at all. You were part of that first team try, which was ace! Without that, we might not have gone on to win, you know. I hope you're okay, though. Will you be up to playing a bit later, do you think?'

'I'm not sure. I hope so, but I don't know, Karo. I feel so weird; not sure *what's* going on. I'm so sorry.'

'It's all right, seriously. Just see how you feel, yeah? I'm just sorry you're missing the thrill of playing out there. It's awesome! The crowd's wicked! Such an adrenaline rush. I wanted you to be part of that, but you're still part of the squad, yeah? And that win,' she says, breathless. She pats me on the shoulder.

If you ask me, *that's* how you captain a team right there. She's the best captain we could have had, if you think about it and everything. She looks across at the squad, who've now huddled, and sees Barry in the middle of the group.

'Oh God, he's only going and giving them a team talk. Come, come, you guys! Come and join the team talk,' she says to us on the bench, jogging backwards towards the group.

I manage to jog slowly to the group where Karo gathers us in a circle, linking arms.

'Brilliant play, guys. You left it all on the field, but at the end of the day, I think we still have plenty in the tank for the next matches, yeah? MVP for this match? Who do you reckon, Coach Dave?'

'All credit to *all* of you, if I'm honest! You're all our most valued players. But this time I think Warren took it to the next level out wide, yeah?'

'Good shout,' says Karo. Warren blushes and grimaces, shooting his shoulders up to his ears and shimmying his eyebrows up and down. He kicks his feet forward and looks to the ground.

'Ah, you guys! Cheers,' he says, with a double thumbs-up and a big rectangular grin.

'Okay, guys. We've got a bit of a wait now until our next match. Hydrate, and get some energy. *Healthy* food. I want you back here before the end of the next match, yeah? We need to check out how the other teams play. You're making me proud, guys. *So* proud. Hands in for The HAMP!' says Coach Dave.

We do the hands in before running off in different directions. Storm and Barry jog past me and Storm says something about murdering another hot dog. Sounds about right.

Chapter 31

Jamie and I head for the stand for the next few matches. It might feel a little less painful sitting there than on the bench, not able to play.

'I'm starving, Rags. Do you want anything?' Jamie says, pointing to a food van.

'I've got zip appetite,' I say. 'But you go ahead, and I'll go up and keep a seat for you, okay?'

'Cool. See you now now,' he says, giving me a hug. 'Sorry you're feeling so grotty, Rags.'

I sit alone, trying to avoid my colleagues' eyes. I can feel Wendy's eyes boring into the side of my head, and she whispers something about "south east London" and something about "Zimbabwean" to Lance. What the hell that has to do with playing rugby, I have no idea, but that irritates me so much.

Everything's making me feel a bit over-the-top emotional today. I'm missing my parents all of a sudden. They used to love watching rugby and I can't imagine what they'd have thought to know I was playing and everything. That I was actually playing and in such a big festival as this. Well, not that I'm actually playing now, but anyway; I was *meant* to be playing.

This is what I'm starting to become:

1. Maudlin.

I have to snap out of it, and just enjoy the rest of the day from the stands. It's a huge thing that The HAMP is part of. I don't want to miss another minute by being pathetic and feeling sorry for myself and everything, which I'm now world champion at.

Jamie comes back with a massive chicken burger and chips, and a beer. He's brought me a bottle of sparkling water, which is perfect. I grab a tissue from my backpack, spray some deodorant into it and hold it against my nose. Anything to kill the smell of the chicken burger and chips, and to stop me from throwing up and everything.

The next few matches are amazing and exciting to watch. Some of the other teams' performances are formidable, but we've got a good spread of natural talent in our side, and I'm confident of our chances when we go back on. Coach Dave has been doing a brilliant job corralling us into a proper team.

Richard seems unable to stay in his seat during any of the other matches. Despite the security guards asking him to sit down, he keeps jumping up and showing off his entire repertoire of dances. If the cameras come near him, he's up on his feet, doing the sprinkler. (That one seems to be his favourite, and the one he wants most to be filmed doing.) The crowd is loving him and the more enthusiastic he gets, the more they egg him on.

'Oy, blue boy! Show us your moves!'

'Mr Blue Sky, where'd'you get those moves?'

Also, the more encouragement he gets, the more cringey his dancing becomes. He's far more animated than any of the other mascots, and is loving the attention from the crowd and the cameras and everything.

If there's an award for mascots today, he'll have to be in the running for it, for sure. I kind of hope he does and I kind of hope he doesn't win the award. It'll be great if he does and everything, and brilliant for The HAMP, but I'm not sure I could cope with the endless play-by-plays and replays we'd get back at the office. I'm exhausted thinking about it, to be honest. But to be a good sport, I really hope he does win it. Sort of.

The crowd suddenly goes mad. Jamie jumps to his feet and is yelling for the corporate guy breaking through the opposition to score a cracker of a try. Three minutes to go, and the teams are neck and neck.

'Number seven, you beauty!' yells Jamie. 'Do it again, mate!'

The number seven looks up at our stand, and gives us a thumbs-up.

'Did you see that, Rags? Did you see that?' Jamie yells into my face. 'He heard me!'

In any ordinary day, I bet you anything you like Jamie would *not* go wild if Robert, the print company salesperson, gave him a thumbs-up. It's amazing the difference an amped-up crowd and a few pints of beer can make in a huge stadium.

One more game to go before we're back on. Karo starts rounding the squad up again, and I feel another pang of disappointment I'm still not up to joining them. Karo asks Storm to wait until after the match before having another doughnut and, when Karo turns away, Storm gives the doughnut to Barry and the middle finger to Karo.

We win our next match and make it through to the next round play-offs. The excitement is starting to make me feel better, but I don't want to risk it and get all pumped up about joining the squad on the field for the next match and everything. Not that I'd be selected for that match anyway; we have to win the next match to stay in the tournament. Coach Dave and Karo will want to field their full-strength, best squad and everything anyway, which is what they do.

I'm proud and nervous and sad and emotional as Team HAMP runs on to the field for the play-off match. We're all up on our feet singing *Song Sung Blue* and clapping and shouting and whooping and whistling. We also shout 'Britain Loves a Trier! HAMP! HAMP!'

Richard is going berserk on the field. He doesn't know what to do with himself. He's running around in such tight circles, he keeps falling over. He gets back up on his feet and almost runs into the stand. He stops and steadies himself, before doing the funky chicken again. He's shouting something, but you can't hear what it is over the roar of the stadium.

We're up against a civil service side this time, and they look scary. One of Karo's amazing strengths is her ability to stay calm, and she's good at calming the team down too. Just breathe, she'll be telling them. I'm telling myself that too. Just breathe. It seems to help keep the queasy feeling at bay too.

Two minutes after kick-off, Karo gets the ball and charges down the middle of the field. Warren is just on her outside, ready for the offload as Karo draws her man. Warren cracks on the pace and barges through the defence to score right under the posts. Ash kicks over a quick conversion.

Oh. My. Word. Warren runs towards our stand and throws himself into a knee-slide, arms outstretched. His hero moment. I'm so thrilled for him. Karo and the rest of Team HAMP run over to him and jump around him, hugging him and beating him on the back and everything. The crowd goes mad. Richard goes madder. Coach and Coach Dave go madder still. They high-five and hug each other and scream something at our stand. What a moment!

The other team replies straightaway with a converted try and we go into half-time, neck and neck. The second half begins with messy play. Both sides are nervous and start to make silly mistakes. Cali scores a soft try in the corner in the dying minutes, and the crowd roars. She's a real favourite out there today. It's a tough shot at posts for Ash, right from the sideline, and he shanks it. But it doesn't matter – we've won the match and we're through to the semi-final. *Woohoo!*

Jamie and I yell into each other's faces. He's almost lost his voice. The rest of our stand goes crazy. So do hundreds of other supporters around the stadium. It's amazing to feel so much love and everything coming our way; that will work in our favour in the next match too.

The stadium announcer shouts out the result, and says, 'Oh, and you'll have seen another great try from the great Cali Shannon, ladies and gentlemen. You wouldn't want to get on the wrong side of her, mind!'

There's a sharp intake of breath right across the stadium, and we all look to see if Cali has heard what he said. She has. She smiles, gestures that it's okay, and waves for everyone to calm down. The crowd applauds her good humour, and it hits me that what just happened is probably the best, most spontaneous and most authentic advert for the work of The HAMP we could ever have hoped for.

The announcer goes on.

'Cheers, Cali! You see, The HAMP does important work, ladies and gentlemen. Please watch this video clip again, and you'll see the huge difference the charity has made in Cali's life. Not long ago, she might have reacted very differently to what I just said. But, with the help and support of The HAMP, she took it in good humour, which is exactly how it was intended. SORRY, CALI! CHEERS FOR BEING A CHAMP, BUDDY!

'And remember, folks. Every penny you donate today will help The HAMP help more people deal with anger management problems. The world will be a better place when more people can get the help they need, when they need it. Thank you.'

Most people are staying in their seats to watch the video clip, and quite a few take out their phones to donate to The HAMP. Coach would offer the stadium announcer a role as our director of comms, if we had such a role and everything.

We're playing in the second semi-final, against a civil service side, and an NHS side is playing a corporate side in the first one. It's excruciating to sit through the first match; too nerve-wracking for words. Both teams look huge and their play is super slick. The corporate side wins, ending the run of the NHS teams in *BLAT*. Holding thumbs we'll win our semi-final match but, if we do, we're up against that corporate team in the final, and they look flipping terrifying, if you ask me.

My stomach churns as our team runs on for the biggest match of our lives. Nerves, for sure, but my insides also feel like a washing machine. The civil service players look like giants next to our team, but I bet they don't have our grit, determination and, I hope, the support of the crowd. The cool thing about being the underdog and everything is that you have nothing to lose. You won't disappoint anyone if you lose, and you will amaze everyone if you win.

'Hey Rags, it looks like the civil service side has fielded their weaker side. They're probably saving their best players for the final. Bet they're expecting to walk all over us. Bring it on!' Jamie's voice is now super husky.

The ref blows his whistle and the civil service side kicks off. Warren runs for the ball and so does his opposite number, taking him down hard. There's a huge 'oof!' from the crowd.

The ball is free and the other team's wing scoops it up and flies down the field. Karo runs and dives after him, tapping his ankle, and he spills the ball forward. Our scrum.

I can't cope with this match. I also feel like I'm about to be sick again. I bury my face in my hands and fall against Jamie's shoulder. I peep through my fingers to see Warren running with the ball. He sidesteps a few attempted tackles and touches the ball down between the posts. Ash converts and we're not only on the scoreboard; we're ahead. The crowd goes wild.

The match is super close. Each side replies quickly to the other's score and when the other team misses a conversion, we go into half-time two points ahead. Coach Dave looks amped. Coach doesn't know where to turn, and Richard tries a clumsy combo of the funky chicken and the sprinkler, and falls over on to the grass. He jumps up, looks around, shakes his head and laughs, and dives straight into his *Greased Lightning.*

'We're on fire, hey Rags?' says Jamie.

'For sure. It's so hard to watch, though. I think I'm on my last nerve.'

'Ah, don't use that one up, Rags! You'll need it for the final.'

I shake Jamie's arm. I'd love and hate us to go through to the final. Not sure I can bear watching it and everything, though.

Jasper is in the squad for this match. He should be listening to Coach Dave's half-time talk, but he's looking around the stadium and running his fingers through his hair, trying to soak everything in. Something like this won't happen again for any of us.

The second half begins and I don't want to take my hands away from my face. I force them on to my lap and I sit up.

Ash kicks off deep into the far right corner. The ball bounces backwards, away from the wing running for it, and into Karo's hands. Cali flies up on the outside and takes the flat pass. She storms through the gap and on to the try-line to dot the ball down next to the posts. Our stand goes bonkers and the whole crowd is up on its feet. Coach runs up and down the sideline, arms outstretched, screaming and everything. Coach Dave jumps up and down, yelling and punching the air.

Our players on the bench jump up, hug, chest bump each other and jump around in circles and scream. I should be there. I can't believe my body has chosen this weekend of all weekends to go on strike. I fall against Jamie's shoulder and he puts his arm around me.

I bring my focus back to the game as the other team's wing takes advantage of a favourable bounce and she runs in an outstanding try. Team HAMP looks baffled and Karo gathers everyone around her to calm them down. And to talk strategy, I reckon. A conversion gives the other side a three-point advantage, and there are two minutes left on the clock. There's all to play for, as they say, in these dying minutes.

As play restarts, I peep through my fingers as The HAMP crew all jump to our feet to watch Team HAMP execute a perfect set piece that ends in a Warren try under the posts. That puts us two points ahead. It doesn't matter if Ash converts this or not; we just need the clock to run out.

Ash looks confident as he kicks the ball high but it hits the upright and bounces back into play. The other captain scoops it up and runs back to the halfway for a quick kick-off. The ball bounces high, Warren jumps for it but knocks it into the hand of the civil service wing. She looks around and takes a gap down the sideline. Cali sprints after her and throws herself on to her, five metres from the try-line. She catches her foot and she spills the ball forward. It would be our scrum, but the ref blows the final whistle. Team HAMP goes crazy on the field, on the benches, on the sidelines, in the stands. Everywhere. We're through to the final. We've beaten the civil service side. Whaaaaat?

Jamie and I jump up and down and hug each other and everyone in front, behind and next to us. *Song Sung Blue* sounds just perfect.

There's an excruciating half-hour wait for the final. The *BLAT* organisers use this time for a battle of the mascots. *Eye of the Tiger* roars out on the field and the camera teams run from mascot to mascot. The crowd has to make some noise for each mascot and the one who gets the loudest roar wins the 'Mascot of the *BLAT* festival' award. Richard looks fit to burst and everything.

He watches the other mascots break-dancing, hip-hopping, crunk-ing, popping and locking, bouncing and snapping. When the cameras get to him, he gives them his best sprinkler with an extra dash of

Elvis. The crowd loves him, and the roar goes on for ages. The other mascots watch him, and laugh as he plays to the camera. He's loving the spotlight; he was made for this moment. He doesn't even notice Pat any more.

When the stadium announcer declares Richard the winner, the crowd roars again.

'And folks, if you haven't done so already, now is a good time to donate to The HAMP. You'll find their lovely volunteers around the stadium with big blue buckets, or you can text to donate; the details are up on the screen right now.'

(It doesn't really matter that the announcer didn't call the buckets "medium turquoise". Does it?)

Richard's a great sport and exactly what our team, and a day like this need. I couldn't imagine a better mascot for The HAMP. And I can tell you this for free: he's going to dine out on this moment and his 'Mascot of the *BLAT* festival' award and everything for the rest of his life. That's for jolly sure.

Jamie and I go down to the field to wish the team well for the final. Karo thanks me, and pats me on the shoulder. She looks nervous, of course. She's about to lead her best team on to the field, with all of us cheering them on from the bench and the stands and everything. Team HAMP supporters and most of the crowd are behind us too. We'd hoped but hadn't imagined for one moment we'd actually get this far.

Storm whispers something into Karo's ear and pats her on the shoulder. Karo looks her in the eye and hugs her. Coach Dave gathers the team around him and shouts some encouragement to them, before leaving it to Karo to say her final words to the team before they run on.

Coach invites me to sit on the bench for the match and, when Jamie turns to go back to the stand, Coach calls him back to come and sit with us. What an honour. Storm, Tracy, Robyn and Mason join us as the others run on to the field. Barry comes over too and asks Storm to "shove up" to make room for him on the bench too.

I watch the match from behind my hands again. The tension is too much to bear. It seems our nerves are getting to us this time. The corporate side we're up against has won every match today by a huge margin. We don't want to let anyone down, but we have to be realistic and everything. We may not match them in talent, but we've worked flipping hard to get here. Okay, maybe we've had a bit of luck and huge support from the crowd. It's been a hell of a wave to ride.

'Come on, you guys! Focus, focus, focus!' yells Barry.

'Barry, we've spoken about this,' says Storm. 'Only positive affirmation for this game, yeah? They know they have to focus; they know they're under pressure. Only supportive words, yeah?'

Barry rolls his eyes, and nods like a petulant child.

'Great work, guys! Super. You're doing fantastic!' He looks at Storm. 'That better, oh supreme one?'

Storm laughs and pushes Barry. He uses his crutch to stop himself falling off the bench.

Coach Dave is pacing up and down the sideline, stopping every now and then to tuck in his shirt and pull up his trousers.

'Look at him, poor little fucker,' says Tracy. 'You feel for him, obviously. He must be proper nervous and all.'

We're two converted tries down in the first half before we trouble the scoreboard with a soft try right in the corner. It's an impossible angle and we don't convert, going into half-time nine points adrift. Coach Dave and Coach go on to the field to speak to the team. When Coach walks away, the team hold their heads a bit higher. She always knows what to say: kind and generous words of encouragement. She's absolutely awesome.

'You know what, Morag?' says Tracy.

'What?'

'I was a bit sceptical about getting involved in *BLAT*, you know. As a fundraiser, I thought it was a bit of a stretch to play rugby sevens to raise funds. But you know what?'

'What?'

'Some of the volunteers doing bucket collections have had to empty their buckets already today. I've never heard of that happening anywhere. Ever. We're going to smash our target today, I tell you. Ker-ching, ker-ching!' She pretends to pull a slot machine lever. 'And you know what?'

'What?'

'Something has kind of like, I don't know, moved this crowd to support us today. Maybe it's Cali – obviously she's been immense on that field. Or it's the passion that our team has out on that field.' She's counting the options off on her fingers. 'Or maybe it's that crazy fucker dancing on the field! Or …'

'You mean Richard?'

'Yeah. He's a proper nutter, isn't he? Wait till he gets indoors! His family will proper wind him up and all. But this crowd obviously loves him. The more they egg him on the more nuttier he gets!'

'Sorry, guys.' Karo has run off the field, panting. 'I need you, Tracy. Jasper has a cramp and says he can't manage the second half. Is that okay?'

'I'll bloody say! I've only gone and waited my whole fucking life for a moment like this, obviously.'

Tracy jumps up and throws her warm top on the ground, does a few stretches and runs across to join the squad. I feel envious and everything but you know what? I'm super chuffed for her.

The second half is even more stressful to watch than the first. We start strong, with a try from Karo in the second minute. Ash converts the try, putting us within striking distance of a win, but that turns out to be our last good move. The other team dominates possession and runs all over us, scoring three more tries in quick succession. They convert two, and it's an agonising wait until the final whistle. Nerves have got the better of us, but they other team has also outplayed us.

The final whistle goes and the crowd roars. We all jump up to our feet and run over to the squad on the field, with a lot of head-cocking and stiff-armed aah-wells and hugs and everything.

'Wasn't meant to be, yeah?' says Barry. 'Fair play to yous, though, you left it all out on the field, right enough.'

Karo gathers all of us around her and calls Coach Dave and Coach into the middle of the huddle.

'Team HAMP, you've been awesome,' she yells. 'Not only today, but in the build-up to today. Every practice, every meeting, every moment. I'm beyond proud of you guys. You put some vulnerability on the table, but we were never going to win against that side! You believed we could. And that belief carried us through to this point, to the final of *BLAT*. You guys totally rock!' It's so loud in the stadium, we have to lip-read most of what she says.

Coach Dave hugs her close to him. 'I'll save my words for the dressing room after, yeah?'

'Just quickly – super exciting news!' shouts Karo, slapping Warren on the back. 'They've just told us Warren is Channel 53's Player of the *BLAT* festival. That's out of *everyone* playing today. Ace choice, right?'

With his best awkward look, Warren shoves his hands in his pockets, looks at his feet and kicks them forward.

'Thanks, guys,' he says, looking up from under his eyebrows.

'They're waiting for us over there,' says Karo, pointing to the camera crews in front of the sponsor banners.

'Hoo, boy,' says Warren. 'Just as well I'm a gifted public speaker.'

'Brilliant, Team HAMP, go and do what you have to do! I need you to jog on to the cameras, ja?' Coach shoos us away.

Richard is already at the sponsor banner, craning his neck to get into shot behind the winning side's captain. When he hears the music, he launches into all of his moves. It's amazing he's still going, I have to say.

I spot a familiar figure in a suit striding towards us; it's Chester. You have to give him his dues; this is a bold move. After leaving the charity under a cloud, actually under *seven* clouds of shame and everything, you have to wonder what the hell he's doing here?

We get to the camera crew before Chester gets to us. His hands fly on to his hips as he stands and watches Karo speak to the reporter.

'Yeah, it's an amazing day for The HAMP. I'm super proud of the team, yeah.' Karo has one hand on her hip and pushes her hair back with the other.

Richard walks around trying to get into shot behind her, but the sponsor banners are in his way.

'The guys gave it their all today. Left it all out on the field. We had tons of self-belief and it blew our minds that we got through to the finals. And we're here today and, at the end of the day, we did this for our supporters, you know. For everyone who struggles with managing their anger.

'Yeah, to be honest, the other team was the better one at the end of the day. We were hungry; we wanted the win. But you know what, we have to take this on the chin. When all's said and done, we're a charity team, you know, and we held our own against a cracking side. Like everyone, we had players in our team who were new to the game, they'd never even played before, so to do what we've done today, I couldn't be any more prouder. It's been epic. Awesome.'

Karo looks at us all and claps at us.

'Sorry? Oh, right. Yes, absolutely. All credit to Cali. She gave it her all. Look, I don't know what we would have done without her support. She's been a role model for our team, and for our supporters, if I'm honest. She's added a new dimension to the game for us, yeah. Cheers, thanks very much.'

The crowd roars and Karo steps around and waves in every direction as she moves away from the sponsor banner.

'And now our Channel 53 Player of the *Britain Loves a Trier* festival – the HAMP's very own Warren Rankin!'

The crowd goes wild. Warren makes a "who me?" face, and fills his cheeks with air as he slides over to the reporter, his hands shoved deep in his pockets.

'Cheers, I appreciate it, yeah. Thanks.' He nods and his eyebrows shoot up, as his mouth opens into his harmonica smile. 'Yeah, I was pleased with the way we played. Top-notch captaincy from Karo, for sure. I should share this award with her, really. Her distribution of the ball, her leadership – yeah, she deserves this as much as anyone. Our whole team, to be honest.'

Warren looks down and his eyes peep up at Karo.

'Thank you very much. Yes, I will put the award in our office, where we can all see it. Thanks. Cheers.'

He gives us all a double thumbs-up before sliding over to hide behind Ash.

Chester comes over to us as we're about to set off on a lap of honour.

'Couldn't resist being here to watch The HAMP team play. Great effort, everybody,' he says, pulling his hands off his hips to clap. 'Smashing it onwards!' A quick glance at his fingernails, watch, and a nudge of the tie.

'Oh, hey, thought I spotted you striding over here, Chester. How wide's the field?' Ash can't resist a cheeky dig.

'What do you mean, Ash?'

'Ah, nothing, Chester, just being silly, yeah.'

'Oh, right, good one! I saw you had a good few minutes on the field, Morag. You'll be a hero in Zimbabwe, yeah?'

'I doubt it, but thanks anyway. Wish I could have done more.' I can only manage a small smile.

'Hey ho,' Chester says. 'Cali, you had a good game, yeah? Not sure if you've heard of me, but I'm Chester Proudfoot. I used to work at The HAMP. Finance director, for my sins.'

Cali must come across people like Chester all the time. She hesitates, and looks around the stadium. 'Cheers, Chester. Nice to meet you. It helps to be part of a brilliant team, yeah?'

Chester steps forward for a high-five, but Cali has already turned away.

'Excellent,' says Chester, clapping hard and pretending that's what he was going to do with his hands all along. 'Being part of a brilliant team is *everything*. I was about to say that. Sorry, Cali.' He moves over and taps Cali on the shoulder. She turns around. 'Has The HAMP team treated you well?' He's never been good at reading the room.

'Yeah, brilliant,' says Cali, turning away again.

'Would you like a quick shot together?' Pat asks Karo, pointing at Chester.

'Nah, you're all right, cheers Pat,' says Karo, waving for us to follow her.

With her hand on Warren's shoulder, Karo moves us on. Richard runs alongside us, his enthusiasm unmatched, his dance moves unnatural.

'No problem. Excellent. Great. See you guys afterwards? Super. Good to meet you, Cali. And good to see everyone else. Keep cracking onwards, you're smashing it. Crack onwards.' Chester waves.

He swings his forearm forward and claps fast, watching us and his final hopes of any vicarious glory from The HAMP's performance today fading forever into the distance.

We make our way around Cardiff Arms Park like rock stars. Lots of people have left already but those still there applaud us warmly. I am so proud of us. We showed up, we made our mark. The HAMP made its mark. We did this. We actually did this. I'm starting to make myself cry, and not just because I'm thinking in clichés and everything.

Coach Dave, Coach and our squad of supporters are waiting for us and applaud us into the dressing room when we finish our lap of honour. They gather us around them.

'HAMP, HAMP, HAMP! What a team! The champions of champions, ja? Every single one of you, ja!' says Coach, moving around the huddle and slapping us all on the shoulder.

'You're right, Coach Pauli, these guys are something else, yeah?' says Coach Dave. 'You played with heart for every minute of every match. Fair enough, we didn't win at the end of the day, but you took it down to the wire. You made it *possible* we could win. You believed in yourselves, and you can't put a price on that. The other side was the better team on the day, but when it comes to heart' — punching his chest — 'you were the bigger team. No question.'

His lip trembles.

'If I ever hear the word "proud" again,' he says, holding his hands up in surrender, 'I'll think of you. I have never, *ever* felt so proud. Guys, I don't even know what else to say. I'm finished.'

'Three cheers for Coach Dave!' shouts Barry, ever the schoolboy. 'Hip hip!'

We all jump around the room and cheer Coach Dave. Coach puts her hand up.

'Team HAMP, I conclude with everything Coach Dave has said now and what your brilliant Captain Karo said out there too. You all gave it your all; you went the extra miles, left it all out on the field, and made actually very very proud this average Austrian rugby player.

'We dreamed it, and we achieved it, ja? You *all* gave hundred and ten percent. Not only today, but every day since we decided Britain could love *this* team of triers. And they did. We did ourselves proudly. And we did our supporters proudly. We dug deep and although we didn't grind out a win, we ground out support from a whole lot of people here today. That's a big win in my books, ja?

'Cali, Team HAMP landed with our noses in the butter when you said you'd play for us today. You've made really a difference to the team, and to us all. I know that without you we wouldn't have got all the support we got today. The crowd loves you. *We* love you. And that love from the crowd has turned into financial support. What is it you say, Tracy – ker-chief, ker-chief?'

'Ker-ching, Coach!' says Tracy, laughing. 'But your one works too, obviously, yeah?'

Cali blushes and looks at her feet. 'Thanks, Coach, that's all right. I only did what anyone in my position would have done, guys. And believe me, I've gained so much from joining your team. You've helped me to feel more confident about my game again, about myself, and I've made a whole lot of new, special friends. It's been a privilege, and something I'll carry with me for the rest of my life.' Cali puts her hands to her heart.

'You've made actually a big difference for our charity too, Cali.,' says Coach. 'All the money in the world couldn't have helped us raise more awareness for our work, in a more authentic way, than you did actually for us today, and in these past few months. I don't know sincerely where I, I mean, we'd be without you, ja? Thank you, Cali, thank you. On behalf of me, The HAMP and all of our supporters.'

We all clap and whoop for Cali. And for Coach, to be honest.

'And team, remember,' says Coach, 'we've got our own awards – our Cloud Sevens awards – that we'll hand out at work next week, ja?'

Karo gives Coach a double thumbs-up.

'Wait a second, Karo. Guys,' says Coach. 'Just one more thing from me. A few months ago you all put forward yourselves for this challenge, ja? For *Britain Loves a Trier*, ja? And today you've shown me, you've shown the charity, and *all* these people here today, just how trying you can be, ja?

'And if any of you ever doubted yourself, I hope you've recognised that you raised nicely up yourselves to the challenge and you clocked it in the face. I'm proud of you. I'm *so* proud of you. You make leading this charity every day a joy and a privilege.'

She takes a breath and puts her hand to her mouth. She wraps her arms around Cali, and pecks her on the cheek.

Three things to know about this:

1. Coach is getting so emotional she may even cry. That's huge.
2. Coach and Cali might be going public with their relationship. They're perfect together and everything and I'm so happy for them.
3. I love the way Coach pronounces the "b" in "doubted".

Chapter 32

'Wow, you slept well, Rags. Do you remember getting out of the car and into bed last night?' It's Sunday morning, and Jamie wakes me up with a cup of coffee.

'Vaguely. I was *so* tired. Thanks for helping me, and for the coffee,' I say, stretching and yawning.

We left Cardiff last night, straight after the team talk. The whole day had been so much fun. The crowd's support was immense – we all felt like celebrities. I felt a bit of a fraud, really, not having played much and everything, but as Barry reminded me and himself, I guess: you all stand and fall as a team. At least he also had his crutches to stop him from falling.

The rest of the team travelled back to London on the train last night, and it must have been some journey. I send Karo a text at midday:

'Hope you're okay, Karo. Huge congrats again for being an amazing captain. Hope the journey back was good, M xx'.

'Gr8, cheers. Not long awake. Lots to tell you. Feeling a bit tatty today. My cats too loud. Thanks 4 everything. C u Tuesday x'.

'Sounds fun. Look forward to hearing about it. Might be in late. M xx'.

'Cool. C u then x'.

Coach has given everyone Monday off to recover from the *BLAT* weekend. I spend the whole day sleeping and reading and trying to feel normal again. I also call to book an appointment to see my GP and I get one on Tuesday morning, first thing. Jamie asks me to call him straight after. The waiting room is empty so I get to see her straightaway, and call Jamie once I'm on the bus to work.

'Hey, Rags, how're you doing? What did she say?'

'I'm feeling okay, thanks. A bit overwhelmed and everything, really. I can't get my head around what she said. Jamie-James, it's a lot to take in. Are you sitting down?'

'Yes. Yes? Why? What did she say? You're scaring me, Rags. Do you want me to meet you somewhere? Are you okay, Rags? Hope you're okay. *Please please* don't be sick, hey. Please *please*!'

'Don't panic, my Jamie. It's okay. Really. You ready?'

'Yes! Tell me, Rags. I can't bear it. What is it?'

'I'm expecting.'

'Expecting what? More tests? What, Rags?'

'I'm pregnant, my Jamie.'

'Whaaaaaaaaaat?'

'I know, hey?'

'Whaaaaaaaaaat? How, my Rags? How can that be?'

'Well …'

'I know *how*. I just mean: how did this happen? How did this happen now?'

'I don't know, hey. I guess we just stopped trying. The doctor said sometimes this happens; when you stop trying and everything. She's quite surprised though, she said, because, you know, I'm in my forties. So she wants to monitor me closely, and …'

'How far are we, Rags?'

'About ten weeks, she reckons.'

'Whaaaat? So that means baby's due in …'

'The winter, as they say here. But January, hey, right at the end of January.'

'Oh, wow! Shall I take a sabbatical from work? I'll drop everything. I'll do everything you normally do, Rags. I'll, I'll cook healthy meals, I'll paint your fingernails, I'll paint your toenails. I'll give you back massages, I'll brush your hair. *All* those things you love, and ...'

'Jamie, slow down! I'm pregnant, not sick, or dying or anything! You don't need to take a sabbatical. Well, some paternity leave obviously. But let's talk about all that later. We'll do this *together*. This is new for both of us and everything, and to be honest, I'm so excited I think I could burst.'

'Me too! But don't do that, my Rags. *Please* don't do that! Not yet, anyway.'

We laugh, kind of hysterically. I guess we're both scared and everything. And, if I'm totally honest, I'm more than a little terrified. What if we lose the baby? Again. What if we *don't* lose the baby?

'Let's meet up for a meal after work, hey Rags. Let's go to that Greek restaurant in Soho. We can share a big salad. What do you think?' Jamie is going to fixate about healthy meals for the rest of our lives. Heaven help me.

'That sounds great, Jamie. I'll see you then.'

I can't believe this is happening. We *never* thought we'd be able to have children of our own. All those years of trying, and hope and disappointment and heartbreak and everything. And tears. And more tears. I've got a good feeling about it this time, but I'm even scared to say that out loud. But you *have* to stay positive and everything, hey?

When you've been here before, and you know how all of those stories have ended, you just can't *bear* another disappointment. Especially when you've given up on the idea of having a family. And especially when you've pushed it all out of your mind and tried to carry on with a life that doesn't include a family and everything.

If only my mom and dad were still around. They're the only other people I'd want to tell right now. They'd be so excited, and nothing but encouraging.

They were so kind to Jamie and me every time we experienced another disappointment. They didn't always have the words or the tools to know how to comfort us, but they made us meals and sent us flowers and called us to tell us about the rugby or the cricket or the latest films they'd watched. They'd invite us to go for scenic drives with them. My dad would tell us his lame jokes. That was their language of love. It was beautiful, and practical, and sweet and everything, and I miss it. I miss them every single day.

When my dad got sick about eight years ago, he told me he was going to fight it with everything he had. And he did, until he couldn't any more. I couldn't bear to see my strong dad growing weaker every day. He'd always handled *everything.* He'd always made the world feel like a safe place to be. And he gave me hope that I could find my own safe place in it.

Throughout my life he'd wipe away my tears with his big white hankie. He did that the day he told me about his diagnosis, and again at the end, as I wept at his bedside. He looked so sad and everything. He wanted to carry on being there for my mom and me. *With* us. He didn't want to leave. He wasn't ready to go, but the cancer had other ideas. It ripped through him fast, without a thought for any of us.

My mom and Jamie and I were with my dad the day he died. We held his hands and told him it was okay for him to go. We didn't want him to suffer any more, but we didn't want to lose him or anything. We knew the world would never be the same without him. Of course, it was much harder for my mom than it was for me. I had Jamie and everything, and she was going to be alone.

She hated being alone. From the moment my dad died, my mom couldn't find her way clear to define a life for herself without him. She'd forgotten that once, long ago, she'd had a life without my dad, but she couldn't remember what it was like. The sorrow ripped through her and, even though she wasn't that old, it robbed her of her strength and health and everything.

Jamie and I could never fill the hole my dad had left in her heart. It was a shape that only my dad could fill, and we were never going to be my dad to her. We tried to keep her busy, to make her smile, to help her live and find some joy again and everything. But my mom just couldn't feel anything but bereft, and it broke our hearts.

It was less than a year after my dad died that my mom took her last breath.

My dad died from the cancer. My mom died of a broken heart. But the cancer took her too, if you think about it and everything.

It wasn't long after we'd lost both of them that we decided to move to the UK. We told everyone we were following a job opportunity for Jamie, but in truth we also wanted a fresh start. To get away from the disappointment of failed pregnancies and everything, but also to get away from the constant reminder that I'd become an orphan.

Most of the time I can keep the sadness at bay, but I'm struggling a bit today. My haywire hormones can't be helping me either.

I sit in a coffee shop near the office for a bit and try to pull myself together and everything before I go to work. I grab a chocolate croissant and a rooibos latte. The one cancels out the other, right? *Please* don't tell Jamie about the croissant.

The office is super quiet. Lucozade bottles on desks a clue as to how everyone's feeling. It must have been some party on the train home – there's been two whole days in between and everything.

'Oh hey,' says Mason, looking up at me briefly. 'All right?'

'Ja, cool, thanks,' I say, as if today is an average Tuesday. 'Still pretty tired after the weekend, hey. How about you?'

'Exhausted!' he says, dropping forward on to his desk.

'Me too,' says Storm, with a mouthful of flapjack.

It's so weird. Everything in the office feels normal, but my whole world has turned upside down – in a good way and everything – in the last few hours. I can't say anything to anyone yet. I have to keep this to myself. And I have to keep this baby too.

'Oh, Morag, *so* glad you're here,' says Madison. 'Hope you're feeling better, my love?'

'Yes, kind of. It's been ...'

'Oh, I'm *so* glad to hear that. *So* glad. So I really need to pick your brain, if that's okay?'

There has to be another reason for a disingenuous enquiry about my health from Madison.

'No worries.' I can be disingenuous too.

'Super. I *really* need to get this marketing copy to this corporate company by twelve today, yeah. They're putting it into their email newsletter and pushing that out to their *whole* database. *So* soz about the rush, but they've only just asked me for it.' (If I were cynical, I'd guess that meant she'd only just remembered about it.)

'Would you mind having a look at my draft and adding your marvellous magic to it? I *love* your magic, Morag. You're *such* a star! Best. Writer. Ever. Tha-anks.' Madison turns around to bash her keyboard to death.

'I hate it when they give you such short notice, don't you? Anyway, send it through to me and I'll take a look. Not sure how much I can add to it, though ...' I say to the back of Madison's head.

The email arrives and it's not anything like a draft for me to add my magic to. Madison has forwarded me the email from the corporate company, with their questions for us to answer. Also, I notice they sent the original email two weeks ago, and have chased Madison twice since then.

'Um, Madison? Sorry, I thought you were sending me your draft? I think you sent me the wrong email, hey?'

'Yeah, sorry. That's the draft they sent us. We just need to tailor it with our messaging, yeah? Things have been *so* manic for me recently, I haven't been able to give it the attention I'd hoped to.' (Or any attention at all, by the looks of things.) 'And, like I said, I've only just received it.'

'Um, Madz, it looks to me like they emailed you two weeks ago and have chased up twice since then.'

'Oh, really? I only saw the email from this morning,' she says, glancing at me before she turns back to her screen.

She's on the Ticketmaster website, and there's a ticking clock in the middle of her screen.

'What are you booking for?'

Madison minimises the window and laughs. 'I wish! I *wish* I had the time to book something.' She shrugs one shoulder.

'Come on, Madz. Spill. Which gig?' says Mason.

She ignores Mason. She's aware I'm watching her and she's desperate not to lose her place in the queue.

'Sorry, Madz, I won't have time to do this today,' I say. 'I've got loads to do so this has to be a no-can-do.' (That's the first time I've ever said "no-can-do" in my whole life. I'm embarrassed I've used such a stupid term, but sometimes you just have to speak to Madison in her language, to be honest.) I hold my hands up like I'm stopping traffic.

'The thing is,' Madison replies, 'we stand to earn some good money from this, Morag. If we don't get the copy to them in time, we'll lose out. Do you want me to go ahead and raise this with Storm?'

'Sure. Go for it,' I say. 'But Madz, it's unfair for you to put this on me. Don't you think?'

As Madison stands up, Storm looks up and puts her hands up.

'I've heard everything, Madison, and Morag is one hundred percent right. It's not fair. I've seen you do this time and time again, and we've chatted about it, haven't we? We need to hold each other to account, and this is about your planning and time management, yeah?'

Madison says nothing.

'You can't just spring something on *anyone* like that and expect them to turn it around for you. Sure, there are exceptions when we have to respond quickly and drop everything to support each other. And Morag is always flexible – not just for you, but for our whole team. But this isn't one of those exceptions. I'm sorry, Madz, you're on your own with this,' says Storm. 'As Morag says, it's literally a no-can-do for you today.' Storm looks at me, and adds, 'Sorry to speak for you, Morag my love. Is that okay?'

'Perfect, Storm.'

'That it was.' Mason makes his funny trumpeting sound. 'A. Perfect. Storm.'

I'm a bit blown away, I have to say. Storm hasn't supported me like that before, even though I've needed her to and everything. I'm not sure what's going on with her; I do like Storm 2.0.

But also, I don't know what's going on with me either, if I'm honest. Not sure where I got the courage and everything to say that to Madison. We have our values to hold each other to account, and I've wanted to say that to her many times, you know, but I usually end up saying "no worries" and muttering under my breath. Or going home and whingeing to Jamie about her. But you know what? I'm so proud of myself for doing that today. Is that because I'm going to be a mom? Has that given me extra courage? Maybe I'm really growing a pair of balls. Whatever it is, I have to say, it feels bloody brilliant.

Barry arrives at Storm's desk and brings me back down to earth.

'Oy, oy, oy, team comms! How're we all doing?' he says, looking to the far end of the office.

'Good, thanks, babe,' says Storm. 'How about you?'

'Not bad, if I'm honest,' he says. 'Babe, I've just crunched the numbers and as it happens, the bottom line is, you owe me £14.37 for the sundry refreshments over the weekend, all right? I've kept all the receipts, right enough, in case you need them for tax purposes?'

'Oh, wow, thanks, that's super detailed, Bazza,' says Storm, grabbing the receipts from Barry. 'Can I transfer this into your account?'

'Of course, babe, whatever suits you. But if you've got a twenty,' — he takes a handful of coins out of his pocket — 'I've got the right change to give you now. But whatever you decide, babe, as long as you settle within thirty days, mind, or I'll start charging you interest.'

'Hilarious,' says Mason.

'Well, can *you* afford to lend out money willy-nilly and not charge interest? You must be a richer man than me, I reckon,' says Barry.

Mason makes a trombone sound.

'Leave it with me, Bazza,' says Storm. 'I'll sort this, yeah?'

'Right enough, babe. Back to the grindstone to earn some more of these,' he says, clinking his handful of coins and chuckling to himself. He astounds himself with his awesomeness.

It's the end of the day and I'm about to log off when an all-staff email pops into my inbox from Karo. (Spelling errors all her own.)

Hello Team HAMP, please join us in the Scrum Room tommorrow afternoon at 5pm o'clock for our HAMP award ceremony. I am sure your looking forwad to hearing about our performance at the Britain Loves a Trier rugby sevens festival over the weekend. Me and Coach want to tell you all about it and to share some bubbels with you too. Your all welcome. Thanks, Karo.'

Sounds like fun. Another email pops into my inbox straight after. This one's from Warren.

'Can we have some make-up bubbles too then? Soz for yesterday. I didn't mean what I said.'

There's a collective intake of breath as hands fly to mouths and

Tracy's strident laugh rings across the office. Everyone turns to look at Warren.

'What?' he says, shrugging.

'You've only gone and replied all, you goon,' says Tracy.

Warren groans and buries his face in his hands.

It's a rite of passage in any office to hit "reply all" when you mean to hit "reply" to an all-staff email. I've done it before and you feel so embarrassed and everything. Everyone turns to look at Karo, who just stares at her screen and taps at her keyboard.

When I get to Soho to meet Jamie, he's waiting for me outside the Greek restaurant. He hugs me tight and holds me as though I'm about to fall over.

'I haven't been able to think about anything else today, my Rags!'

'Me neither.'

'I couldn't concentrate at *all*, at work. People kept asking me if I was okay. I just told them I was hungover from the weekend. We're going to have a *baby*, Rags! We're going to be a mom and dad!'

I nod and cry and nod and cry and sniff and snuggle into his shoulder. I've had to keep this all to myself for the whole day, and it's a relief to be able to share the joy and tears and everything with him.

When we turn to walk into the restaurant, Jamie links his arm into mine and holds me under my elbow.

'Jamie! I know I'm a bit of a wimp and everything, but I'm not sick, hey. And you don't need to wrap me in cotton wool!'

There will be a lot for us to start thinking about. We need to absorb all the information the GP gave me about what I can and can't do, what I can and can't eat, what sort of exercise I should do and what I should avoid. Jamie's also trying to do the right thing and everything, but I hope he chills out a bit. I mean, good grief: I can manage a few stairs up to the restaurant, for crying out loud.

Years ago, my mom – the queen of the euphemism – told me about when she found out she was "expecting" me. Those were the days before home test kits and stuff like that, and even though she didn't have any problems like we've had, she had to go to her doctor to do a test.

'When I got there, I had to, you know, go down the passage.'

My mom mouthed the words, "down the passage", in case anyone knew she'd had to go to the toilet to give a urine sample.

When Dr Powys told her the test was positive, she asked him for some advice. She told him she didn't know what she was supposed to do because she'd never expected a baby before.

He laughed, leaned back in his chair, and told her to live her life as she always had. He said if she were a smoker, he'd suggest she stop. But other than that, he told her to stay healthy, eat well, keep doing her health and fitness classes and everything, and playing her tennis or golf as long as she felt comfortable to do so. He told her to go back and see him if she had any problems. But he reminded her the baby would be there before she knew it.

'Just go and enjoy this time,' he told her.

And so she did. She didn't see Dr Powys again until I was born.

It's so different from how things are today. I turned out pretty well, given the doctor's rudimentary advice to my mom and everything. But would I have been any different – healthier or cleverer or more accomplished – had I been born today? I'm not sure, really. Maybe I would have been; maybe I wouldn't have been. It's weird. In some ways, I wish life were simpler again and we didn't have such an overload of information and choice and dos and don'ts and everything. But after the roller-coaster ride Jamie and I have been on, trying to start a family, I'm really glad the wealth of knowledge is there. I guess that's the whole point of progress, hey?

I manage to get Jamie to slow down to a panic about our pregnancy, and we enjoy our meal together. He says he won't have any wine because I can't, which is quite sweet and everything, if you think about it.

We talk fast and lots about having a baby and imagining our future as parents, and then there are long pauses where we're both thinking the same thing. What if this ends in disappointment again?

Jamie breaks one of those long silences.

'Rags?'

'Ja?'

'I'm a bit scared to say this, my love.'

'What?' I'm nervous.

'I don't know what it is, Rags, but I just can't help it. The whole day today, I've just been feeling that this is *it*, you know. I don't know about you but I'm scared shitless, I really am. But at the same time, I can't help feeling this is our time. That it's going to be okay.

'Remember when we had our twelve grapes at midnight in Valencia last year? At the time, prosperity for me was that we would get to have a family. I didn't know how we could get there after everything, you know, but now we're pregnant.'

'Ah, Jamie, that's amazing. You know what? I had exactly the same thoughts and hopes and everything. I didn't say anything to you …'

'Because you didn't know whether I still wanted children?'

I put my hand to my mouth and nod. I can't find any more words, but the tears flow.

'Me too. It's been so long and I thought you might have given up hope. But this must be our time, don't you think? It feels real, like our wish is coming true.' Jamie speaks through tears of his own.

'I never gave up hope, Jamie. It was easier to keep that hope to myself, but I'll share that hope with you now, if you will too.' The tears are now pouring from my eyes.

'Absolutely, my Rags.' Jamie wraps his arms around me. His tears fall on to my head. We hold each other for what feels like ages before Jamie pushes himself away to look at me.

'Hey Rags, I've been thinking too – if our baby's a boy, I have the perfect name for him.'

'Awesome! You're way ahead of me. What?'

'Chester.'

'Ah, Jamie! Can you imagine? He'll arrive wearing a suit and referring to himself in the third person and everything!'

'Oh, my word!'

'Okay, let's think of names we actually like.'

'Fair enough,' says Jamie, nodding.

He frowns and takes a deep breath.

'So, how's this one, Rags? You know how we always say we met because we were just light for each other?'

'Ja,' I say. I have no idea where this is going.

'Well, if it's girl, let's call her Ellie-Dee. As in LED.'

'Oh, Jamie! It would be so hilarious to call our child a pun. But we can't really, can we?'

Jamie shrugs and pulls me close to him again. We both laugh.

This is going to be a long, never-ending conversation, and I can't bloody wait.

Chapter 33

When we get into the Scrum Room for Karo's meeting, Coach, Coach Dave and Karo are there already. Cali walks in behind me, and there are hugs all round.

The room is filled with medium turquoise balloons, with bottles of non-alcoholic sparkling grape juice on the table (we're not allowed alcohol on the charity premises), along with bowls of Wotsits, crisps and Hula Hoops, a few supermarket cakes, paper plates and plastic cups.

Karo is fiddling with the keyboard and trying to open something on the big screen. She asks me to call Warren to help her.

Warren is still sitting at his desk, which is unlike him. He's usually one of the first to get to any meeting.

'You okay, Warren?' I say.

'Yeah, cool. Just busy. *Suuuuper* busy.'

'Karo's asked if you can go and help her with the big screen.'

'Yeah? She asked for me?'

I nod.

'Okay, I'm on my way,' he says, shuffling a random pile of upside-down papers on his desk and trying to look super busy.

No one knows what was going on between him and Karo. It seems they haven't resolved whatever it was either.

'Warren said he's a bit busy, but he's on his way,' I tell Karo.

'He's literally right behind you, Morag,' she says.

The two of them faff with the keyboard and talk to each other in muted tones, as people stream into the Scrum Room around them. Richard walks in and waves to the room.

'Oy, oy, oy!' he says, grabbing a handful of Wotsits.

He jumps as the big screen blasts into action.

Warren and Karo laugh, and Wendy screeches.

'I'm glad I'm not the only one! Richard, that was *so, so* funny,' says Wendy, slapping her thighs.

'Well, that's one way of getting your attention, ja,' says Coach, closing the door. 'It's 5pm and we might as well get started. Please, help yourselves to some non-alcoholic bubbles, ja, and there should be a slither of cake for each and every one of you too. Coach Dave, Cali, Richard – thank you for coming. Please make absolutely yourselves at home.'

There's a run for the bubbles, a few whinges about 'no alcohol' and a few mutters of 'hey ho'.

Coach taps a bottle of non-alcoholic bubbles with her pen.

'Thank you, everybody, for coming here today. It's a celebration of all-sorts, ja? We'll be handing out our Cloud Sevens awards for the performance excellence of our team. I've been hovering literally over cloud seven since the weekend – you made absolutely us all proud.

'And I also have some very exciting news about the funds we raised over the weekend with the bucket-shakes and the text-to-donations. And another little surprise too,' she adds. 'But firstly, let me hand you over to Coach Dave who wants to say several words.'

'All right, everyone? Hi. It's good to be here, yeah. Never been to your offices before. To be honest, I never thought you lot did any work – thought you was all mouth and no trousers, so to speak. Now I've seen some of you at your desks, and you've proved me wrong, and all. Unless, like Barry or Tracy, you're all just *pretending*.'

'Nice one, Coach,' says Tracy. 'We can obviously count on you to keep us humble, yeah.'

'Cheeky fucker,' she adds, under her breath.

'Cheers, Coach Dave! I'll take one for the team, shall I?' says Barry, lifting up his cup.

'Right, to be serious for a bit, I do have a few things to say to you all. And I suppose it makes sense to start at the beginning. When Pauli – Coach – asked me if I'd be interested in taking you on for the *BLAT* challenge, I said yes without really thinking. After our first training session, I couldn't work out why I hadn't stopped to think about it first. No easy way to say this, guys: you were rubbish! Your performance didn't exactly fill me with confidence!

'Fast forward a few weeks, and I could see the hunger in your eyes. You weren't taking this on to win; you were taking this on for The HAMP. Big difference, guys. With that kind of motivation, I realised you could do *anything*. You played to the whistle at every training session. You dreamed it and *you* achieved it. Hundred and ten percent, as Coach says.

'I asked and you answered the call, and you did that without giving me any lip. It's rare that happens, yeah? We had no egos in the team and, as your captain reminded us, there was no *i* in our team. I think that's all down to your leader – your Coach. Before I go on, can we just thank her for everything?'

We clap and jump to our feet. Coach nods and smiles and puts her hands to her heart. Warren's sniffing and wiping his nose on the back of his hand.

'You're a legend, Coach!' he shouts. 'A bloody legend.'

Barry, ever the head prefect, leads us in singing 'For she's a Jolly Good Fellow'.

'Thank you, once and for all,' Coach says, putting her hand in the air. 'Thank you. I feel humble. Now please stop it, before I start to feel proud.'

She gestures for us to sit down.

'See what I mean?' Coach Dave says, looking at Coach. 'Now I've got just one more thing – no, two – to say to you. Thank you, team, for your hard work and dedication, and for making me a very proud coach at the end of the day. We didn't go into *BLAT* with hopes of winning; we wanted to show up for The HAMP's supporters, and throw everything we had at every match we played. But you: *you* went one further. You got results. To get to the final in a festival where, to be honest, I thought we had a snowball's chance of winning any matches ... I have no words. No words. Thank you, you lot. Come up to the front, team, and let's thank you all for leaving it all out there, and for giving your all for The HAMP. Nice one, guys. Nice one.'

Coach Dave and the rest of the room clap as Karo waves us forward. Warren shuffle-steps and leads us up to the front, and Coach Dave shakes hands with each of us. We bask in a few minutes of glory, and a standing ovation from our colleagues, before returning to our seats.

'My final words are for you, Karo. Oh captain, my captain! You wore the armband well. You knew it was going to be a marathon and not a sprint, so on the day and from the off, you led from the front, by example. And in our post-mortems in Cardiff, you brought me solutions, not problems. And those solutions showed up on the scoreboard at the end of the day, when it counted.

'What a leader! Good leadership yields results. You can't ask for more than that now, can you? It's my privilege to present to you the Pauli Gerber Leadership Award for Outstanding Captaincy. Let's give it up for Karo. Karo!'

There's another standing ovation. Karo blushes and nods and looks down to read the little engraved plaque on her tiny trophy. The font must be minute, if you think about it and everything. She dabs her eyes before looking up again, gesturing for us to stop and sit down.

'Thank you, guys. That means a lot,' she says.

Coach thanks Coach Dave and applauds him back into his seat.

'Well, that follows nicely on to the next person. Karo?'

'Thanks, Coach. I think we're going to do this together, yeah?'

Coach nods, and waves her hands for Karo to carry on.

'Okay, this is the fun part of the day. Coach mentioned on Saturday that we'd be handing out our own Cloud Sevens awards to the team, yeah? Well, the time has come.'

'The walrus said, to speak of many things,' says Barry.

'Shut it, Poet Laureate! Who asked you?' says Tracy, laughing.

Sometimes we really sound like children. But I rather love the banter too.

'So, we've had a bit of fun with these awards, yeah? They're mostly serious, but we've decided to take the mick a bit with some of them too. Just to wind you up, yeah?' says Karo, to murmurs around the room. 'So, without any further *adieu*, as our beloved Coach says, the first award we have is for Richard. All of our awards come to you with huge gratitude from The HAMP and from all of our supporters. Just to get that out of the way upfront, yeah?'

'So Richard, you absolutely nailed it being The HAMP mascot on Saturday. You also won the Mascot of the *BLAT* festival on Saturday, so that's an indication of how good you were. So Richard, thank you for being the best HAMP mascot we could have imagined. You get an A for enthusiasm, an A star for the joy and fun and energy you brought to us and the whole stadium, and a jolly good effort mark for wearing more medium turquoise than we've ever seen in one go, ever. But you also get top marks for your range of, quite frankly, precocious dance moves and the expert way you executed them.'

'More like murdered them!' says Barry.

'Oy, you!' says Richard, winking and pointing at Barry. 'Challenge accepted.'

'So, Richard, please come forward and get your Mr Bean Dance Award from The HAMP.'

'Mr Bean? Insult my dance moves, why don't you?' Richard jumps up and moonwalks to the front.

After shaking hands with all three, he holds his tiny trophy in the air like he's just won the Premier League. Pat films the awards, and Richard savours the moment by smiling into the camera and doing the sprinkler, the trophy dangling from his pinkie finger.

And so the award ceremony continues, with each of us getting a fun or serious – or both – award and citation. Coach, Coach Dave and Karo must have had fun with these:

1. Cali – The Celebrity Player
2. Warren – The Most Modest Player
3. Binny – The Most Northern Player
4. Ash – The Golden Boot
5. Jasper – The Best Dressed Player
6. Charlie – The Quietest Player
7. Storm – The Cordon Bleu Player
8. Tracy – The Most Potty-Mouthed Player
9. Mason – The Best Learner Player
10. Morag – The Most Southern Player
11. Robyn – The Player That Counts the Most
12. Barry – The Man from Ankle

Coach presents The Best Coach Award to Coach Dave, and Karo and Coach Dave present The Best CEO Award to Coach, along with a bonus wooden spoon award for 'creative use of the English language'.

'Oh, gosh,' Coach says. 'Does that mean I don't sound really like a local? I thought I'd given it enough wellington.'

'It's welly, Coach, welly!' says Tracy.

'Well, as long as you know what I mean, ja? Thank you everybody, this is very special. I will cherish this opportunity, these awards, and I'll carry always with me these memories.

'Okay, now that's done, I told you I also had some exciting news to share with you, ja? By getting to the final, we were awarded the runner-up prize of £200k. Between the bucket collections and the text donations, we raised also a little over £30k. And you know that team we played in the final? Well, their CEO contacted actually me on Monday, for two reasons.' Coach grabs her pinkie finger. 'First, he wanted to donate £100k of their prize money to us! That smacked absolutely me in the gob, as they say, ja?'

'You're kidding me, Coach? That's wild,' yells Storm, as everyone around the room whoops and whistles.

'It is, ja. I still can't believe it actually. It is wild. But the second thing, ja' — she grabs her thumb — 'is that their Cardiff branch wants to partner with us after seeing us at the stadium on Saturday. They said they loved actually our performance, the huge amount of support we had, and the clear and strong work ethic they could see at play. All that from a sevens festival, our Cloud Sevens festival, ja? Isn't that the best news, team?'

We all clap and whoop and whistle again.

'And so this will help us do more of what we do, for more people struggling with anger management problems, ja? All the new funding is unrestricted, which means we can choose where best to use it. So we're going to use it to expand our outreach programme, right across the country. We can train more people to help more people. I can't believe actually how awesome is this all. Ja? It ticks nicely even more boxes than we had,' says Coach.

'But that's not all, folks' says Tracy. 'That company's coming in to meet us next week, right, and because they've got a big comms team, they kind of like want to make a film about the impact of the whole

BLAT experience on our charity's work. They want to share the film to, I don't know, reach more new customers in Wales or something, so it will need to focus quite a lot on our Cali. Smashing, yeah?' says Tracy.

'Smashing, absolutely, Tracy. Thank you. They also love Cali and everything she stands for. Who doesn't, ja? And they have great ideas of other promotional and fundraising opportunities for us, with her. They will keep actually you busy, Cali, ja?'

Cali smiles and nods.

'So when they come in next week, I want them to meet each and every one of you, ja? Our *whole* HAMP team, ja? Warren will invite you to a meeting, and we'll send you information about what we know so far.

'So that's what I wanted to say. Isn't that all super exciting? Out of a Chester disaster rises a phoenix, a world of new opportunities, and a beautiful healing that can only come through sport. Ja? Thank you, Cali, thank you Team HAMP. I'm proud of you all.' Coach is holding back tears as she claps at all of us.

'Jasper, your hand's up. Do you want to say something?'

'Thanks, Coach. Do you think we could start a social rugby club?'

'Good idea, Jasper. I'll leave that with you all to discuss at the pub later, ja, and let me know what you decide.'

'Get in!' Jasper jumps up and pumps the air.

'Storm? You want to say something?'

'Thanks, Coach, I just wanted to add some more good news, if that's okay. You know when *Chestergate* hit, that young Scottish influencer McKayla was kind of caught in the crossfire? Well, I took the opportunity at the time to reach out to her to see if she wanted to work with us, to see if we were vaguely in her lane. Yeah? Her brother, who's her agent, told me she was involved with other charities and wouldn't be able to get involved with us too. Well, she's just DM'd me on Twitter to say she watched us play in the *BLAT* festival, and she asked if there was anything she could do for us. How's that?'

'She's dating a Scottish rugby player, tbf,' says Mason.

'Oh right, that makes sense then!' says Storm. 'Well, she and I have had a bit of back-and-forth, yeah, and she said she'd like to train to become a HAMP volunteer. Isn't that awesome? And maybe when the Rugby World Cup is on, her boyfriend can tweet about us, or something. We'll have to give that a bit more thought, but we can get *so* much mileage out of that, can't we? Especially in Scotland,' she adds, storm-clapping.

'That's fantastic, Storm! I hope she'll get as much out of this as we will, ja?' says Coach.

'Of *course*, yes. That's what I meant,' says Storm, waving and pfffting.

'This is a good day. Thank you, everybody, thank you. It's all of your efforts that have brought us to this good day, ja? I appreciate you and value you and your hard work,' says Coach, to a collective "aah" around the room.

'I've kept you long actually in the office, and I don't want to hold you back from getting to the pub, so you're now free to go. I'll see you there.' (This is how Coach pronounces pub: *pup*. I love it.)

She's about to blow the full-time whistle, but remembers something else she wanted to say.

'Guys, sorry, one more thing before you go. I'd like to get the band back together again soon – maybe you can come even to mine – to watch our *BLAT* games, ja? I taped them all. And all of the back stories, ja? Good idea?'

Everyone claps and whoops, as Coach calls time and blows the full-time whistle.

It's a fun and festive evening at the pub. I manage to bat away any questions about not drinking alcohol, saying my stomach still isn't quite right. It's also an excuse to pop outside a few times; the fresh air helps to keep me awake.

'Jamie obviously doing the cooking again, lolz?' says Gennypha, laughing.

With the wine and beer flowing, the conversation gets louder and louder in our corner of the pub. When the shot trays start arriving, thanks to Kevin and Tracy, I call it quits and go home. I'm feeling super tired too, and am struggling to keep up with the pace of conversation. It's weird, but the more sober you are and everything, the less funny everything seems.

Of course I'm the first one to leave, and *everyone* hugs me goodnight, says they can't wait to see me tomorrow and everything. Most people also tell me they love me, which is really funny, if you think about it. It's not even our Christmas party or anything, but I guess it's kind of the same.

On my walk to the station to get the tube home, I reflect on all the things I've seen or heard tonight:

1. Kevin sings in a chamber choir. I'm not sure which Kevin is the singer, though: the blunt, earnest office version or the hammered one. Either way, Kevin has invited Tracy to audition for the choir next week, and she's going to go. Kevin has told her to wear her weekend shoes. Things must be getting serious.
2. The rugby season has birthed and nurtured a few relationships: Coach and Cali, Storm and Barry, Karo and Warren, and it looks like there are actual sparks between Mason and Jasper too.
3. Even a few wines in, Madison is still annoying.
4. Gennypha is bloody brilliant at pool.
5. Warren and Karo's argument started over something petty, as fights usually do, and escalated when Warren told Karo he wasn't crazy about cats. (That *is* petty, if you think about it

and everything.) He apologised, but it took Karo a few days to accept his apology. She thought not loving cats was crossing a line. From what I saw this evening, it looks like he's found his way back to the right side of that line. That's a relief, I have to say. I love those two together.

6. It's not a great idea to let Richard near the karaoke machine. But in fairness to him, he gave 'Bohemian Rhapsody' his tuneless best, even though he got a bit breathless from dad-dancing.

7. Wendy took a selfie with everyone and posted on Facebook that she was out with the best rugby sevens team in the UK. She loves to boast and exaggerate and everything, and claim things that might not be true, but I'll forgive her this one. She might just be right.

8. You sure learn loads when you go outside with the smokers.

Chapter 34

The next two months at The HAMP bring big changes to our team. Gennypha starts them off when she announces she's going to leave the charity to join Cali's team. She's been thinking about it and everything for some time, but she feels now is the right time to go. She says she learnt a lot from leading the work with Cali's team, and this boosted her confidence to take the leap to go and work in celebrity publicity and promotion, as she's always wanted to do. She and Storm have healed their relationship and Gennypha is now happy she can leave on good terms, and on her own terms and everything.

I'll be sorry to see Gennypha go, but it won't be long before I'll also be leaving The HAMP for a while.

Not long after Gennypha announces she's leaving, Jasper applies for her role and gets it. He's been waiting for a role like this, he says, and it's a good opportunity for his career. And then Storm tells us she's leaving too, to pursue a career in counselling.

'Since that blowout with Gennypha, guys, I've been doing some work on myself,' she tells us, when she calls us into the Scrum Room for a catch-up. 'I also started to pay more attention to the work our volunteers were doing with people with anger management issues. And after that drama with Tom, I realised how much I really love doing *real* work like that. Helping people, resolving issues, you know. To be honest, I think there's more synergy between that work and my personality, yeah?'

'Amazing, Storm. Would you say there's more synergy between that work – you know, counselling – and your personality?' says Madison.

'Yes, Madison, I've literally just – never mind. You're quite right. And another thing, which may or may not be news to you guys,' she continues, her mouth now full of chicken tikka wrap, 'you know, working with your partner is never a good thing. Barry and I are going to be moving in together, so I thought I'd grab life by the horns and start my studies. So I'm going to leave The HAMP, do some freelance work to keep my hand in, and start at counselling school. I finish up here at the end of December.'

She seals her decision with a Storm-clap. For the first time ever, we all join her.

'Brill, Storm. Makes sense,' says Mason, giving her a thumbs-up. 'Always saw you doing that, tbh.'

'Oh, Stormz, that's just amazing. I'm *so* thrilled for you. Congrats. You'll be so fab. Do you mind if I pick your brains quickly, though?' says Madison, clapping long after everyone else has stopped.

'Sure. Do you want to catch up later, or is it something I can help you with here?' says Storm.

'Here's fine, Stormz, no worries. I was wondering, do you know if they're going to recruit for your replacement internally before putting it out on the external channels?'

'Asking for a friend?' says Mason.

'Oh, absolutely. I'm asking for a friend,' says Madison, in her best west country accent. She throws her head back into a false laugh and flicks her hair.

'Not sure, if I'm honest, Madz,' says Storm. 'I've only just handed in my notice, to be fair. Why don't you go ahead and ask Coach?'

'Marvellous. Will do, tha-anks,' says Madison. '*Really* thrilled for you, though, Stormz. You'll be brill.' She squeezes in those last words before her screensaver rolls back up.

My pregnancy seems to be progressing well, although I don't really want to say that out loud and everything. I have to have lots of precautionary check-ups and scans because of my age. It feels a bit insulting to discover I'm what's known in medical terms as an *elderly primigravida*. Why can't they just say I'm a tiny bit on the older side for having my first baby? Anyway, I get it and I'll take being called anything that will end in being called a mother.

Everything indicates the baby's growing well and nothing unusual is happening. I disguise my hospital appointments as a range of general check-ups and no one at work is any the wiser, I don't think. Not sure what they must think of my growing waistline, even though I'm working hard to disguise it.

I need to start talking about it at work, though, because you know how much I hate keeping secrets and everything. A lot of people have commented on my being quiet, and I'm starting to wonder if they think I'm terminally ill or something. If you think about it and everything, being quiet and having loads of hospital appointments could add up to bad news.

I haven't been sure how or when to share my news. And then the perfect opportunity arises when I get to work today and find a bright yellow envelope on my desk, with *Morag Williams* handwritten on the outside.

'Oh, hey,' says Mason, looking up and making a trumpeting sound. 'You got one of those too?'

'Ja, what is it?' I tear the envelope open.

'Wait and see.' He watches me as I take a beautiful, hand-etched card out of the envelope.

Please join us at our wedding!
Cali and Pauli ...

'Whaaaat?' I say. 'That's amazing, hey. Wow! I didn't see this coming – well, not this soon. Did you?'

'Nah, thought it'd be another year or so. But I guess when you know you know, yeah?'

'Definitely! That's such cool news. I have to go and speak to her!'

I run to Coach's office with the card in my hand.

'Coach, this is brilliant! I'm so happy for you. Cali is perfect; you're perfect; you're perfect together. Thank you so much for inviting me to your wedding. Wow, that's such a privilege and an honour and everything. I'm so, so excited!'

Oh boy, I may be over-gushing here. But I've never really been able to assimilate the British reserve, to be honest. I've always failed. I'm going to churn this over and over for the next twenty-four hours but I guess there are worse things to feel terrible about than being heartfelt and enthusiastic.

'Thank you, Morag. That means a lot. We're both hovering over cloud seven ...'

'Nine,' I say. 'Coach, the saying is *to be on cloud nine.*'

'Haha! That's so funny. I never understood anyway cloud seven, but cloud nine still doesn't make sense. But it's at least higher, ja? We're both very happy. I hope you can join us, ja?'

'We'd love to, thank you.'

'You saw you can bring a plus one, and it'll be nice to have you and Jamie there, ja?'

'Yes, I did, thank you. Actually, Coach, I'm also hovering over cloud nine, or seven as you say, and I was wondering, do you think I could maybe bring a plus-two?'

Coach cocks her head at me.

'A plus-two? What do you mean? Will you have a friend staying with you? I can check and I'm sure it can actually be fine, but what do you mean?'

'Well,' I say, stroking my slightly-bulging tummy. 'I do have a little friend staying with me for a few more months. Can I bring him or her?'

'Oh, Morag! This makes so much my heart full. I'm so happy for you! For you and Jamie too,' she says, putting her hands to her mouth. 'You'll be actually brilliant, beautiful parents. I'm absolutely happy for you both. When is baby scheduled?'

'Haha, baby's not a flight, Coach! Baby's due in late January, so I'll be really big at your wedding. I didn't know how else to tell you … I've been wanting to tell you for a few weeks now.'

Coach comes over to the other side of the desk. She punches my arm, and puts her hand on my shoulder.

'Can we have a hug, Coach?'

'Absolutely,' she says, wrapping her arms around my waist and burying her head in my neck. She whacks my back super hard a few times before she pulls away.

'Thank you for telling me. I feel actually honoured. I'm not sure who else knows, but why don't you tell the rest of your team the same way? It's a beautiful way to share your news.'

I sink my head against her shoulder.

'Thank you, Coach. I will do.'

I turn to leave her office, and swing back round to look at her. She's smiling the widest smile ever.

'Coach? I just wanted to say thank you. For everything. You've been everything, the best leader, just what I've needed. You've really made my time in London and at The HAMP special.'

Coach gives me a thumbs-up and winks and smiles at me again. Her eyes are glistening, and I feel like I'm on top of the bloody world.

My tummy grows over the next few months, and I often forget to make room for it. I have to imagine there's another person in front of me, and I guess you could say there is, if you think about it and everything.

I took Coach's advice and told my colleagues about taking a plus-two to Coach and Cali's wedding. Here's how they've all reacted and have been since I've told them:

1. Storm gave me the biggest hug ever and congratulated me over and over. She also said she hoped we could become friends, and hoped we'd stay in touch. I had no words; miracles seem to be happening everywhere I look.

2. Wendy has gone overboard giving me advice about being pregnant. And about having children and how they ruin your life, your body, and your career. She's what Jamie and I now call a 'JW': a 'just wait' person. 'Just wait till your heartburn starts. It'll kill you, I'm telling you.' Or 'Just wait until baby's here. It will change your life. No more nights out, no more social life. Enjoy your freedom while it lasts.' I'm learning to filter out her crap and take in only the bits of value and truth I can find. It's no different from how I treat *any* Wendy information, if you think about it and everything.

3. Madison? Well, I've tried four, maybe five times, to tell her the news – rather, to tell it to the back of her head. She still hasn't heard but I guess one of these days she might notice I'm no longer there and she has a new pod-buddy.

4. Warren heard the news the first time I mentioned it to the back of Madison's head. He and Karo are thrilled for me, and Warren keeps asking me for updates. His enthusiasm and encouragement are the sweetest ever.

5. I made an appointment to meet with Kevin to tell him I was pregnant and to start planning my mat leave and everything. He was sweet and kind and enthusiastic in a Kevin sort of way. 'Yes, good. That *is* good news. Splendid news. Good. Do you

know my older sister was pregnant last year? She got hugely overweight and is still trying to get rid of it. The baby fat, that is, not the baby. She quite likes him and thinks she'll keep him. Good. Yes. I'll send you all the paperwork and you'll have to send it back to me promptly. Good.'

6. Tracy hugged me and cried when I told her I was pregnant. 'That's one lucky little fucker, I tell you, Morag, having you for a mum. You'll obviously be ace and all. Proper chuffed for you, my love. I don't know, mate, I'm fucking made up.'

It's late December, and my mat leave is due to start soon. Mason calls me into the kitchen for a send-off. I have to sit in the middle of the room, while everyone looks at me and says things about me and everything. People who leave the charity usually say they dread this, but I've always found it to be a special tradition. But then again, I'm from southern Africa and I've never minded that kind of positive attention.

I do feel a bit shy and everything, though, but not in a bad way. Storm says some lovely things about me, which a year ago would really have surprised me and everything. She thinks I've grown and, without going into details about the recent Madison-moment, says it was well-deserved that I was on Coach's chalkboard last month for the "AHAH-er of the month".

She also says she's enjoyed working with me, and I've decided this time to believe her. She *has* changed, and I don't believe she would say things just for show any more.

When Storm hands me a card and a gift bag, I take it and I blush and say thank you. When I start to open the card, Mason says I can save it for later, but I have to open the gifts now. I dig into the gift bag and pull out a tiny Springbok rugby jersey.

'Ah, so you reckon this little one's going to be a world champ, just like the Boks, hey?' I say.

'Don't rub it in, all right?' says Barry, laughing.

There's more in the gift bag. I pull out a white onesie with the words 'Mommy's sunshine and everything' on the front. I hold it up and I can't stop laughing.

'You guys!'

'We had it made especially for you ... and everything,' says Mason.

That's pretty awesome, if you ask me. I have no words, and my laughter turns to tears. Happy, happy tears that pour down my face.

'Ooh, look! She's going, she is. She's proper welling up,' says Tracy, pointing at me and pulling two tissues out of her shirt cuff. She gives me one and dabs her eyes with the other.

I am welling up. And everyone's watching me as the tears roll down my face, but I don't mind one single bit. I soak everything in. I want to take a picture of this moment and keep it somewhere where I can look at it always. At everyone in this room; this group of random, weird, annoying, kind, grumpy, flawed, hilarious and special, special people.

And it suddenly dawns on me that this bunch of colleagues here in London have not only become my friends, but they've also become my family. My sweet charity.

Jamie and I start to plan, for the first time ever, to become a family. We pick out baby clothes and toiletries and fluffy toys and everything, and learn about Moses baskets and cuddle chairs and research baby monitors. We buy a car seat, and paint the spare room in our flat.

When we finally let go of our fear and replace it with hope, it's a wonderful, scary and liberating release, to be honest. It looks like next year will be a good year for us; maybe our best yet.

I read and re-read the wishes my colleagues wrote in my baby card and sometimes even find myself missing them a little. Sort of.

I've added some new words to the lists of words I hate:

1. Swollen ankles.
2. Just wait.
3. Visceral.

Here are some new ones I love:

1. Bye, Madison.
2. Blossoming.
3. Doula.

And these are my new favourite words of all time and everything:

1. It's a boy.

Acknowledgements

I carried the seed of this book with me for years. I carried it in notebooks, in scribbled observations, in random social media posts, and in sharing with friends and family the absurdity of the everyday things I noticed in the world around me. I owe so much gratitude to my husband and my two sons, who have endured my stories over the years and my longing to weave them into a book. *Sweet Charity* has been two years in the writing and more than 25 years in the brewing.

Thank you, sweet family of mine, for loving me and encouraging me through this long birthing process, and for being my cheerleaders from day one. To my husband, for pushing me to get going with this jolly book of mine, when I had no idea where to start. 'At the beginning,' you said. Duh. It sounded much easier than it was, but thank you for getting me to my beginning, and cheering me on to the end. You were also my favourite first reader in the whole wide world.

And to my boys, for being my favourite rugby consultants in the whole wide world. After twelve years of Saturdays watching you play rugby in Cape Town, I knew you'd know what you were talking about. Thank you for helping me bring BLAT to life and make it sound like a festival that could happen. And for answering my endless and random questions with grace and patience, even when you had no idea why I was asking you! You're superstars, you're hilarious, and you're two of the kindest human beings I've ever known.

I'd also like to thank my extended family and my community of friends for your interest and encouragement and, in some cases, your nagging! You made me believe people might actually buy my book.

I'm grateful to have worked with the amazing editors, Rob Matthews and Janie Brayshaw, of Betterwrite. I learnt so much from you both, and I hope my book shines a little bit brighter because of your gentle and superbly encouraging guidance. You helped me believe I could do this, that I could birth a book, and I hope I can get to work with you both again.

And to my friend and champion designer, Debs Waters, thank you for sprinkling your unique creative magic to bring my book cover to life. I'm blown away by your talent and the way you approach every task. Thank you.

About the author

If you ask Ruth Martin where she comes from, you'll always get a long story. (You can say the same about anything you ask her, really.) The youngest of four, Ruth was born to South African parents in the then-Rhodesia. She and her family moved to Zambia when she was four and back to Bulawayo when she was twelve. After completing high school in Bulawayo, Ruth studied at the University of Cape Town, where she graduated with a BA, and a boyfriend who became her husband. She's always loved writing and, as long as she can remember, has found humour in the absurdity of everyday life. 'My mom says I'm very noticeable,' said five-year-old Ruth. Her mom probably said 'observant'.

Her debut novel, *Sweet Charity*, reflects the observations she's gathered over many years of working in the non-profit sector in Cape Town and London, and watching the world around her wherever she's been. While the novel is set in a charity, Ruth has created her cast of characters from everywhere she's lived, worked and travelled.

Ruth currently lives in London with her husband, and the two of them travel back to Cape Town whenever they can. They have two adult sons.